WITHDRAWN
D0386425

THE REFERENCE SHELF VOLUME 39 NUMBER 3

CENSORSHIP IN THE UNITED STATES

EDITED BY

GRANT S. McCLELLAN

Editor, Current Magazine

THE H. W. WILSON COMPANY

NEW YORK 1967

THE REFERENCE SHELF

The books in this series contain reprints of articles, excerpts from books, and addresses on current issues and social trends in the United States and other countries. There are six separately bound numbers in each volume, all of which are generally published in the same calendar year. One number is a collection of recent speeches; each of the others is devoted to a single subject and gives background information and discussion from various points of view, concluding with a comprehensive bibliography.

Subscribers to the current volume receive the books as issued. The subscription rate is $12 ($15 foreign) for a volume of six numbers. Single numbers are $3 each.

Library of Congress Catalog Card No. 67-17466

PRINTED IN THE UNITED STATES OF AMERICA

PREFACE

How prevalent is censorship in the United States?

Although there are many state and municipal laws involving the censorship of printed materials and of the theater, films, and other public activities, there are few such Federal statutes. The stark simplicity of the language of the First Amendment to the Constitution* tends to prevent the proliferation of censorship legislation and rulings by the courts—but not completely.

Within the last decade the Supreme Court has spoken with ever greater clarity against censorship of the press, films, and speech. Even so, the most forthright condemnations of censorship remain in some of the dissenting opinions of members of the highest court.

It is obvious to the average reader and theater- and moviegoer that there is more freedom of expression now than there was a decade ago. At the same time, many subtle—and not so subtle—censorship activities (often private in nature) have flourished since World War II, activities such as the extremist attacks on schools, teachers, and libraries. This is nothing new in American life; indeed it is traditional. Often such censorship is backed by majority public opinion; we are still too close to the rampant arguments of the Cold War to overlook that. Furthermore the wave of protests about the war in Vietnam, and the counterthrusts by our highest officials, have yet to subside. The restlessness and protests of the college generation and the often agonized efforts of educational authorities to deal with them are with us too.

The constant theme of our history, the struggle for order with freedom, is now being played at dramatic pitch. It is this theme which unifies the materials brought together in this compilation.

Central to the unfolding of the theme, as always, are the judgments made by the Supreme Court regarding censorship cases, issues

* "Congress shall make no law respecting an establishment of religion, or prohibiting the free exercise thereof; or abridging the freedom of speech or of the press; or the right of the people peaceably to assemble, and to petition the government for a redress of grievances."

centering on fair trial versus free press, and the like—all of which are discussed here. The part other Government agencies and regulations play in withholding information from the public is also dealt with. More broadly, this compilation shows how our freedom to read and freedom of speech are currently affected by censorship activities, public or private. There are no final conclusions, however; there never can be in this ever-changing sphere of discussion and action.

The editor wishes to thank both the authors and the publishers of the following selections for permission to reprint them in this volume.

GRANT S. MCCLELLAN

May 1967

CONTENTS

Preface 3

I. Censorship: The Current Debate

Editor's Introduction 9

1. The Current Scene

A Year's Censorship Harvest .... Publishers' Weekly 10

2. Pornography: Toward a New Understanding

John Henry Merryman. The Fear of Books .. Stanford Today 14
Howard Moody. A New Definition of Obscenity ....
.... Christianity and Crisis 20
George Steiner. Pornography or Privacy .... Encounter 24
Joseph A. Schneiders. Christianity and Pornography ....
.... Crane Review 28

3. The Case Against Pornography

George P. Elliott. On Behalf of Censors .. Harper's Magazine 32
O. K. Armstrong. Dealing With the Smut Business ....
.... Reader's Digest 49

II. The Supreme Court: More Freedom or Less?

Editor's Introduction 54

1. The Supreme Court on Obscenity Cases

Ralph I. Lowenstein. The Legal Testing of Obscenity 55
William J. Brennan, Jr. The Ginzburg Majority Opinion ... 68
Hugo L. Black and William O. Douglas. Two Dissents in the
Ginzburg Decision 75

A Protestant View of the Ginzburg Decision .... Christian Century 80
Confusion on Obscenity: A Catholic View .... America 83
A Conservative View .... National Review 84
A Liberal View .... New Republic 85
Jason Epstein. More Freedom or Less? .... Atlantic Monthly 87

2. *Fair Trial Versus a Free Press*

A Recent Supreme Court Decision .... Social Education 94
Fred P. Graham. American Bar Association Proposals ...... New York Times 99
Sidney E. Zion. Views of the American Newspaper Publishers Association .... New York Times 103
Sidney E. Zion. Views of the Association of the Bar of the City of New York .... New York Times 106
American Civil Liberties Union's View 110

3. *Extending Freedom of Speech*

The Julian Bond Case .... New York Times 118

III. Censorship and Politics

Editor's Introduction 120
John D. Pomfret. A New Law .... New York Times 120
A Journalistic Reaction 122
Geoffrey Wolff. The Government as Publisher: The USIA .... Washington Post Book Week 124
Reed Harris. The Government as Publisher: A Reply ...... Washington Post 129
Arthur Greenspan. Government Subsidies to Publishers .... New York Post 130
James Reston. The Press, the President and Foreign Policy .. Foreign Affairs 132
Clifton Daniel. A Footnote to History .... New York Times 140
Freedom and the Press .... New York Times 149

IV. Censorship and Intellectual Freedom

Editor's Introduction 151
The Passing of the Index of Forbidden Books .... Christian Century 152
Elizabeth Bartelme. Let It Be Printed .... Commonweal 153
Vincent Canby. A New Movie Code .... New York Times 158
Self-Censorship of TV .... Newsweek 161
An Attempt to Rewrite History 164
Irwin Karp. Writing History on Approval .. Saturday Review 168
Kathleen Molz. The Role of the Public Librarian .... American Scholar 173
David Dempsey. Advice to Librarians .... Saturday Review 182

V. Censorship and Education

Editor's Introduction 180
Henry Steele Commager. The Nature of Academic Freedom .... Saturday Review 189
Richard M. Nixon. Four Academic Freedoms .... Saturday Review 197
Fred P. Graham. Academic Freedom Is Free Speech .... New York Times 202
Philip Gleason. The Problem Facing Catholic Colleges .... America 205

Bibliography 214

I. CENSORSHIP: THE CURRENT DEBATE

EDITOR'S INTRODUCTION

Any one year's harvest of censorship controversies could set the stage for a discussion of censorship in the United States. The year 1966 was especially dramatic, for the Supreme Court dealt with the matter in several landmark decisions as important as its epoch-making decision in the 1957 Roth case, until then the leading case concerning bans on obscene materials. It was a year which also saw the attempt by private individuals to control the writing of history, notably in the much-publicized controversy over William Manchester's *The Death of a President*. A round-up of the year's events from *Publishers' Weekly* opens this compilation.

The remainder of the section deals with the nature of pornography and obscenity. This discussion is presented at the outset for two reasons. First, the question of what constitutes obscenity, the publication of which is banned by the Supreme Court, has been reopened in recent years by many literary and social critics, as a result of changing social and sexual mores in the Western world. Second, the problem of definition is central to much else in this compilation; the new concern about obscenity informs later materials included in the volume.

In "The Fear of Books" a professor of law maintains that censorship is socially more harmful than the material it seeks to ban. The search for a new definition of obscenity is illustrated by the article by Howard Moody, minister of the Judson Memorial Church in New York City, for whom the greatest obscenity is simply man's inhumanity to man. A new look at pornography is found in the two following selections. Literary critic George Steiner questions the literary pretensions of "high pornography" and emphasizes its monotony and deadening effect. A Unitarian minister, Joseph A. Schneiders, evaluates traditional Christian concepts about pornography in the light of today's moral standards.

The section closes with what may be called the case for censorship. The American novelist and essayist George P. Elliott is admittedly of two minds, but he singles out a genre of pornography to which he objects—that which is nihilistic. That there is a good deal of what we have long called "smut" for sale in America is evidenced by the final selection by a former United States Representative, O. K. Armstrong, who also suggests a few measures which can be taken to curb the "smut business."

1. The Current Scene

A YEAR'S CENSORSHIP HARVEST [1]

Early in 1966, proponents of the freedom to read received a major setback when the United States Supreme Court upheld publishers' censorship convictions in two out of three cases on which it had held public hearings late in 1965. Of the three Supreme Court verdicts, by far the most sweeping was the one in which the court upheld the sentence of publisher Ralph Ginzburg (*Eros* magazine) to five years in jail and $28,000 in fines for having sent three of his publications through the mails. The Court, accepting the Government prosecutor's admission that reasonable doubt existed about the alleged obscenity of Mr. Ginzburg's publications, nevertheless held that Mr. Ginzburg was guilty because his advertising and promotion of his publications constituted "titillation" and "pandering" —something with which he had not been originally charged. The Court thus departed from its traditional position of judging a book as a book and put the publishing community on notice that henceforth it might well look at a book not just as a book but as a whole package of advertising, publicity, promotion and publisher's intentions.

In the second case, the Court upheld the conviction of Edward Mishkin, a longtime New York City publisher and seller of books and pamphlets which could most charitably be described as "borderline." Mr. Mishkin, in his defense, raised the issue of illegal police search-and-seizure procedures which allegedly had taken place at

[1] From "Censorship and the Freedom to Read." *Publishers' Weekly*. 191:50-2. Ja. 30, '67. Reprinted by permission.

his firm's warehouse. Sometimes in the past, this issue has been sufficient for the Supreme Court to throw out a censorship case, but this time the Court ignored the issue and upheld Mr. Mishkin's sentence of a $12,000 fine and three years in jail.

In the third decision, the Supreme Court overturned Massachusetts' ban on the sale of *Fanny Hill* and thus presumably brought to an end the trials that the two-hundred-year-old erotic classic had undergone since its publication in a modern edition by G. P. Putnam's Sons.

The Supreme Court's decision in the Ginzburg case in particular was generally seen as repressive, a retreat from the liberal anti-censorship position which the Court had taken in recent years, a broadening of the area of permissible censorship and an invitation to local units of government to engage more widely in censorship activities. . . .

Local censors, professional and amateur alike, were encouraged by the Ginzburg decision, and the balance of the year saw a spate of censorship legislation at the state level. This generally took the form of establishing a dual standard for the alleged protection of youth—i.e., books permissible for anybody and books "for adults only"—for the Supreme Court in earlier cases had hinted its willingness to condone such a dual standard. New York State has two such statutes, which somewhat contradict each other, on its books, and in October the United States Supreme Court declined to review them. Meanwhile, the New York State Legislature enacted a so-called "obscene premises" act, which would have barred minors from premises "where objectionable literature is sold." The way in which the act defined "objectionable" would probably have covered any bookstore or library that attempted to represent modern literature, any museum or gallery with a comprehensive collection. Governor Rockefeller vetoed the measure, calling it neither necessary nor constitutional.

CLEAN's Proposition 16 Campaign in California

At the state level the year's greatest concentration of censorship activity was in California. There, an organization called the

California League Enlisting Action Now (CLEAN) succeeded in putting on the November ballot a measure, Proposition 16, which would have done away with just about every existing safeguard for the freedom to read and would have put the vigilante private citizen firmly in the driver's seat with respect to censorship prosecutions.

A group of authors and librarians was unsuccessful in a court move to get Proposition 16 off the ballot. Proposition 16 began looking like a winner; it was endorsed by Ronald Reagan, Republican candidate for governor, who also was looking like a winner. Opposition to Proposition 16 was mustered by every book trade, library and author group in the state—one wag suggested that all these groups should unite as one organization called DIRTY (Decent Inspirational Reading for Today's Youth). And when the ballots were counted, it developed that while Mr. Reagan was indeed a winner, Proposition 16 had been defeated.

Other Censors Active

San Francisco in 1966 became a prominent center of censorship activity. Three booksellers were arrested for selling a privately published book of erotic poetry, *The Love Book* by Lenore Kandel. And the San Francisco Board of Permit Appeals denied a Berkeley bookseller's petition to open a branch store in the city because, it said, the store would attract "an undesirable element" and would bring a Berkeley taint to the shabby genteel confines of San Francisco's Haight-Ashbury section.

Across the country, a Connecticut circuit court enjoined the sale of Hubert Selby's novel *Last Exit to Brooklyn* (Grove Press), in all or maybe only part of the state (there was considerable difference of opinion on this last point). There was some speculation that prosecution of the book was in part inspired by the fact that an election was imminent. Whatever the inspiration, the election was held, and the case against the book stood still; no one involved in the action got very excited about it.

Attempted censorship of another kind—through the laws of libel and invasion of privacy—was much in the news in 1966 as prominent people in various walks of life tried to suppress books that had been written about them or their relatives. Folk singer Bob Dylan was unsuccessful in trying to stop a forthcoming Citadel Press biography of him. Multimillionaire Howard Hughes—though he tried harder than Mr. Dylan did—was unable to stop Random House from publishing *Howard Hughes: A Biography* by John Keats. Mr. Hughes' agents took the case all the way to the United States Supreme Court, which declined to hear it. Mary Hemingway was likewise unsuccessful in her court fight against publication of a book about her late husband, *Papa Hemingway* by A. E. Hotchner (Random House).

Libel and Privacy Codes Used for Censorship

Former baseball pitcher Warren Spahn, however, won another round against publication of *The Warren Spahn Story* by Milton J. Shapiro (Messner, 1958), when New York State's highest court upheld his contention that the book contained misstatements and fictitious episodes and constituted an invasion of his privacy. But a United States Supreme Court decision early this year—upholding *Life* magazine's portrayal of the real people upon whose experiences Joseph Hayes based his novel and his play *The Desperate Hours*—cast some doubt that the Spahn verdict would be upheld on appeal. [It was not upheld.—Ed.]

In an action still pending at year's end, Helen Clay Frick, daughter of the late industrialist Henry Clay Frick, went to court in Pennsylvania to try to stop the distribution of *Pennsylvania—Birthplace of a Nation* by Sylvester Stevens (Random House), which, she said, contained defamatory passages about her father. The case drew wide interest from historians, who saw in it the likelihood that all historical writing could be inhibited by the threat of lawsuits brought by relatives of deceased historical figures. . . . [Miss Frick's suit was dismissed by the judge trying the case.—Ed.]

Last but far from least in this chronicle of censorship in 1966 was the year's biggest censorship attempt which resulted in the year's biggest backfire. "The Battle of the Book," the press called it:

Jacqueline Kennedy's effort to censor the book about President Kennedy's assassination which she herself had "authorized": *The Death of a President* by William Manchester . . .[which was condensed and serialized by *Look* and published in book form by Harper & Row in April 1967]. . . .

Mrs. Kennedy got the deletions she wanted, it was said, and so speculation centered on the nature of these deletions. The Kennedys claimed that they were entirely of a personal and not a historical nature. Others speculated that they might be political, reflecting the Kennedys' attitude toward President Johnson. . . . One result of the whole episode was that everyone within reach of newspaper, radio or television coverage knew—or thought he knew—what it was that Mrs. Kennedy did not want to have known.

2. *Pornography: Toward a New Understanding?*

THE FEAR OF BOOKS [2]

The fear of books seems, at one time or another, to have affected most literate societies. It appears in aggravated form (bibliophobia compounded by pyromania) in the person of the book burner. If he burns only his own books (and takes certain elementary precautions against the spread of fire) he is harmless. If he tries to persuade me to burn my books he is, at worst, annoying. But when he tries to burn my books, without my consent, he had better have some good reasons.

For book burner read censor. The analogy holds. If he is afraid of a book, he need not read it. If he is ready for a good argument, he can try to persuade me not to read it. But when he tells me (and others) what I am and am not permitted to read, he moves into a very sensitive area. There is a heavy burden of proof on him—or should be.

I stand in reluctant admiration of the smooth way in which the censorious have brought about a reversal of this burden of proof. They have managed to get laws enacted which require the rest of

[2] From an article by John Henry Merryman, a member of the law faculty of Stanford University. *Stanford Today*. p 14-17. Autumn '66. Reprinted from *Stanford Today*, Autumn 1966, Series 1, No. 17, with the permission of the publishers, Stanford University.

us to prove that the books they want to suppress have "literary value" or "redeeming social importance" or some similar pretentiousness. Those of us who can take our books or leave them alone are compelled to defend our choices. The burden of proof has moved mysteriously, to us.

Eventually these laws work their way through the courts. Some are declared unconstitutional; others are held valid, and then the courts face the hopeless task of application. In the process of applying an incogitant statute to a concrete situation, a justifiably puzzled judge cannot expect to look his best. The opinions in censorship cases are, on the whole, a sorry lot. How could they be otherwise?

Let us consider a particularly interesting class of bibliophobia—the perennial fear of dirty books. Here the authority of the state, in the form of obscenity laws, is squarely behind the censorious. There are three groups of questions which must be answered in any balanced appraisal of such censorship in the United States.

The first group might be summed up this way: What is there to fear? If there is any rational basis for the fear of obscenity it must be the assumption that what people read influences them toward socially undesirable behavior. This is an easy assumption to make, but the advocates of censorship have yet to produce any evidence which gives convincing objective support to it. There is more persuasive evidence to the effect that no such relation exists. Studies of juvenile delinquency show that those who get into trouble, and are the greatest concern of the advocates of censorship, are far less inclined to read than those who do not become delinquent. Sheldon and Eleanor Glueck, who are among the country's leading authorities on the causes of juvenile delinquency, list approximately ninety factors that might lead to or explain delinquent behavior. Reading matter is not one of these.

Impressive empirical evidence *against* a causal relation between reading and action is provided by those who seem most certain that it exists. What censor, what activist in the cause of increased governmental control of dirty books, after steeping himself in obscenity in the line of duty, has consequently become a sex criminal? Yet these are the people who affirm most confidently that the word leads inevitably to the deed.

A strong argument can be made to the effect that those who favor censorship have reversed cause and effect. The fact that sex maniacs read pornography does not mean that they became what they are because of their reading, but that their reading became what it is because of them. Their personalities probably were basically formed before they learned to read. Reading does not create the appetite, it feeds it, whether the reader be sex criminal or compulsive censor.

What Loss to Society?

A second group of questions has to do with the loss to society, if any, if dirty books are censored. The point of view that there is no loss has been clearly put by Mr. Justice Brennan of the United States Supreme Court in the Roth case. "Obscenity," he said, "is utterly without redeeming social importance."

We are entitled to ask whether the state can ever be allowed to make this kind of judgment. Some would argue that freedom of expression means little if those who govern are allowed to suppress what they deem to be "socially unimportant." Mr. Justice Brennan appears to believe that he knows social unimportance when he sees it, but others are not so sure. How can one predict the effect on society of suppressing what now may seem utterly useless? Lacking prescience, one can only guess. And this, in the words of Mr. Justice Black, dissenting in the Ginzburg case, "is a dangerous technique for government to utilize in determining whether a man stays in or out of the penitentiary."

Why should a different set of standards apply to discussions or portrayals of sexual matters? We rightly tolerate a full range of discussion of science, politics, economics, and many other subjects, regardless of how banal, whether of demonstrable benefit to society or not. The potential for social harm is at least as great in those fields. Given the startling discoveries of the past fifty years concerning the role of sex in human behavior can we confidently say that sex is socially less important than politics?

But the matter need not rest here. Reputable psychiatrists believe that aggressions and frustrations that might otherwise lead to violence are dissipated by reading. According to this theory obscenity provides readers with an outlet for feelings and emotions that could otherwise express themselves in the form of antisocial behavior. This observation is fortified by the evidence previously mentioned that delinquency is concentrated among the group who do very little reading. It is possible that those who do read dirty books would be delinquent if they did not. In this way, obscenity may, indeed, have redeeming social importance.

The third group of questions concerns the appropriateness of legal controls. Let us assume that dirty books are a serious social problem; does it follow that the law should try to control them? Those who move easily from premise to conclusion ignore the inherent limitations of the legal process, and they fail to count the social cost of ill-advised legislation. Consider these factors:

The record of censors is, on the whole, bad. As Mr. Justice Douglas said, in his dissent in the Roth case: "If experience in this field teaches anything, it is that censorship of obscenity has almost always been both irrational and indiscriminate." [See "The Legal Testing of Obscenity" in Section II, below—Ed.] One need only scan a list of books censored as obscene in the United States in the past few years to make the point. There are several reasons why we can predict similar performances for the future.

It has been suggested that the paranoid personality is drawn to censorship. This is too hard, but the psychology of censorship *is* a curious thing. The demand for censorship does not come from persons who wish their own morals protected. Censorship, in the words of Goodwin Watson, "represents the White Soul's Burden." The censorious want to save the rest of us, not by persuasion, but by imposition. They are zealous, self-righteous missionaries in the service of a militant faith. However carefully and temperately a law is drawn its enforcement will come into their intemperate hands. They are the ones who care.

Balance aside, how qualified is the typical censor? The post of censor is not likely to attract the individual with the kind of literary training and ability that will make it possible for him to judge books in the proper context. Few censors are really prepared to do their job well. . . .

But even if he is balanced and qualified the censor can be expected to abuse his office. The function of a censor is, after all, to censor. He has a professional interest in finding things to suppress. His career depends on the record he makes. When in doubt he will err on the side of the angels. The greater outcry would come from his constituency if he let a dirty book slip through than if he suppressed a safe one. The pressure is, inevitably, in the direction of overcensorship.

The Effect of Censorship Laws

Since obscenity as a legal term bears no meaning, the operation of censoring laws is bound to be varying, perverse, and unpredictable. One man's sex is another man's obscenity, and there is no objective standard against which to measure. Censors and judges, like the rest of us, lack the ability to apply such terms objectively or consistently. Thus laws and judicial decisions in the obscenity area produce legal uncertainty and social insecurity.

Law enforcement in disregard of individual rights is a major civil liberties problem in the United States. One effect of censorship laws has been to increase the opportunities for this kind of abuse. Policemen, taking advantage of the law's vagueness, can use the threat of prosecution as a means of coercing citizens who are confused about their rights, who wish to avoid the undesirable aspects of prosecution or who are, as so many are, dependent on the tolerance of officials for their continued business existence. Official censorship can easily be used repressively even though the forms of legal procedure are observed, since these cases never come to court.

Censorship laws also provide opportunities for private persons and groups to force their own standards on the community. Some church-derived groups, in particular, have used police pressure and threats of prosecution as weapons against bookdealers, distributors, and publishers, even when the publications in question probably are not legally obscene. This is clearly wrong. The right of such groups to urge their position is unquestioned, but they have no right to abuse the law to achieve their ends. The inherent irrationality and uncertainty of antiobscenity laws makes such abuse possible.

The problems created by censorship, although on a smaller scale, are similar to those created for the nation under prohibition. The demand for pornography exists, is substantial, and is met by bootleggers. The law does not successfully limit their activity. It merely determines the channels that activity will follow. Meanwhile the illegality of allegedly obscene publications adds to their glamour, creates a criminal subgroup which exploits them, and otherwise actually magnifies rather than diminishes the problem it is supposed to control.

But while censorship makes money for the pornographer and the opportunists and criminals who exploit his works, it has a debasing and distorting effect on the work of art. A book which has been banned is subsequently approached with curiosity focused on its wickedness, and its value as literature suffers. A sort of Gresham's Law operates where the censor is active. As bad money drives out good, so trash fills the vacuum when honest works of art are driven out or degraded by censorship.

At bottom our reaction to obscenity is a complex, subjective thing based in part on taste, morality, and religion. Are these matters ideally suited to legal control, or are they better left to the family, the school, and the church? Does not the existence of these laws tend to justify us in abdicating our responsibilities as parents and teachers? An excellent judge has said, in discussing Faulkner's *Sanctuary* and Caldwell's *God's Little Acre:*

> It will be asked whether one would care to have one's young daughter read these books. I suppose that by the time she is old enough to wish to read them she will have learned the facts of biologic life and the words that go with them. I should prefer to have my own three daughters meet the facts of life and the literature of the world in my library than behind a neighbor's barn, for I can face the adversary there directly. If the young ladies are appalled by what they read they can close the book at the bottom of page one; if they read further they will learn what is in the world and in its people, and no parents who have been discerning with their children need fear the outcome.

What Can Be Done?

Thus logic and experience contradict the censorious on every point: on causation, on the social value of obscenity, and on the wisdom and effect of censorship legislation. I am not the first to point this out. The book burners are clearly and decisively refuted in every forum in which reason governs, yet they march serenely on. What can be done?

First, we should insist on the obvious but often ignored distinction between criticism and censorship. The critic of dirty books who seeks to persuade others to alter their reading habits is exercising his constitutional right to free expression. He is operating competitively in the marketplace of ideas in the best American tradition. But censorship is the reverse of the free marketplace; it is state control over ideas.

Once we see this distinction clearly we can set about restoring the burden of proof to those who advocate censorship. We can insist, before we approve state intervention in the realm of ideas, that those who would repress dirty books prove three things: (1) that there is a genuine prospect that such books will lead to socially undesirable behavior; (2) that little or nothing of social value will be lost by their repression; and (3) that the method of legal control advocated is not likely to cause more social harm than it will prevent. When that case is made, all of us should join in the campaign for censorship. Until that case is made, all of us should restrict ourselves to criticism. We should try to influence others in their choice of reading matter, but we should resist laws that would deprive them (and us) of the power to choose.

Mr. Justice Stewart, dissenting in the Ginzburg case, said, "Censorship reflects a society's lack of confidence in itself. It is a hallmark of an authoritarian regime." I would put it in a slightly different way. In a free society a citizen has the power to choose, and bears responsibility for the choices he makes. Censorship laws deprive us of choice and responsibility. They diminish us, and they diminish our society.

A NEW DEFINITION OF OBSCENITY [3]

It was no accident that one of the issues in the presidential campaign [of 1964] was the "breakdown" of morality and the "de-

[3] From "Toward a New Definition of Obscenity," by Howard Moody, minister of the Judson Memorial Church in New York City. *Christianity and Crisis.* 24:284-8. Ja. 25, '65. Reprinted by permission.

terioration of decency." We are obviously in the midst of what is simultaneously a moral and an artistic revolution, and it is usually difficult to tell where one leaves off and the other begins....

In the last few years slick paper sex magazines like Ralph Ginzburg's *Eros*, as well as classics like *Fanny Hill*, have been banned and unbanned with disarming regularity. More recently the new wave of off-beat film makers experimenting with weird and strange themes have been arrested and their films banned from public places. Everything from topless bathing suits for women to bottomless bathing suits for men . . . are subjects for legal action. . . .

Though the Puritans have often been blamed for "blue laws" and censorship, they actually were a great deal freer than they are often given credit for. . . . As a matter of fact, our first antiobscenity law did not come into existence until the nineteenth century. Our forefathers, the Revolutionists and fashioners of the Constitution, did not seem so concerned with obscenity or pornography (and don't think there wasn't plenty around . . .). Their concern is contained in the words of the First Amendment about Congress making no law abridging freedom of speech, religion and the press. The real beginning of censorship—the establishment of prudery by legal sanctions—was the work not of Puritans and Pilgrims but of nineteenth century Protestants. . . .

Since the higher courts keep refusing to make irrevocably clear what is obscene, censors are driven to vigilante tactics that are extralegal, highly undemocratic and probably unconstitutional. Self-appointed citizens' clean-books councils are springing up all over the country. Their tactics are intimidation, and their appeals are sloganeering. Operating under the very appealing objective of "keeping filth and smut from our children," they move on to cleaning from libraries such books as *Brave New World*, *Black Boy*, *Catcher in the Rye* and others. . . . The question that comes to the Church and to individual Christians at this point is what should be *our* posture in the midst of these revolutions? . . .

At least two of the important grounds for censorship are "dirty words" and "sexual subjects." Relative to the matter of vulgar language, what righteous indignation can we Christians muster about our Anglo-Saxon forebears? Can we really pretend that the use of "coarse" and "vulgar" words is somehow tantamount to an affront to God Almighty? (Do we have to be so ashamed of the "bawdy" talk of Martin Luther?) Vulgar speech and four-letter words are not blasphemous or immoral, and our shame and prudery over them are basically class matters. (Even the derivation of the word *lewd* is interestingly traced to a *lewdefrere,* a lay brother; unlearned, unlettered, rude, artless, belonging to lower orders.) Vulgar and bawdy language may well be objected to on the basis of esthetics and social manners, but it is hardly justifiable to make a moral or theological case against raw language as the Church has tended to do. . . .

The true profanity against God is to refuse to take him seriously; the truly "dirty" word is the one used to deny and to denigrate the humanness of another person. Language is symbolic, not literal; when a person speaks in raw language he may be trying to say something that nice and prosaic words will not communicate. My point here is that, from a theological or ethical perspective, "dirty words" are a terribly inadequate base from which to write a definition of obscenity.

In the same way, we do not do justice to the Christian perspective upon human evil and immorality if we see *sex* as the dominant and determinative factor in the judgment of what is obscene. Sex, by our understanding of creation, is vital and a potent force in human behavior, though shot through with human sin and distortion. To make sex the sole determinative factor in defining "obscenity" or "pornography" or "filth" is to relegate it to the shadowy regions of immorality (depending on who says it in what community and how much). This completely fails to explain what all Christian faith and tradition teaches us is really *obscene* in this world.

For Christians the truly obscene ought not to be slick paper nudity, nor the vulgarities of dirty old or young literati. . . . What is obscene is that material, whether sexual or not, that has as its basic motivation and purpose the degradation, debasement and dehumanizing of persons. The dirtiest word in the English language is . . . the word *nigger* from the sneering lips of a Bull Connor. Obscenity ought to be much closer to the biblical definition of blasphemy against God and man. . . .

I do not conceive that a picture is "dirty" because sex is its dominant theme. . . . The "lewdest" pictures of all—more obscene than all the tawdry products of the "smut industry"—are the pictures of Dachau, the ovens, and the grotesque pile of human corpses.

A New Christian Definition

Let us as Christians write a new definition of obscenity based on the dehumanizing aspects of our contemporary culture. Can we not see the hypocrisy of our prudery when we spend time, words and money trying to prevent the magazine *Eros* from going through the mails and never raise an eyebrow about the tons of material that vilify human beings and consign whole ethnic groups to the lowest kind of animality? Do we not have to admit the duplicity that allows our police to *guard* George Lincoln Rockwell as he mouths blasphemous obscenities of the most inhuman order on public streets, while the same police are used to *harass* Lenny Bruce in the confines of a night club while he vulgarly satirizes our human hypocrisies?

Should we not, as Christians, raise a new standard of "obscenity" not obsessed with sex and vulgar language, but defined rather as that material which has as its dominant theme and purpose the debasement and depreciation of human beings—their worth and their dignity. Such a definition might include some material dealing with sex but this would be a minor aspect of pornography. The "words" that would offend us and from which we want our young protected would not be "Anglo-Saxon" but English, French, German, which carried within their etymology and meaning outrages against human individuals and groups.

The pornographic pictures would be those that showed humans being violated, destroyed, physically beaten. . . .

All the resources of our Christian teaching and tradition, all the theological armament in the Church could be called up in the warfare against "the new obscenity." The significant concomitant of this is that it would lessen the distortion and perversion of sex in our society that the present definition of obscenity has created. A further advantage to this new understanding would be that the Church and many literary critics would be saved the embarrassment of having to defend every mediocre form of literature and art against the wild attacks of the book-banners. . . .

If it is asserted that this position skirts dangerously close to "license" and the accompanying breakdown of moral order, I can only reply that it is one of the hard truths of Christian tradition that we have been released to a freedom whose burden is a terrible risk. This freedom of the Christian man has already sent Christians in our time against the law to prison and even to death. With this new definition of obscenity we will run a risk by allowing our children and ourselves to see "obscene pictures" of the instant destruction of 200,000 persons at Hiroshima with one bomb—the risk that we may come to accept this as a natural and realistic way of solving conflicts between men and nations.

This is a real danger, but the alternative is mental slavery, a restricted thought process, a closed society. Consequently, in the battles of censorship in a pluralistic society, Christians may find themselves coming down regularly against the inroads of censorship at the risk of being called licentious and immoral.

It may be, as some politicians claimed in the past campaign, that this nation is in a state of moral decadence. If so, I am convinced that the evidence of this is not to be found in salacious literature, erotic art or obscene films but in the "soul-rot" that comes from the moral hypocrisy of straining at the gnat of sexuality and swallowing the camel of human deterioration and destruction.

PORNOGRAPHY OR PRIVACY [4]

Despite all the lyric or obsessed cant about the boundless varieties and dynamics of sex, the actual sum of possible gestures, consummations, and imaginings is drastically limited. . . . This is the obvious, necessary reason for the inescapable monotony of pornographic writing. . . .

[4] From "Night Words," by George Steiner, professor of humanities at New York University, writer and critic. *Encounter*. 25:14-19. O. '65. Reprinted by permission.

Above the pulp line—but the exact boundaries are impossible to draw—lies the world of erotica, of sexual writing with literary pretensions or genuine claims. This world is much larger than is commonly realized. It goes back to Egyptian literary papyri. At certain moments in Western society, the amount of "high pornography" being produced may have equaled, if not surpassed, ordinary *belles-lettres*. . . .

Obviously a certain proportion of this vast body of writing has literary power and significance. Where a Diderot, a Crébillon *fils*, a Verlaine, a Swinburne, or an Apollinaire write erotica, the result will have some of the qualities which distinguish their more public works. . . . Nevertheless, with very few exceptions, "high pornography" is *not* of pre-eminent literary importance. It is simply *not* true that the locked cabinets of great libraries or private collections contain masterpieces of poetry or fiction which hypocrisy and censorship banish from the light. . . . What emerges when one reads some of the classics of erotica is the fact that they too are intensely conventionalized, that their repertoire of fantasy is limited, and that it merges, almost imperceptibly, into the dream-trash of straight, mass-produced pornography. . . .

The plain truth is that in literary erotica as well as in the great mass of "dirty books" the same stimuli, the same contortions and fantasies, occur over and over with unutterable monotony. In most erotic writing . . . the imagination turns, time and time again, inside the bounded circle of what the body can experience. . . .

What needs a serious look is the assertion about freedom, about a new and transforming liberation of literature through the abolition of verbal and imaginative taboos. . . . Censorship is stupid and repugnant for two empirical reasons: censors are men no better than ourselves, their judgments are no less fallible or open to dishonesty. Secondly, the thing won't work: those who really want to get hold of a book will do so somehow. This is an entirely different argument from saying that pornography doesn't in fact deprave the mind of the reader, or incite to wasteful or criminal gestures. *It may, or it may not.* We simply don't have enough evidence either way. The question is far more intricate than many of our literary champions of total freedom would allow. But to say that censorship won't work and should not be asked to, is *not* to say that there has been a liberation of literature, that the writer is, in any genuine sense, freer.

On the contrary. The sensibility of the writer is free where it is most humane, where it seeks to apprehend and reenact the marvelous variety, complication, and resilience of life by means of words as scrupulous, as personal, as brimful of the mystery of human communication, as the language can yield. The very opposite of freedom is *cliché,* and nothing is less free, more inert with convention and hollow brutality than a row of four-letter words. Literature is a living dialogue between writer and reader only if the writer shows a twofold respect: for the imaginative maturity of his reader, and in a very complex but central way, for the wholeness, for the independence and quick of life, in the personages he creates.

Respect for the Reader

Respect for the reader signifies that the poet or novelist invites the consciousness of the reader to collaborate with his own in the act of presentment. He does not tell all because his work is not a primer for children or the retarded. He does not exhaust the possible responses of his reader's own imaginings, but delights in the fact that we will fill in from our own lives, from resources of memory and desire proper to ourselves, the contours he has drawn. Tolstoy is infinitely freer, infinitely more exciting than the new eroticists, when he arrests his narrative at the door of the Karenins' bedroom, when he merely initiates, through the simile of a dying flame, of ash cooling in the grate, a perception of sexual defeat which each of us can relive or detail for himself. George Eliot is free, and treats her readers as free, adult human beings, when she conveys, through inflection of style and mood, the truth about the Casaubon honeymoon in *Middlemarch,* when she makes us imagine for ourselves how Dorothea has been violated by some essential obtuseness. These are profoundly exciting scenes, these enrich and complicate our sexual awareness. . . . There is no real freedom whatever in the compulsive physiological exactitudes of present "high pornography," because there is no respect for the reader whose imaginative means are set at nil.

And there is none for the sanctity of autonomous life in the characters of the novel, for that tenacious integrity of existence which makes a Stendhal, a Tolstoy, a Henry James tread warily around their own creations. The novels being produced under the new code of total statement shout at their personages, strip, fornicate, perform this or that act of sexual perversion. So did the S.S. guards at rows of living men and women. The total attitudes are not, I think, entirely distinct. There may be deeper affinities than we as yet understand between the "total freedom" of the uncensored erotic imagination and the total freedom of the sadist. . . .

Respect for Privacy

Sexual relations are, or should be, one of the citadels of privacy, the nightplace where we must be allowed to gather the splintered, harried elements of our consciousness to some kind of inviolate order and repose. It is in sexual experience that . . . two human beings in that attempt at total communication which is also communion, can discover the unique bent of their identity. . . .

The new pornographers subvert this last, vital privacy; they do our imagining for us. They take away the words that were of the night and shout them over the rooftops, making them hollow. The images of our love-making, the stammerings we resort to in intimacy, come prepackaged. . . . Sexual life, particularly in America, is passing more and more into the public domain. This is a profoundly ugly and demeaning thing whose effects on our identity and resources of feeling we understand as little as we do the impact on our nerves of the perpetual "suberoticism" and sexual suggestion of modern advertisement. . . .

Because there were words it did not use, situations it did not represent graphically, because it demanded from the reader not obeisance but live echo, much of Western poetry and fiction has been a school to the imagination, an exercise in making one's awareness more exact, more humane. My true quarrel with . . . [the new *genre* of erotica] is not that so much of the stuff should be boring and abjectly written. It is that these books leave a man less free, less himself than they found him; that they leave language poorer, less endowed with a capacity for fresh discrimination and excitement. It is not a new freedom that they bring, but a new servitude.

CHRISTIANITY AND PORNOGRAPHY [5]

Sex is the bugaboo of Christianity. Other religions and their cultures can take men and women as they are, separate and distinct, male and female, but joyous in union. Hinduism, for instance, the father of most contemporary important religions, the religion which has survived longer than any other, is not ashamed to depict the most intimate relationships between men and women on its temple walls (pictures of which are smuggled into this country and sold at exorbitant prices as pornography). Ancient Hellas, father of our own culture, origin of our drama, art, science, philosophy and most of our Christianity, depicted its gods and goddesses in the most lascivious of encounters, and its chief god, Zeus, was depicted as the supreme lecher of all time. Even contemporary Islam depicts Paradise as a place of the most delicious carnal delights. And it is interesting to note how popular and what prominent place in our bookstores is given to the Hindu, Greek and Islamic "classics"—manuals on sexual maneuvers (a religious part of these cultures but sold as pornography here)....

Christianity has been the one religion which could not let sex have its own common everyday importance among men and women....

If religion is anything (and by etymology this *is* its meaning) it is that one common endeavor which men use to bring themselves into a natural and orderly relationship with their fellow man and with their environment. And so it is disturbing that one of the two or three basic human drives should be eliminated as a continuing suitable topic for open discussion in our churches. Instead of quoting St. Paul as such an omniscient eternal authority, there should be at least an occasional reference to the theories of Sigmund Freud, and some continuing reference made to the change and development of these theories.

[5] From "The Persistence of Pornography," by Joseph A. Schneiders, minister of the First Unitarian Church of South Bend, Ind. *Crane Review*. 8:118-24. Spring '66. Reprinted by permission.

A Place for Pornography

But our specific subject is pornography. Like most bad words in our culture—atheism, communism, socialism—pornography is a relativism. It is pornographic in the state of Mississippi in the United States to show a white man shaking hands with a Negro man on a public billboard—while in India it is not pornographic but religious to portray all kinds of (what we call) sexual deviations in temple sculpture. The Rev. Dr. Israel R. Margolies told his congregation in the People's Temple in New York City this recently when a few clergymen put on a campaign against pornography: "Far more children are damaged by the inhuman conditions in which they are compelled to live than by any pornographic material to which they are exposed." He called slums worse than smut. (And so—the only clergyman or social reformer with whom I will engage in a discussion over the ill effects of pornography is one who is willing, also, to work by my side with equal intensity at the elimination of illiteracy, war, poverty, disease, segregation and other *proven* cripplers of children's minds and bodies.)

Few would advocate that the mere, lurid so-called obscenities be forced upon children, even though there is no proof that the healthy child is ever hurt by them. The Hindu child taken to the temple at an early age, does not necessarily become a sex pervert because he is exposed to a complete range of "deviant" practices depicted vividly on temple walls. Also, there *are* studies made in America which indicate that the healthy child is not seriously affected by being exposed to the pornographic language and art of our society. It has been legally established that criteria of what is or should be acceptable within our society are to be determined not by the weaknesses of the sick but the strengths of the healthy. (Do we prevent the sale or use of alcohol—despite the increasing number of alcoholics?) By using illness as the determinant, the normative factor, we aggravate the illness—to be explicit, to make such a to-do over pornography is to make a societal value judgment which says that those who do not regard such materials as evil are evil themselves, and by extension to create even greater feelings of worthlessness, of guilt within those who already have sensitively responded to our culture's preconditioning that this is so. The person who is already imbued with severe guilt feelings because he has been unable correctly to evaluate or interpret his sex urgings, must necessarily have increased feelings of guilt when he is exposed to all this judicial and clergy activity.

Nor is it desirable to deny to otherwise normal and societally acceptable men and women their right to fulfill the visually or literarily stimulated erotic needs which so many men and women within our society obviously have—or why is pornography such a profitable business? In fact, there is a fairly large and responsible body of psychologists who maintain that pornography actually is a social good, that it drains off and uses up energies which might otherwise be manifested in many persons by violence and force. One of our great problems today, divorce, as any counselor knows is largely the result of the ultimate clash between fantasy and reality. Sex in our society is always portrayed without its "sweat, blood and tears." It is the sweat, blood and tears of sex which we call pornography or obscenity. If our children were exposed to this reality sooner, certainly much sooner than the inevitable confrontation in marriage, is it not possible they might be prepared for reality and not expect the fantasy—and marriage would be much more successful?

The Church and Pornography

In summary then I suggest the following.

First, all censorship should be opposed because there is never any guarantee that once it is made a tool of society it won't be used to suppress *all* unpopular ideas within that society. And this includes censorship of so-called pornography which is a simplistic approach to the problem (if it is a true problem). Rather than removing these materials from the surface of society (where there is at least some minimal control) and driving them underground (where there is no control) a more fruitful approach would be to make honest attempts at scientific analysis to determine quantitatively and qualitatively the needs and the effects of pornography. For instance, it would be interesting to know the kind or kinds of persons who need it, how deeply the need is felt, the effects resulting from the suppression of the need, and actually how many needs it represents.

(Even a cursory examination of pornographic materials, so-called, reveals that this represents not a single category, but that it is a generic term which covers several different categories.) Pornography, like alcoholism, may represent the best adjustment which the individual can make to the psychological and biological tensions of his society; as with alcoholism, its removal may uncover a deep otherwise unadjustable mental illness.

The censorship of pornography provides a too easy focus of so-called religious involvement and a too obvious goal of supposed social reform. Clergymen and social reformers can expectedly energize themselves and their followers against this minor target (of pornography) whose ill-effects are exaggerated and unproven, while ignoring the larger and indisputable evils of disease, war, poverty, illiteracy and segregation.

In addition we can legitimately suspect the motives of the Comstocks who are willing to submerge themselves in all this "filth" in order to act as guardians for the rest of the community. An interesting corollary of this is how these guardians of our morals create pornography out of materials which are not pornographic (as an example, the California group which distributed a list of all the dirty words which were found in a reference book . . .).

It is true that pornography is a possible evil in a true religious sense if and when it becomes the only outlet for sexual energies, when it debases sex into an "I-It" relationship, making the other person, other persons, or one's self an object merely to be used. But if the churches were doing their designated job—that of showing men and women how to live effective and meaningful lives—then they would be devoting a major portion of their time and efforts to this prime concern and energy of men and women, would be teaching us how most effectively to manifest its language and to develop its energy so that our sexual relationships would be "I-Thou" relationships, for an "I-Thou" relationship is the optimal definition of love, and love is what religion is all about (or should be).

In other words, pornography *is* bad—when and if it inhibits or becomes a substitute for, the rich fulfilling experience of true sexual love. This is the only concern churches should show about pornography. It *is* the task of the churches to show us how to transform "I-It" relationships into "I-Thou" relationships. It *is* they who can do something realistic about the persistence of pornography; not as they have been doing and are doing—by trying to eliminate it as a manifestation of something evil—but by trying to understand and transform its basic energies so that men and women will be able creatively to use these energies in that perhaps highest of all human experiences and human potential—human love.

3. *The Case Against Pornography*

ON BEHALF OF CENSORS [6]

Pornography is like a squalid, unnecessary little country which owes its independence to a vagary of history. But, though pornography is seldom of much importance, it may be of considerable interest, for to talk about it is unavoidably to talk about the Great Powers adjacent to it. Pornography speaks the language of Art; in recent centuries it has come within the sphere of influence of the Law; Psychology and Morals have vested interests in it. Moreover, occasionally pornography becomes genuinely important—when it is used as a seat of operations by the erotic nihilists who would like to destroy every sort of social and moral law and who devote their effective energies to subverting society as such. One who undertakes to discuss pornography finds himself, willy-nilly, falling back upon some of his ultimate positions in matters esthetic, social, psychological, ethical. If a reader agrees with these opinions, he is likely to view them as principles; if he disagrees, prejudices. Here are some of mine.

Before plunging ahead, I had better indicate two mutually antagonistic dispositions, one liberal, the other conservative, in my opinions on pornography. On the one hand, I favor the liberal view that the less power the state and the police have over us private citizens the better, that the less the state concerns itself with the individual's thoughts, entertainments, and sexual actions the

[6] From "Against Pornography," by George P. Elliott, novelist and former teacher at the Writers' Workshop, the State University of Iowa. *Harper's Magazine*. 230:51-60. Mr. '65. Copyright © 1965, by Harper's Magazine, Inc. Reprinted from the March, 1965 issue of *Harper's Magazine* by permission of the author.

better, and that we should do what we can to keep from drifting toward totalitarianism. In other words, let us have no censorship because it strengthens the state, which is already too strong. Also let us have none because most of the things that in fact get censored are less harmful than some of the things that do not—for example, large-circulation newspapers and magazines.

Society is harmed far less by the free circulation of a book like *Fanny Hill* than it is by routine and accepted practices of the daily sensationalist press: let a man inherit ten million dollars, pour acid on his wife, or win a Nobel Prize, and reporter and photographer are made to intrude upon him and his family and then to exhibit to public view in as gross a manner as possible his follies, shames, or just plain private affairs. Such invasions of privacy are not only allowed, they are allowed for the purpose of letting the public enjoy these same invasions vicariously, all in the name of freedom of the press. I believe that this accepted practice has done more damage to society as a whole and to its citizens individually than massive doses of the most depraved pornography could ever do. So much for my liberal views.

On the other hand, I favor the conservative view that pornography exists among us and is a social evil, though a small one. That is, in a good society of any sort I can imagine—not some daydream utopia where man is impossibly restored to sexual innocence but a society populated with recognizable, imperfectible men—in a good society there would be active opposition to pornography, which is to say, considerable firmness in the drawing of lines beyond which actions, words, and images are regarded as indecent. Furthermore, the opinion that pornography should not be restrained I regard as being commonly a symptom of doctrinaire liberalism and occasionally an evidence of destructive nihilism.

A liberal suspicion of censorship and a conservative dislike of pornography are not very compatible. Some sort of compromise is necessary if they are to live together. Their marriage will never be without tensions, but maybe the quarrel between them can be patched up well enough for practical purposes....

Pornography is the representation of directly or indirectly erotic acts with an intrusive vividness which offends decency without esthetic justification. Obviously this definition does not just describe but also judges; quite as obviously it contains terms that need pinning down—decency, for example. But pornography is not at all a matter for scientific treatment. Like various other areas of sexual behavior in which society takes an unsteady, wary interest—homosexuality, for example, or fornication or nudity—pornography is relative, an ambiguous matter of personal taste and the consensus of opinion. The grounds for this definition are psychological, esthetic, and political.

The Criterion of Distance

Psychologically, pornography is not offensive because it excites sexual desire; desire as such is a fine thing, and there are happy times and places when desire should be excited and gratified freely and fully; moreover, even in inappropriate times and places there is plenty of free-floating desire abroad in the world; it doesn't take pornography to excite excesses of desire among young men and women. Nor is pornography offensive because, in its perverted and scatological versions, it excites disgust; in the proper context disgust serves the useful function of turning us from the harmful. Psychologically, the trouble with pornography is that, in our culture at least, it offends the sense of separateness, of individuality, of privacy; it intrudes upon the rights of others....

Pornography also raises esthetic questions, since it exists only in art—in painting, literature, sculpture, photography, theater—and my definition implies that it is offensive esthetically. The central esthetic issue is not whether certain subjects and words should be taboo but what distance should be maintained between spectator and subject. Because of our desire to withdraw from a man performing private acts and our doubly strong desire to withdraw from a man performing acts which are not only private but also disagreeable or perverted, we wish esthetically to remain at a certain distance from such acts when they are represented in art. Nothing whatever in human experience should, as such, be excluded from consideration in a work of art: not Judas betraying Christ nor naked starved Jews crowded by Nazi soldiers into a gas chamber nor a child locked by his parents in a dark closet for months till he goes mad nor a man paying a whore to lash him with barbed wire for his sexual relief nor even husband and wife making love.

Nothing human is alien to art. The question is only, how close? But the criterion of distance is an extremely tricky one. Esthetically, one good way to keep a spectator at a distance from the experience represented by an image is to make the image artificial, stylized, not like us. If it is sufficiently stylized, it may be vivid and detailed and still keep a proper distance from the viewer. One would normally feel uneasy at being with a lot of men, women, and children engaged in every imaginable form of pleasurable erotic activity. Yet the vivid throngs of erotic statues on certain Indian temples create in the viewer no uneasiness but are simply delightful to look at. The viewer is kept at a considerable remove by the impossible poses and expressions of the statues; he cannot identify with the persons performing the acts. For the statues do not represent lustful, passionate, guilty, self-conscious, confused people like you and me, but pure beings to whom all things are pure, paradisal folk who are expressing their joy in generation and the body by erotic acts: these are stylized artifices of blessedness. . . .

The Erotic Used—and Misused

There is a special problem raised by realism, because it aims to present people as they actually are. How can a realistic artist be true to his subject if he is forbidden direct access to an area of human behavior which is of considerable importance? The esthetic problem is for the realistic artist to represent these actions in such a way as to lead to understanding of the characters without arousing disgust against them or a prurient interest in their activities. When he can accomplish this very difficult feat, then he is justified in including in a realistic work of art representations that would otherwise be pornographic. . . .

The esthetic problem has been stated succinctly by Jean Genet. As a professed immoralist and enemy of society, he has no compunction about using pornography and in fact he once made a pornographic movie. But as a writer, he has this to say about his art (in an interview in *Playboy* magazine for April 1964): "I now think that if my books arouse readers sexually, they're badly written, because the poetic emotion should be so strong that no reader is moved sexually. In so far as my books are pornographic, I don't reject them. I simply say that I lacked grace."

Nothing said thus far would justify legal suppression, official censorship. The effect of pornography in a work of art is esthetically bad, but it is no business of the state to suppress bad art. The effect of pornography on an individual psyche is that of an assault, ranging in severity from the equivalent of a mere pinch to that of an open cut; but in the normal course of things one can avoid such assaults without much trouble, and besides the wounds they make are seldom very severe one by one, though they may be cumulatively.

To be sure, there are people who want and need pornography just as there are those who want and need heroin, but such a secret indulgence is not in itself socially dangerous. Here again, the state has no business intruding: a man's soul is his own to pollute if he wishes, and it is not for the state to say, "Be thou clean, be thou healthy, close the bathroom door behind you." It is only when pornography becomes public that, like dope, it takes on a sufficiently political cast for censorship even to be considered. It is unlike dope in that it sometimes acquires political overtones by being used ideologically, when put in the service of nihilism. But in one important respect it is like dope: it usually becomes public by being offered for sale, especially to the young.

Sell It Under the Counter

The classic example of pornography is a filthy picture: it is ugly; it is sold and displayed surreptitiously; it allows the viewer to intrude vicariously upon the privacy of others; it shows two or more men and women posing for money in front of a camera, in attitudes which sexual desire alone would lead them to assume in private if at all. An adult looking at such a picture is roused to an excitement which may lead either to revulsion or to satisfaction, but whatever his reaction, he should be left alone to decide for himself whether he wants to repeat the experience. The state has no legitimate political concern with his private vices. But the effect on young people of such a picture, and especially of a steady diet of such pictures, is another matter. A common argument against allowing young people to have unrestricted access to pornography runs somewhat as follows.

About sex the young are curious and uncertain and have very powerful feelings. A filthy picture associates sexual acts with ugly, vicarious, and surreptitious pleasure, and helps to cut sex off from love and free joy. At the most, one experience of pornography may have a salutary effect on the curious, uncertain mind of an adolescent. To be shown what has been forbidden might provide him a considerable relief, and if he has feared that he is warped because of his fantasies. he can see how really warped are those who act on such fantasies. Moreover, by his own experience he can learn why pornography is forbidden: experience of it is at once fascinating, displeasing, and an end in itself, that is to say, perverse. However, too many experiences with pornography may encourage the young to turn their fantasies into actions ("in dreams begin responsibilities") or to substitute fantasies for actions, and so may confirm them in bad habits.

Whatever the validity of this argument, it or something like it is the rationale by which our society justifies its strong taboo against exposing children to pornography. For my own part, I would accept the argument as mostly valid. The state has no business legislating virtue; indeed, one of the symptoms of totalitarianism is the persistent attempt of the state not just to punish its citizens for wrongdoing, but to change their nature, to make them what its rulers conceive to be good. But patently the state has the obligation to protect the young against the public acts of the vicious.

This means that, in the matter of the sale and display of pornography, the state, the apparatus of the law, should have two effective policies. It should strictly forbid making pornography accessible to the young: "No One Under 18 Admitted." But as for pornography for adults, the law should rest content with a decent hypocrisy: "Keep it out of the marketplace, sell it under the counter, and the law won't bother you."

An assumption underlying such policies is that a certain amount of official hypocrisy is one of the operative principles of a good society. It is hard to imagine a civilized society which would not disapprove of adultery, for the maintenance of the family as an institution is one of the prime concerns of society, and adultery threatens the family. Yet, on the other hand, imagine living in a country in which the laws against adultery were strictly enforced—the informing, spying, breaking in upon, denouncing, the regiment of self-righteous teetotalers. What is obviously needed here is what we have: unenforced laws. Only an all-or-none zealot fails to distinguish between the deplorable hypocrisy of a man deceiving his neighbors for his own gain and the salutary hypocrisy of a government recognizing the limits beyond which it should not encroach upon its individual citizens. Another assumption underlying these recommendations is that the censorship of simple pornography for adults will never be very effective. There is a steady demand for it, and it is not important enough to prosecute at much expense. The main function of laws against adult pornography is to express disapproval of it.

Clearly the logic of this argument leads to prohibiting certain books and works of art that are now legally available in some parts of the country. For example, in some localities the courts have refused to prohibit the sale of *Fanny Hill.* This refusal seems to me quite irresponsible on any grounds other than a general refusal to censor pornography, for by any meaningful definition *Fanny Hill* is pornographic. Such story as there is in the novel exists for no other purpose than to provide occasions for detailed accounts of sexual encounters, and these accounts are the only passages in the book with power to stir the reader's emotions. The characters are very simple types without intrinsic interest, and Fanny herself is little more than a man's fantasy of female complaisance and sexual competence. The one literary quality which has made the book celebrated is a certain elegance of style; compared to most simple pornography it reads like a masterpiece, but to anyone familiar with eighteenth-century English prose it reads like several other third-rate novels. Surely the world is not in such need of third-rate eighteenth-century English fictional prose as to allow this consideration alone to justify the public sale of a work of sheer pornography. What else would justify its sale is hard to imagine.

To deny that the book is pornographic or to say that its literary value redeems its pornography, is to blur distinctions, and for an august court of law to do so is for the state to abrogate one of its functions. An essential and conservative function of the state is to say, "Thou shalt not," to formulate society's taboos. Unless I am seriously mistaken, in this instance the court, speaking for the state, has refused to draw a clear line which corresponds to society's actual customs. In our culture the place for nudists is in a nudist colony, not on the city streets, and the way to sell books like *Fanny Hill* is under the counter, not over it. In the name of enlightenment and sexual permissiveness, the state is violating an actual taboo, and the reaction to many such violations may very well be a resurgence of that savage fanaticism which burns books and closes theaters. . . .

What to Censor, and Why

The censoring of unquestionable pornography is of little interest; it pretty directly reflects what decent society considers indecent at a given time; it is custom in action. But the censorship of borderline pornography demands discrimination and philosophy, without which censorship can degenerate into puritanical repressiveness of the kind there has been quite enough of during the past two or three centuries.

Thus far, my argument on what to censor and why has led to a legal position which is at least within hailing distance of common practice in the United States now. To purveyors of raw pornography our practice says in effect: bother your neighbors, especially children, and you will be punished; leave others untroubled by your vice and you will be viewed with disapproval by the law but left alone. This attitude is fine till one gets down to cases, but once it is a matter of wording and enforcing a law, the question must be answered: how is one to distinguish between pornographic and decent art? Still, such lines must be drawn if there are to be laws at all, and they must, in the nature of things, be arbitrary. As I see it, a more manageable form of the question is this: who should do the censoring? Whatever the answer to this question may be, whatever the best method of censoring, one thing is clear—our present method is unsatisfactory.

As things stand, an object is banned as pornographic on the judgment of some official in customs or the postal service or else by some police officer prodded by a local zealot. In most cases this judgment presents little difficulty: even civil-liberty extremists who are opposed to all censorship on principle blanch when they are confronted with genuine hard-core pornography, the unarguably warped stuff, the bulk of the trade. But sometimes there is the question of assessing the value of a work of art, and for this task the bureaucrats and policemen who are presently empowered to decide are unqualified.

Should *Fanny Hill* be offered to the public freely? When society has said no for generations and when judges and literary critics cannot agree on the question, it is wrong to allow a police sergeant to decide the matter. If a duly constituted public authority says, "*Fanny Hill* shall not be sold in this state," then the policeman's duty is clear: arrest the man who displays it for sale. But to leave to bureaucrats and policemen the task of making all the delicate discriminations necessary in deciding whether the novel should be censored in the first place, is genuinely irresponsible of society at large and of legislators in particular. To be sure, cases are brought to court. But the laws offer such vague guidance that far too much depends on the quirks of the judge or jury at hand. *No censorship might be preferable to what we have now.*

In fact, a strong case can be made for removing all censorship of pornography. Here are six arguments for abolishing censorship. The first three seem to me valid. (1) No law can be framed so as to provide a clear and sure guide to bureaucrat, policeman, judge, and jury. (2) It is very hard to demonstrate that pornography does in fact injure many people severely, even adolescents, for if the desire to break taboos is satisfied imaginatively, it is less likely to issue in antisocial acts. (3) The less power the state and the police have the better.

There are three further arguments against censorship which are commonly used but which I find less persuasive. (1) Decent citizens can by their very disapproval segregate pornography without assistance from the state. But, in an age as troubled as ours and with so much private indiscipline and theoretical permissiveness in sexual matters, there is little reason to suppose that the moral disapproval of decent citizens would actually stop the public distribution of pornography. (2) It is arguable that some people are rendered socially less dangerous by having their sexual tensions more or less satisfied by pornography, tensions which unrelieved might well lead to much more antisocial acts. True, but pornography, if it is to help those who need and use it, must be outside the law, clearly labeled *shameful;* if society has any respect for them, it will sternly assure them that what they are doing is nasty by passing a law against it, and then will pretty much leave them alone. (3) In the past, censorship has not succeeded in keeping books of literary value from being read but has only attached an unfortunate prurience to the reading of them. But the prurience attached to reading pornography derives less from breaking a law than from violating the taboo which caused the law to come into existence.

There is another argument, more important and erroneous than any of these six, which is commonly advanced in favor of abolishing censorship. It hinges on a mistaken liberal doctrine about the nature of sexual taboos. According to this doctrine, sexual taboos, like fashions in dress, are determined by local custom and have as little to do with morality as the kinds of clothes we wear. However—the argument goes—people frequently mistake these sexual taboos for ethical rules, and pass and enforce laws punishing those who violate the taboos. The result is a reduction of pleasure in sex and an increase of guilt, with an attendant host of psychological and social ills. The obvious solution is to abolish the taboos and so liberate the human spirit from its chief source of oppression and guilt. . . .

[This doctrine] presents a considerable difficulty: by supposing that the potent and obscure emotions surrounding sexual matters derive from unenlightened customs, it holds out the hope that enlightened views can liberate us from those customs so that sex in every form can become healthy and fun for all. This is a cheery, optimistic view, not unlike the sweet hopefulness of the old-fashioned anarchists who thought that all we have to do, in order to attain happiness, is to get rid of governments so we may all express our essentially good nature unrestrained. . . .

Conceivably the First Amendment will be taken literally ("Congress shall make no law . . . abridging the freedom of speech or of the press") and many or all legal restraints against pornography may in fact be removed. But I believe that so far from eliminating sexual taboos, such an official undermining of them would only arouse the puritans to strengthen the bulwarks; the taboos would be made more repressive than ever; and many of the goods of liberalism would be wiped out along with and partly because of this utopian folly. Decent people had better learn now to censor moderately, or the licentiousness released by liberal zealots may arouse their brothers, the puritan zealots, to censorship by fire.

Feasible Restraints

A civilized method of censoring is feasible. One does not have to imagine a utopian system of extirpating pornography through some sexual revolution—an Eden of erotic innocence in which prohibitions will be unnecessary because social relations will be as they should be. In our actual, historical United States, in which perversions and pornography flourish, one can imagine a better method of restraining pornography, which is yet within the framework of our customs and procedures. It would operate somewhat as follows.

All decisions about what is legally pornographic in any of the arts are in the custody of boards of censors. A board is elected or appointed from each of three general categories of citizens: for example, a judge or lawyer of good repute; a professor of art, literature, or one of the humanities; and a social worker, psychologist, or clergyman. These are not exciting categories; but in them, if anywhere, are likely to be found citizens whose own opinions will reflect decent social opinion and who are also capable of making the various discriminations the task calls for. Obviously it is necessary to keep sexual anarchists off the board; just as a person is disqualified from serving as a juror in a murder case if he is against capital punishment, so one would be disqualified from serving on a board of censors if he were against censoring pornography.

A board of censors must never look to a set of rules of thumb for guidance—not, as now, to the quantity of an actress's body that must be covered. Is a burlesque dancer's breast indecent from the nipple down or is it only the nipple itself that offends? That way foolishness lies. Rather, the censors must look only to their own personal experience with a given work of art for only in such experience can art be judged. For this reason, the censors should be people for whom society's taboos are part of themselves, not something in a code external to them. No photograph, drawing, book, stage show, or moving picture is banned by the police except at the instruction of this board. Its decisions, like those of every quasi-official public agency, are subject to appeal to the courts, but the Supreme Court would do all it could to dodge such cases. *The banning is deliberately hypocritical: out of sight out of mind, so long as children are not molested.*

The esthetic and moral principles guiding the board are roughly these: distance and effect. At the distance of a movie close-up, a kiss between husband and wife can be pornographic. If a child and adult are sitting side by side watching a stage performance of a witty Restoration comedy of adultery, they are at altogether different distances from the play, the adult closer than the child; but at a marionette performance of a fairy-tale melodrama they reverse distances, the child closer this time and the adult farther away. As for effect on the spectator, this consideration is only slightly less tricky than distance. The question to be asked is whether a story intrudes on the privacy of its characters in order to give the reader vicarious and perverse sexual excitement or in order to provide him with a sympathetic understanding which he could have got in no other way. These criteria of distance and effect—these rubber yardsticks—apply to the parts as well as to the whole, so that a novel or a movie of some esthetic merit may be judged as censorable in part. In a movie the part is excisable with more or less esthetic harm to the movie as a whole; with a book, if the board decides the gravity of the offense outweighs such literary excellence as the whole book may possess, the book is banned —not burned, just no longer offered for public sale.

This system is scarcely watertight; it presents plenty of opportunity for contradictions and revisions; it has tensions built into it. But it would not be likely to become troublesome politically; for, without strengthening the state, it provides a better way than the present one for our society to enforce certain inevitable taboos. Civilization behaves as though men were decent, in full knowledge that they are not.

A Weapon of Nihilism

The last aspect of the subject I am going to deal with is the use of pornography as a weapon of nihilistic destruction, especially by two important writers currently using it in this manner, Genet and Henry Miller. Such a writer as William Burroughs is less important because more successful; that is to say, the very thoroughness of his solipsistic nihilism defeats his purpose, for finally his novels are not only repetitious and revolting but also pointless, so that their failure as art keeps them from being a threat to society.

In this general context, the term nihilism signifies a great deal more than it did originally. In Turgenev's *Fathers and Sons,* where the word was given political currency, nihilism was quite idealistic; it held that a given society (Russia, in that case) was so corrupt or wicked that it should be destroyed, but destroyed so that a better society could emerge from its ruins. Those nineteenth-century Russian nihilists were extreme revolutionists, and quite high-minded; they did not advocate murder but political assassination, not promiscuous lust but free love. Among us now, James Baldwin is rather like those old-fashioned nihilists; he preaches destruction in the name of love. To be sure, the images of sexual love Baldwin offers are at once vacuous and indecent, and the images of disgust and blame are strong. Still, compared to the thoroughgoing destructivists, he and his books are not so wild. They are tamable enough, at least, to become the fashion, for they are interpreted—against his intention, or at least against one of his intentions—as preaching little more than a local rebellion, the righting of the injustice which American Negroes have endured for so long. However, there is a nihilism which is not against this or that unjust society or social injustice but against society as such; its rage is not just political but metaphysical as well; and pornography is one of its weapons.

Genet sometimes strives to be this sort of nihilist. But in his best work, *The Balcony* especially, he is too good an artist to succeed as a total nihilist. *The Balcony* creates an imperfect but strong image of the corruptness of modern Western societies, a satiric exaggeration which the audience can recognize as the truth distorted mostly for dramatic effect. Genet the sexual pervert and social criminal sometimes wants to destroy society, though as a criminal of intelligence he knows that he needs the law his enemy; but as a dramatic artist he makes meaningful works which by their very structure oppose destruction. And the potential pornography of the works serves a dramatic end. Furthermore, he has made them to be presented in a theater, that most social of artistic forms. As a result, whatever Genet himself wants to say, a play such as *The Balcony* says to the audience, "Look how monstrously you have warped your society." So we look; and it is true, we have warped it monstrously. But this is moral art, this is not the assault of sheer nihilism. To see a performance of *The Balcony* drives one to serious contemplation of the nature of society and law. What this contemplation leads me to is the conclusion that we must improve our society and firm up our laws, for the alternatives that now appear to be open to us in the way of other social arrangements are not worth the agony and risk of attempting a revolution. The play does not arouse a nihilistic zeal to destroy society, any more than it arouses sexual desire.

The Case of Henry Miller

Of nihilistic fiction, Henry Miller's *Tropic of Cancer* is currently the most widely read and the best spoken of. Miller is not only a fairly good writer, but the personality he projects in his book is attractive. When he stands stripped of his civilization—stripped down to his language, that is—the savage that is left is not exactly noble but he is at least honest about himself, self-indulgent, energetic, beauty-loving, and interested in the world, not a cold-hearted, torturing pervert. . . . Miller's prose is usually vigorous and sometimes splendid, and he is the best writer of "the character" since Sir Thomas Overbury.

Should *Tropic of Cancer* be censored or not? According to the standards for censorship advanced earlier in my argument it should not be censored for its pornography: as a work of art, it has considerable merit, and it could not achieve its ends without the use of intrinsically pornographic episodes and images. But the conflict of interests in judging this book is acute, for the purpose of Miller's novel is not just esthetic, it is nihilistic as well. The literary value of the book is enough to redeem its pornography but not enough to make one ignore its destructive intention. *Tropic of Cancer* has no structure and is very verbose; it is, like Miller's other books, an anatomy and a segment of his imaginary autobiography, a string of images and actions. But it does have an unmistakable message: society is intrinsically vile, let us return to the natural man. In effect, this return to nature means as little work as possible and lots of loveless sex. Miller has often been mispraised, for example by Karl Shapiro, for a supposedly pagan rejoicing in sex. Miller himself is honest about his intention. Again and again he represents the sexual antics of his characters as evidence of desperation, lurking behind which is the total despair of meaninglessness. He is what he says he is: an enemy not just of the badness of our society, not just of our specific society, but of society as such. To do what he can to get his readers also to become enemies of society, he assaults with persuasive force taboos, especially sexual taboos, which are intrinsic to social order.

Yet a whole new set of justifications are needed if *Tropic of Cancer* is to be banned, justifications having to do with pornography as a destructive social act. As an act against society, to write, publish, and distribute a book like *Tropic of Cancer* is more serious than to write, publish, and distribute a pamphlet which intellectually advocates the forcible overthrow of the government, but less serious than to take arms against the government—about on a par with inciting to rebellion, an act which a secure, free government will watch carefully and disapprove of strongly, but not forbid and punish. In other words, the only plausible argument for suppressing *Tropic of Cancer* would be that its publication is a dangerous political act and not that the book is pornographic, even though its pornography is the main instrument of the book's nihilistic force.

If you want to destroy society—not just write about a character who wants to, but if you want to make your book an instrument for destroying, a weapon—then you need pornography. For since society, at least Western society, is founded on the family as an essential social unit, nihilists and totalitarians must always attack the family as their enemy; conversely, those who attack the family as an institution are enemies of our kind of society. The totalitarians would substitute the state for the family; the nihilists would dissolve both the state and the family in the name of unrestricted gratification of natural appetite. To effect this dissolution, nihilists assault taboos, both because taboos restrain appetite and because they are an integral part of civilized order, of society as such. And since of all taboos the sexual ones are much the most important, pornography becomes for the nihilists (as it does not for the totalitarians, who need taboos) important as an instrument of dissolution; obviously a nihilistic representation of people violating taboos will be effective only if the representation itself also violates taboos. The reverse does not hold: pornography is not intrinsically nihilistic; conventional pornography recognizes and needs the rules it disobeys.

Because most pornography is not terribly harmful, and also because of the prevalence of liberal permissiveness in sexual matters, our society is falling down on one of its lesser jobs—the drawing of firm lines about what is decent. Furthermore, it has not sufficiently recognized that indecency can be and sometimes is put to politically dangerous uses. Society should oppose those who proclaim themselves its enemies and who subvert it by every means they know, not least of which is pornography. But violent repressiveness is not the best way for it to oppose them.

Our Lost Innocence

If one is for civilization, for being civilized, for even our warped but still possible society in preference to the anarchy that threatens from one side or the totalitarianism from the other, then one must be willing to take a middle way and to pay the price for responsibility. As things stand now, so liberal are we that a professor whose salary is paid by the state can speak out more easily in favor of *Tropic of Cancer* than against it, applauding not just its literary merits but also what he calls its celebration of sensuality and antisocial individualism. These are his honest opinions, and he, no more than the book, should be censored for advancing them. But his colleagues should not allow themselves to be cowed by his scorn of what he calls their bourgeois respectability but should rise in opposition to those opinions. In Miller's own presentation, his sensuality would guard against despair but itself becomes a way to despair; his individualism is a frenzied endeavor to compose a self in the vacuum of alienation, an alienation which he childishly blames the absolute villain, society, for imposing on him, the absolute victim; he intends his book to be an instrument for persuading its readers to abandon society, abrogate responsibility to their fellow men, and revert to a parasitic life. He claims that this sensual life is more joyous and fulfilling than any other possible in civilization; but what he describes is not a sensuality which is indeed a fulfillment for adult persons, so much as a would-be consolation for those who aspire to the condition of babies as a remedy to their grown-up woe.

To be civilized, to accept authority, to rule with order, costs deep in the soul, and not least of what it costs is likely to be some of the sensuality of the irresponsible. (In this respect the politically repressed are irresponsible, being denied responsibility. This would help account for the apparently greater sensuality among American Negroes than among American whites, for as a group Negroes have only recently been allowed to assume much social responsibility.) But we Americans, black and white, must be civilized now whether we want to be or not. Perhaps before civilization savages were noble, but, if there is anything we have learned in this vile century, it is that those who regress from civilization become ignoble beyond all toleration. They may aspire to an innocent savagery, but what they achieve is brutality.

At the end of *Tropic of Cancer,* Henry Miller says: "Human beings make a strange flora and fauna. From a distance they appear negligible; close up they are apt to appear ugly and malicious." What Miller says is right enough, but he leaves out what matters most. There is a middle distance from which to look at a man, the flexible distance of decency and art, of civilized society, which defines both a man looking and a man looked at; and from this distance human beings can look pretty good, important, even beautiful sometimes, worthy of respect.

DEALING WITH THE SMUT BUSINESS [7]

Until the early 1950's obscene materials were sold privately. Now hard-core obscenity has emerged into the open. On countless newsstands, paperback books by the score present explicit accounts of sexual perversion. "Stag" movies and slides, records of obscene songs and humor, pornographic pictures and comic books—all are available on the open market, to buyers of any age.

According to Henry B. Montague, chief inspector of the United States Post Office Department, at least 100 million copies of "objectionable" publications go through the mail each year. The Department estimates that a half billion dollars' worth of obscene materials is distributed, by mail or truck and express.

Who produces this filth? Most pornographers are reluctant to discuss their trade. But since many are under indictment, or have been convicted, for violating laws against obscenity, the major facts about the lucrative racket can be established from court records.

According to James J. Clancy, a former assistant district attorney of Los Angeles County who has been active in the prosecution of many big smut peddlers, about 60 per cent of the lewd magazines and paperbacks that circulate in the United States are published by

[7] From "Filth for Profit: The Big Business of Pornography," by O. K. Armstrong, former member of the United States House of Representatives from Missouri. *Reader's Digest.* 88:73-6. Mr. '66. Reprinted with permission from the March 1966 *Reader's Digest.* Copyright 1966 by The Reader's Digest Assn., Inc.

California firms. Two big West Coast producers of magazines or books declared obscene by the courts are Sanford E. Aday of Fresno and Milton Luros of Los Angeles. Aday began publishing paperbacks as early as 1952. Records show that, operating under several firm names, he produced 826,840 volumes featuring lurid sex in one five-month period. He has been indicted numerous times, and he and an associate were convicted in a Federal court in Grand Rapids, Michigan, in 1963, under a law which permits prosecution of a publisher wherever his obscenity is sold. The court assessed heavy fines and imposed a prison sentence, but the case is on appeal. Meanwhile, Aday's firm continues in business.

The companies controlled by Luros turn out a tremendous volume of offensive literature, some paperbacks featuring lesbianism, incest, perversion, sadism and homosexuality. Court records show that from July 1963 through July 1964 Luros also published 2.49 million copies of girlie magazines, retailing for an average $1.50 a copy. In that same twelve-month period, he turned out at least twenty-eight nudist magazines, averaging 25,000 copies of each. His total annual sales approximate $6 million. Luros has been indicted four times, convicted twice. (The second conviction, at Sioux City, Iowa, in January 1966, will be appealed.)

In the New York area, Edward Mishkin has held front rank among numerous publishers and sellers of sex literature. In 1960, New York City police, armed with a search warrant, seized forty-two different titles of paperbacks in one of Mishkin's retail stores. The writers testified that Mishkin had directed them to fill the books with raw sex scenes. Leotha Hackshaw, one of the authors, told the court: "The sex had to be very strong; it had to be rough; it had to be clearly spelled out. He wanted scenes in which women were making love to women, men with men—sex in an abnormal and irregular fashion."

Mishkin was convicted, and the verdict was upheld by the New York Court of Appeals . . . [and by the United States Supreme Court—Ed.].

By late 1965, according to the National Office for Decent Literature (an organization that screens all paperbacks for guidance of Catholic families), the offensive soft-bound books were hitting the market at the rate of about two hundred new titles a month. In addition, magazines for the "homosexual trade" have multiplied. Last fall, I counted nineteen in one bookstore in Washington within a block of the White House.

After the opening of the first "sunbathing" camps in the United States during the early 1930's, a few nudist cults issued privately circulated publications, using photographs taken at the camps. They were not pornographic. "But today the situation is changed," declares Mervin Mounce, editor and publisher of *Eden*, one of the legitimate nudist magazines. "The new so-called nudist publications, which number more than one hundred, are simply girlie magazines." They use pictures of professional models posed to excite prurient interest.

How do the publishers of pornography operate? The going rate of pay to an author of a smutty paperback is $600. The author grinds out a manuscript in about a week. Retail price per copy, when published, is 95 cents. Paper, artwork for the cover, and printing cost a total of about 10 cents. National and local wholesale distributors, retailers and transportation expenses take another 45 cents or so. That leaves 40 cents for the publisher. If all of a standard printing (30,000 copies) is sold, he stands to realize approximately $12,000—minus the $600 for the author.

"And many of these publishers make no capital investment," says Clancy. "Their business is done on credit."

One of the biggest mail-order smut dealers in the nation is John Amslow and Associates, of Culver City, California. Amslow uses an assortment of pseudonyms, selling by direct mail such items as nudist films, pornographic records, pictures and playing cards, and lingerie. One enormous mailing recently went out advertising records that present "the actual sounds of erotic love." During 1965, thousands of families received advertising matter from "X Sales, Winnetka, Calif.," openly soliciting the purchase of stag movies. The films portray the worst in perverted sex.

Printing the magazine and paperback smut is itself a substantial business. At least 25 firms work at the job in the Los Angeles area. Two of these are Nu Cal Litho and London Press, the latter owned by Milton Luros. Gross income for the printer runs about 15 cents for a magazine, 10 cents for a paperback. Also, many small legitimate firms take on print orders for a girlie magazine or two for the extra profit. At one plant I saw presses, which had just completed 100,000 "nudies," being readied for a run of a monthly religious publication.

The final step for the pornography publisher is distribution. Ordinarily he tries to arrange for a wholesaler to handle his wares. "We leave with each retail outlet, on consignment, the number of copies of each publication we think that outlet will sell, based on past performance," a big distributor told me. Most general distributors protest that they do not pressure retailers to take the sexy magazines and paperbacks. But many retailers say: "We have to take the bad publications with the good, or be penalized."

Some big distributors have taken the ultimate step in merchandising: they underwrite their own retail stores. Shops have been opened in many large cities to handle lewd magazines and paperbacks almost exclusively.

If this tide of obscenity is to be beaten back, citizens must recognize pornographic materials as the public enemies they are—destructive of the values essential to a wholesome, law-abiding society. We need not stand by helplessly; the multimillion-dollar smut industry is vulnerable to determined, united effort by concerned citizens. The First Amendment to the Constitution, which guarantees free speech, does not make the smut peddlers immune to prosecution. The United States Supreme Court has declared: "Implicit in the history of the First Amendment is the rejection of obscenity as utterly without redeeming social importance. Obscenity is not within the area of constitutionally protected speech or press."

Here is a program of action that citizens of any community can follow:

1. Speak out. The spread of pornography results from public apathy and ignorance of the problem. Do *not* act as a self-proclaimed censor, but make your voice heard. Examine the paperback books, magazines and films sold in your community. If you think some material is offensive, say so. Ask your town attorney if it violates any law.

2. *Organize community support.* Clergymen, parents, civic, business and labor groups can form an effective committee to demand action from law-enforcement officials. Citizens for Decent Literature, Inc., 3300 Carew Tower, Cincinnati, Ohio, has helped to establish three hundred such committees across the country.

3. *Secure expert legal advice.* The battle against pornography is often won or lost in the courtroom. Convictions depend upon vigorous prosecution backed by strong laws. Make certain that the anti-obscenity statutes in your state are powerful and consistent with the latest Supreme Court decisions, and that your police officials know the proper procedures to enforce them. Urge that all cases be tried in a criminal court before a jury, by an attorney experienced in obscenity law.

II. THE SUPREME COURT: MORE FREEDOM OR LESS?

EDITOR'S INTRODUCTION

The centrality of the Supreme Court in matters tested before it under the First Amendment is obvious. Hence a few of its most recent decisions concerning obscenity, free press, and free speech are dealt with in this section.

As an opener a short history of the landmark obscenity laws and decisions is given by Ralph I. Lowenstein of the Freedom of Information Center, University of Missouri. The sketch recounts the various tests employed by the Court down to the Ginzburg decision of early 1966. Fuller materials on that decision follow.

The Ginzburg majority opinion is given by Justice William J. Brennan, Jr. It is followed by excerpts from dissents by Justices Hugo L. Black and William O. Douglas.

Next, the decision is analyzed in turn from a Protestant viewpoint by the *Christian Century;* a Catholic viewpoint by *America;* a conservative viewpoint by the *National Review;* and a liberal viewpoint by the *New Republic.* Jason Epstein, vice president of the publishing firm of Random House, argues that the Court has on balance probably extended freedom to publish under the Ginzburg decision, despite the strictures against the type of advertising campaign for the materials Ralph Ginzburg offered for sale, strictures which led the majority of the Court to rule against him.

A decision by the Court on the issue of fair trial versus free press is followed by articles about three significant reports on the problem: the proposals prepared by a Committee of the American Bar Association; a report of the American Newspaper Publishers Association; and a report by a committee of the Association of the Bar of the City of New York. The views of the American Civil Liberties Union are given next.

A last entry in the section is an editorial from the New York *Times* on the Court's decision overriding the wishes of Georgia's state legislature to bar seating a member who had been duly elected but whose views on Vietnam and other questions offended the legislators. It was the first decision by the Supreme Court overriding a state legislature on this issue. As such it is historic, and it also affirms the right of free speech of all citizens—the electors who choose a particular legislator as well as the members of state legislatures.

1. The Supreme Court on Obscenity Cases

THE LEGAL TESTING OF OBSCENITY [1]

When the United States Supreme Court agreed to review the lower court obscenity decisions involving Ralph Ginzburg, Edward Mishkin and the publisher of *Fanny Hill,* it set the stage for . . . another landmark ruling in the history of freedom of expression. Those who have rallied to the cause of the three defendants see freedom of the press itself as the issue in contention. Those who support the prosecution say that the issue involved is the right of society to protect itself from the harmful influence of pornography. . . .

What brought the Supreme Court into the obscenity morass? What are the earlier laws and decisions that laid the foundation for the current controversy? What are the issues now in contention before the Supreme Court? This paper will attempt to answer these questions.

Landmark Obscenity Laws and Decisions

There are three major laws and six major decisions that affected the course of obscenity on the Federal level in the United States:

1842—Congress included in the Customs Law a prohibition against the "importation of all indecent and obscene prints, paintings, lithographs, engravings, and transparencies."

1865—Congress passed its first law to make mailing obscene matter a criminal offense.

[1] From "Obscenity and the Supreme Court," by Ralph I. Lowenstein, publications editor, Freedom of Information Center. Publication no 154. The Center. School of Journalism. University of Missouri. Columbia. F. '66. Reprinted by permission.

1868—Lord Chief Justice Cockburn of England wrote the "Hicklin Rule," which became the traditional test for obscenity in both England and the United States. The Hicklin Rule: ". . . the test of obscenity is this, whether the tendency of the matter charged as obscenity is to deprave and corrupt those whose minds are open to such immoral influences and into whose hands a publication of this sort may fall."

1873—Congress passed the famous "Comstock Law," which declared nonmailable any "obscene, lewd, lascivious, or filthy book, pamphlet, picture, paper, letter, writing, print, or other publication of an indecent character." It set up a fine of $5,000 and-or five years' imprisonment for the first offense.

1922—The New York State Court of Appeals, in the *Halsey* case, found that a book could not be ruled obscene because of selected words or paragraphs. The entire work must be considered as a whole *(Raymond D. Halsey v. The New York Society for the Suppression of Vice)*.

1934—The Second United States Circuit Court of Appeals upheld a lower court ruling that *Ulysses*, by James Joyce, was not obscene and could therefore be imported into the United States. In affirming the "dominant effect" standard laid down in the *Halsey* case, Judges Augustus N. Hand and Learned Hand declared: "In applying this test, relevancy of the objectionable parts to the theme, the established reputation of the work in the estimation of approved critics, if the book is modern, and the verdict of the past, if it is ancient, and persuasive pieces of evidence; for works of art are not likely to sustain a high position with no better warrant for their existence than their obscene content *(United States v. One Book Called "Ulysses")*.

1957—The Supreme Court held in the *Roth* and *Alberts* cases that obscenity is "utterly without redeeming social importance" and therefore falls outside the protection intended for speech and press. However, the Court knocked out the traditional Hicklin Rule test for obscenity and set up a new one: "Obscene material is material which deals with sex in a manner appealing to prurient interest, and the test of obscenity is whether to the average person, applying contemporary community standards, the dominant theme of the material appeals to prurient interest" *(Roth v. U.S., Alberts v. California).*

1962—The Supreme Court clarified the *Roth* ruling by stating that a work must have the quality of "patent offensiveness" as well as "prurient interest appeal" to be considered obscene *(Manual Enterprises v. Day).*

1964—In a further clarification of the *Roth* ruling, the Supreme Court declared that obscenity must be judged by "national" community standards and not by individual local standards. It also emphasized that a work "cannot be proscribed unless it is 'utterly' without social importance" *(Jacobellis v. Ohio).*

Two other Supreme Court decisions should be mentioned here, although they played no role in the legal definition of obscenity, as such. These are *Joseph Burstyn Inc. v. Wilson,* 1952, in which the Supreme Court for the first time brought motion pictures under the guaranties of the First Amendment; and *Freedman v. Maryland,* 1965, in which the Court ruled that if a movie is censored there must be procedure for taking the case to the courts almost immediately, with the burden of proof resting on the censor.

Current Obscenity Tests

Although the postal and customs regulations barring obscene matter placed this issue squarely within the jurisdiction of Federal courts, the Supreme Court did not have to face the constitutional problems in regard to obscenity until *Roth v. U.S.* At that time, Justice William J. Brennan Jr., delivering the majority opinion, wrote:

> Although this is the first time the question has been squarely presented to this Court, either under the First Amendment or under the Fourteenth Amendment, expressions found in numerous opinions indicate that this Court has always assumed that obscenity is not protected by the freedoms of speech and press . . . the First Amendment was not intended to protect every utterance. This phrasing did not prevent this Court from concluding that libelous utterances are not within the area of constitu-

tionally protected speech. At the time of the adoption of the First Amendment, obscenity law was not as fully developed as libel law, but there is sufficiently contemporaneous evidence to show that obscenity too was outside the protection intended for speech and press.

Justice Brennan then explained why obscenity, in the opinion of the majority of the Court, could not be considered within the protection of the First Amendment:

All ideas having even the slightest redeeming social importance—unorthodox ideas, controversial ideas, even ideas hateful to the prevailing climate of opinion—have the full protection of the guaranties, unless excludable because they encroach upon the limited area of more important interests. But implicit in the history of the First Amendment is the rejection of obscenity as utterly without redeeming social importance. This rejection for that reason is mirrored in the universal judgment that obscenity should be restrained, reflected in the international agreement of over fifty nations, in the obscenity laws of all the forty-eight states, and in the twenty obscenity laws enacted by Congress from 1842 to 1956. We hold that obscenity is not within the area of constitutionally protected speech and press.

Having laid the constitutional issue to rest, the Supreme Court proceeded in the *Roth* opinion and two subsequent opinions to set up these three tests for judging obscenity:

1. Whether the material is *utterly* without redeeming social importance.

2. Whether to the average person, applying contemporary national community standards, the dominant theme of the material appeals to prurient interest.

3. Whether the material is patently offensive.

The arguments about obscenity in films, books and magazines now range around these three tests.

Is anything *utterly* without redeeming social importance? Ralph Ginzburg was able to produce professors, critics, psychiatrists and at least one minister to testify that his publications had some redeeming social importance.

How can the average juror apply national community standards toward his determination of whether a publication is obscene? Or does this test mean that juries are no longer qualified to hear obscenity cases? Notre Dame Law School Dean Joseph O'Meara recently commented that the Supreme Court should restore local option in obscenity cases and "recognize the jury as the authentic alter ego of the community, reflecting its morals and mores more truly than even the wisest of judges" (*Time,* December 17, 1965).

But even if juries are permitted to try obscenity cases on the community level, how can jurors judge the "dominant theme" of some of the lengthy books that have fallen under the censorship ax? In an Indianapolis criminal court, a judge ruled that the entire 287 pages of *Tropic of Cancer* had to be read to a jury before the book could be accepted as evidence. It took the prosecuting attorney three days to perform this task. The jury then found the book obscene (June 24, 1963) and fined a twenty-nine-year-old divinity school graduate five hundred dollars for selling it in a bookstore.

How does one define "prurient interest"? *Webster's New World Dictionary of the American Language* (World Publishing Company, 1962) gives this definition of prurient: "to itch or long for a thing, be lecherous, 1. having lustful ideas or desires. 2. lustful; lascivious; lewd: as, *prurient* longings. 3. (rare), itching." Charles Rembar, attorney for G. P. Putnam's Sons, publisher of *Fanny Hill,* told the Supreme Court (December 9, 1965): "Our problem is that no one is an expert on prurient interest—that's a question for the court. . . . It's a legal question. . . . The court has to be an expert."

In an earlier statement filed with the Court, Putnam said the prurient interest test "leaves no room for the proposition that a writing may be suppressed merely because it produces normal sexual response in a healthy adult." The publisher added:

> [*Fanny Hill*] is, of course, an erotic novel. It is at the same time a work of art . . . read as a whole, it creates an effect that is primarily literary. . . .
>
> Any legislative attempt to do away with books that may excite sexual thoughts and desires becomes ludicrous when viewed against the realities of contemporary civilization.
>
> An eighteenth-century novel, no matter how much it may be devoted to the act of sex, can hardly add anything to the constant sexual prodding with which our environment assails us.

At what point does material become patently offensive? In the *Manual Enterprises v. Day* case, which involved magazines apparently designed to appeal to homosexuals, the Court indicated that a patently offensive publication was one that went beyond the customary limits of candor—"beyond the pale of contemporary notions of rudimentary decency." The magazines in question, the Court found, would appeal to the prurient interest of homosexuals, but they could not be "deemed so offensive on their face as to affront current community standards of decency. . . ." The Court therefore ruled that the magazines were not obscene because they were not "patently offensive." Justice John M. Harlan wrote:

> In most obscenity cases . . . that which is patently offensive will also usually carry the requisite "prurient interest" appeal. It is only in the unusual instance where, as here, the "prurient interest" appeal of the material is found limited to a particular class of persons that occasion arises for a truly independent inquiry into the question whether or not the material is patently offensive.

According to Attorney Edward de Grazia, the Court was broadly hinting in the *Manual Enterprises v. Day* case that perhaps only "hard-core pornography" could be found patently offensive and indecent (*ALA Bulletin*, August 1965).

The difficulty of applying the tests established by the Supreme Court is spotlighted by the three cases now before the Court for consideration.

The Ginzburg Case

In 1963, the Justice Department charged publisher Ralph Ginzburg with twenty-eight counts of mailing obscene matter. The trial, which took place in a Philadelphia United States District Court, involved three different publications issued by Ginzburg:

1. One issue of *Eros*, a quarterly "devoted to the joy of love"

2. *Liaison,* a biweekly newsletter of current events on matters of sex

3. *The Housewife's Handbook on Selective Promiscuity,* a Tucson woman's sexual autobiography covering her sexual activities from age three to thirty-six. *Handbook* was written by Mrs. Lillian Maxine Serett under the pen name Rey Anthony.

United States District Judge Ralph C. Body heard evidence and argument in the case during five days in June 1963. Prosecuting attorneys said the publications were "patently offensive," went "beyond the customary limits that society tolerates" and were "loaded with shameful, unhealthy, morbid expressions of sex." Ginzburg produced witnesses who testified that the publications had redeeming social and literary importance. A Baptist minister, for example, testified that he used the *Handbook* in "counseling." Literary critic Dwight Macdonald testified that many of the articles in *Eros* demonstrated "considerable literary value."

On June 14, 1963, Judge Body found Ginzburg guilty on all twenty-eight counts, but deferred sentencing until December 19, 1963. On the latter date, he sentenced Ginzburg to five years in prison and fined him $28,000. He fined Ginzburg's three publication companies an additional $14,000. Ginzburg was released on $10,000 bail.

Judge Body said that each of the publications "is a blow to sense, not merely sensibility." Taken as a whole, he said, they are "dirt for dirt's sake and dirt for money's sake."

Ginzburg appealed to the Third United States Circuit Court of Appeals. A year later, this court affirmed the sentence. In a unanimous opinion prepared by Judge Gerald McLaughlin, the court found that Ginzburg had conducted "an operation on the part of experts in the shoddy business of pandering to and exploiting for money one of the great weaknesses of human beings."

Ginzburg then appealed to the Supreme Court. Among those supporting his cause are the American Civil Liberties Union, the Authors League of America and more than one hundred authors, playwrights, editors, librarians, critics, psychiatrists, poets and clergymen. . . .

The Mishkin Case

Edward Mishkin, who operated a bookstore in the Times Square area, is appealing a sentence of three years' imprisonment and $12,500 in fines. He was convicted by a New York court in December 1960 of publishing and selling more than one hundred paperbacks devoted to sadism and masochism. The books bore such titles as *Dance With a Dominant Whip, The House of Torture, Fearful Ordeal in Restraintland, Screaming Flesh* and *Swish Bottom.* Some contained scenes of naked women whipping each other.

Leotha Hackshaw was one of a team of three writers and two artists hired to write and illustrate the books at issue, 17,121 copies of which were seized. She testified at the New York trial that she was told to produce a book "full of sex scenes and lesbian scenes . . . the sex had to be very strong, it had to be very rough . . . (Washington *Post,* April 4, 1965).

Mishkin's attorney, Emanuel Redfield, said in his brief to the Supreme Court, "At worst, these books can be described as trashy and vulgar . . . Instead of stimulating the erotic, they disgust and sicken."

Mishkin apparently is basing his case on the *Manual Enterprises v. Day* ruling, in which Justice Harlan wrote that the "patently offensive" test must be applied to material that is of "prurient interest" only to a limited class of persons. Attorney Redfield argued before the Court that Mishkin's books did not appeal to the average person's prurient interest. "They appeal to the elderly, the impotent and the perverse. Must one be judged by what offends others?" (*Time,* December 17, 1965). Redfield added: "Only obscene books can be proscribed. Are sadism and masochism synonyms for obscenity? If so, there is no end to the literature that may be prohibited."

The "Fanny Hill" Case

In the *Fanny Hill* case, the courts have come full cycle in the course of American obscenity history. According to Morris L. Ernst and Alan U. Schwartz (*Censorship: The Search for the Obscene,* Macmillan, 1964), the first obscenity case in America involving a book occurred in Massachusetts in 1821—and *Fanny Hill* was the book.

Sometimes known by its alternate title, *Memoirs of a Woman of Pleasure,* the book was written by English author John Cleland in 1749. It describes the adventures of a prostitute in an extremely explicit manner, although it manages to do so without ever using the four-letter words so common in modern novels.

Fanny Hill has had its problems in four states. New York's highest court found the book not obscene in July 1964. But trial courts in New Jersey and Illinois, as well as the highest court in Massachusetts, have ruled that the book is obscene.

G. P. Putnam's Sons first published the novel in July 1963. A month later New York Supreme Court Justice Charles Marks issued a temporary injunction against its sale and distribution in New York. At the trial in which the district attorneys of the five counties of New York City sought to make the injunction permanent, Assistant Corporation Counsel Seymour B. Quel gave Justice Arthur G. Klein thirty-five passages of "pure pornography" from the book.

Poet and critic Louis Untermeyer testified that *Fanny Hill* was a "work of art" and was not pornographic. Other experts gave similar testimony. But cross-examining counsel asked each expert if he realized that *Fanny Hill* contained twenty acts of sexual intercourse, four of them in the presence of others; four acts of lesbianism, two acts of male homosexuality, two acts of flagellation and one of female masturbation.

Justice Klein decided for Putnam (August 23, 1963) and vacated the previous injunction against the book. He said the "high literary quality" of the book had been established by the defense, while the prosecution had failed to establish that the book did not have "redeeming social value." The justice mentioned the then-current Profumo case in England and said that *Fanny Hill* could not be called "patently offensive" in the light of current community standards.

The appellate Division of the New York Supreme Court found *Fanny Hill* obscene (February 28, 1964) and reversed Justice Klein's decision. Then the New York Court of Appeals, the state's highest court, overruled the Appellate Division (July 10, 1964) by a vote of 4-3. It said the book could not be banned under the tests laid down by the United States Supreme Court and therefore lifted the injunction.

Stating the opinion of the majority, Judge Francis Bergan wrote:

> The suppression of a book requires not only an expression of judgment by the court that it is so bad, in the view of judges, that it is offensive to the community standards of decency as the Legislature has laid down; but also that it is so bad the constitutional freedom to print has been lost because of what the book contains. The history and tradition of our institutions stand against the suppression of books.

In Massachusetts it was a different matter. In September 1964, Justice Donald M. Macaulay of the Superior Court of Massachusetts, a lower court, ruled that *Fanny Hill* was "obscene, indecent and impure." Justice Macaulay said he had read the book four times and found it to be "hard-core pornography," "patently offensive" and "utterly without redeeming social importance." The opinions of Putnam's defense witnesses, he said, "cannot be substituted for those of average persons in the contemporary national community." He added: "If this classic example of pornography is not obscene, then I doubt if any written matter can be found obscene" (*Publishers' Weekly,* September 14, 1964). The defendants appealed.

On April 22, 1965, the Supreme Judicial Court, Massachusett's highest court, upheld the lower court ruling by a 4-3 vote. The higher court said *Fanny Hill* was in violation of every judicial test currently being used to determine obscenity (*Publishers' Weekly,* August 9, 1965).

It is this decision that Putnam is now appealing to the Supreme Court. In argument before the Supreme Court, Putnam attorney Charles Rembar suggested (December 9, 1965) that the justices would not have to read the entire book to make a decision. Testimony of scholars about the literary and historical value of the book, he said, would present adequate evidence to the Court that the novel passed the social importance test.

But William I. Cowin, assistant attorney general of Massachusetts, urged the Court to consider the book itself. Accepting Rembar's suggestion that testimony itself was enough, he said, would make it practically impossible ever again to ban a book as obscene, because some evidence could always be found in favor of a book's supposed value.

Causal Effects of Obscenity

Tests and precedents aside, at the heart of the obscenity controversy is the belief by some that obscenity motivates certain people to commit antisocial acts. There has been widely divergent testimony by psychiatrists and psychologists, some contending that it does trigger abnormal bchavior, and others contending that it actually serves as a safety valve, allowing people to release their sexual urges and aggressions vicariously. . . .

Even so, there is very little scientific or statistical evidence available so far to support either side. Justice William O. Douglas, in his dissent in the *Roth* case, emphasized this point:

> If we were certain that impurity of sexual thoughts impelled to action, we would be on less dangerous ground in punishing the distributors of this sex literature. But it is by no means clear that obscene literature, as so defined, is a significant factor in influencing substantial deviations from the community standards.

Justice Douglas pointed out that scientific studies of juvenile delinquency show that delinquents are less inclined to read than nondelinquents and that reading is a relatively insignificant influence in the composite forces that lead an individual to deviate from community standards. He wrote:

> The absence of dependable information on the effect of obscene literature on human conduct should make us wary. It should put us on the side of protecting society's interest in literature, except and unless it can be said that the particular publication has an impact on action that the government can control.

The most recent development in the area of information about the causal effects of obscenity was an announcement (September 15, 1965) by Assistant Attorney General Fred M. Vinson Jr. that the Federal Government may begin a scientific study to determine the effect of obscenity on the human mind. He said the Justice Department and the Department of Health, Education, and Welfare were exploring such a proposal.

Vinson told a congressional subcommittee that in addition to laws prohibiting pornography, society needed to develop scientific data measuring the effects of obscene matter. "Such data would clarify the premises underlying our obscenity laws," he said. "It would enable us to accurately describe what it is we are prohibiting."

Obscenity and Youth

Even if it could be demonstrated that there is no causal effect between obscenity and antisocial acts, it is still quite likely that large numbers of American parents would object to obscene materials being made freely available to their children. . . .

During the hearings on *Fanny Hill* in New York, Justice Arthur G. Klein mentioned the objection that parents "would not like the book to be read by their young children." He then quoted Supreme Court Justice Felix Frankfurter in a decision that upset a Michigan statute: "The incidence of this enactment is to reduce the adult population of Michigan to reading only what is fit for children" (New York *Times*, September 24, 1963).

In his decision in the *Jacobellis* case, Justice Brennan addressed himself to this same question. He said state and local authorities "might well consider whether their objectives in this area would be better served by laws aimed specifically at preventing distribution of objectionable material to children, rather than totally prohibiting its dissemination."

The New York State Legislature has apparently followed this advice by enacting two overlapping laws that would prohibit the sale or delivery of pornographic material to minors.

The Hecht Act, which became effective July 1, 1965, makes it a misdemeanor for anyone "knowingly" to sell, lend or give away pornographic materials to a person "actually or apparently" under eighteen years of age. Under its definition of "knowingly," the seller or lender would be responsible for carrying out "reasonable inspection" to determine the character and content of the item. Pornography, according to the act, covers any book, pocket book, pamphlet or magazine "containing details, descriptive or narrative accounts . . . written or presented in such a manner as to exploit lust for commercial gain and which would appeal to the lust of persons under the age of eighteen years."

The Travia Act, which became effective September 1, 1965, defines as a minor anyone under seventeen and as pornographic any material which "predominantly appeals to the prurient, shameful, or morbid interest of minors and is utterly without redeeming social importance for minors." According to the act, an "honest mistake" would excuse the defendant from liability if he made a reasonable attempt to ascertain the true age of the minor (*Library Journal*, September 15, 1965).

The *Library Journal* reported (September 15, 1965) that in the opinion of the American Book Publishers Council, these amendments to the New York penal laws "reflect efforts to draft enforceable laws prohibiting the sale of 'pornography' to minors that would withstand challenge on constitutional grounds. Similar measures are likely to be introduced in other states."

Clear and Present Danger Test

The American Civil Liberties Union, in supporting the appeal efforts of Ginzburg, has asked (October 18, 1965) the Supreme Court to declare that all published material is protected by the First Amendment unless it creates a "clear and present danger" of causing antisocial conduct. The ACLU said the Court's present tests for obscenity are "vague and unworkable" and give judges "a license to adjudicate by whim and caprice."

Precedent for invoking a "clear and present danger" test goes back to 1919, when Justice Oliver Wendell Holmes invented this standard for protecting free speech under the First Amendment: "Is there a clear and present danger that a particular writing or speech will result in the evil aimed at?" But the Supreme Court found in the *Roth* case that there was no need to apply the test of "clear and present danger" since obscenity itself lay outside the protection of the First Amendment.

Dan Lacy, [former] managing director of the American Book Publishers Council, has argued that the "clear and present danger" position is a poor one . . . because it either means too much or too little. If interpreted strictly, he said, no prosecution for obscenity could ever be successful—and the courts would therefore not adopt such a doctrine. If interpreted loosely—and Lacy said this would be likely—the prosecution could almost always produce an expert to testify that a publication was a "probable" danger to lawful conduct (Freedom of Information Center Publication No. 38, September 1960).

The Douglas-Black Dissent

The ACLU is not alone in believing that all published material should come under the protection of the First Amendment. Two justices of the Supreme Court, William O. Douglas and Hugo Black, would go even further than the ACLU and rule that obscene publications fall under the protection of the First Amendment virtually without qualification. These are excerpts from Justice Douglas' dissent, with which Justice Black concurred, from the *Roth* ruling:

. . . if the First Amendment guarantee of freedom of speech and press is to mean anything in this field, it must allow protests even against the moral code that the standard of the day sets for the community. In other words, literature should not be suppressed merely because it offends the moral code of the censor. . . . the test that suppresses a cheap tract today can suppress a literary gem tomorrow. All it needs is to incite a lascivious thought or arouse a lustful desire. The list of books that judges or juries can place in that category is endless.

I would give the broad sweep of the First Amendment full support. I have the same confidence in the ability of our people to reject noxious literature as I have in their capacity to sort out the true from the false in theology, economics, politics, or any other field.

Given the climate of opinion of Congress and the American people, it is unlikely that such a liberal point of view will prevail with the majority of the Supreme Court in the foreseeable future. According to a recent (October 15, 1965) Gallup Poll, 58 per cent of the American people believe that laws regarding the kind of books that can be sold are not strict enough—only 4 per cent believe such laws are too strict. Even among the college educated, opinion is more than 4 to 1 in favor of stricter censorship laws.

The need for a clearer definition of obscenity is obvious. The ACLU is probably correct in describing the present tests as "vague and unworkable." The vagueness of the tests is evidenced by the rash of obscenity cases in the courts of the nation since 1957.

THE GINZBURG MAJORITY OPINION [2]

Mr. Justice Brennan delivered the opinion of the Court.

A judge sitting without a jury in the District Court for the Eastern District of Pennsylvania convicted petitioner Ginzburg

[2] From the Supreme Court opinion by Justice William J. Brennan, Jr., in *Ralph Ginzburg et al, Petitioners, v. United States. United States Reports.* 383 U.S. 463 (1966). Supt. of Docs. Washington, D.C. 20402. '67.

and three corporations controlled by him upon all twenty-eight counts of an indictment charging violation of the Federal obscenity statute. . . . Each count alleged that a resident of the Eastern District received mailed matter, either one of three publications challenged as obscene, or advertising telling how and where the publications might be obtained. The Court of Appeals for the Third Circuit affirmed. . . .

We granted certiorari (380 U.S. 961). We affirm. Since petitioners do not argue that the trial judge misconceived or failed to apply the standards we first enunciated in *Roth v. United States* (354 U.S. 476), the only serious question is whether those standards were correctly applied.

In the cases in which this Court has decided obscenity questions since *Roth*, it has regarded the materials as sufficient in themselves for the determination of the question. In the present case, however, the prosecution charged the offense in the context of the circumstances of production, sale, and publicity and assumed that, standing alone, the publications themselves might not be obscene.

We agree that the question of obscenity may include consideration of the setting in which the publications were presented as an aid to determining the question of obscenity, and assume without deciding that the prosecution could not have succeeded otherwise. As in *Mishkin v. New York*, . . . we view the publications against a background of commercial exploitation of erotica solely for the sake of their prurient appeal. The record in that regard amply supports the decision of the trial judge that the mailing of all three publications offended the statute.

The three publications were *Eros*, a hardcover magazine of expensive format; *Liaison*, a biweekly newsletter; and *The Housewife's Handbook on Selective Promiscuity* (hereinafter the *Handbook*), a short book. The [specified] issue of *Eros* . . . contains fifteen articles and photo-essays on the subject of love, sex, and sexual relations. The specified issue of *Liaison* . . . contains a prefatory "Letter from the Editors" announcing its dedication to "keeping sex an art and preventing it from becoming a science." The remainder of the issue consists of digests of two articles concerning sex and sexual relations which had earlier appeared in professional journals and a report of an interview with a psychotherapist who favors the broadest license in sexual relationships.

As the trial judge noted, "[w]hile the treatment is largely superficial, it is presented entirely without restraint of any kind. According to defendants' own expert, it is entirely without literary merit." . . . The *Handbook* purports to be a sexual autobiography detailing with complete candor the author's sexual experiences from age three to age thirty-six. The text includes, and prefatory and concluding sections of the book elaborate, her views on such subjects as sex education of children, laws regulating private consensual adult sexual practices, and the equality of women in sexual relationships. It was claimed at trial that women would find the book valuable, for example as a marriage manual or as an aid to the sex education of their children.

Besides testimony as to the merit of the material, there was abundant evidence to show that each of the accused publications was originated or sold as stock in trade of the sordid business of pandering—"the business of purveying textual or graphic matter openly advertised to appeal to the erotic interest of their customers." *Eros* early sought mailing privilege from the postmasters of Intercourse and Blue Ball, Pennsylvania. The trial court found the obvious, that these hamlets were chosen only for the value . . . their names would have in furthering petitioners' efforts to sell their publications on the basis of salacious appeal; the facilities of the post offices were inadequate to handle the anticipated volume of mail, and the privileges were denied. Mailing privileges were then obtained from the postmaster of Middlesex, New Jersey. *Eros* and *Liaison* thereafter mailed several million circulars soliciting subscriptions from that post office; over 5,500 copies of the *Handbook* were mailed.

The "leer of the sensualist" also permeates the advertising for the three publications. The circulars sent for *Eros* and *Liaison* stressed the sexual candor of the respective publications, and openly boasted that the publishers would take full advantage of what they regarded an unrestricted license allowed by law in the expression of sex and sexual matters. The advertising for the *Handbook,* apparently mailed from New York, consisted almost entirely of a reproduction of the introduction of the book, written by one Dr. Albert Ellis. Although he alludes to the book's informational value and its putative therapeutic usefulness, his remarks are preoccupied with the book's sexual imagery. The solicitation was indiscriminate, not limited to those, such as physicians or psychiatrists, who might independently discern the book's therapeutic worth. Inserted in each advertisement was a slip labeled "GUARANTEE" and reading, "Documentary Books, Inc. unconditionally guarantees full refund of the price of *The Housewife's Handbook on Selective Promiscuity* if the book fails to reach you because of U.S. Post Office censorship interference." Similar slips appeared in the advertising for *Eros* and *Liaison;* they highlighted the gloss petitioners put on the publications, eliminating any doubt what the purchaser was being asked to buy.

This evidence, in our view, was relevant in determining the ultimate question of "obscenity" and, in the context of this record, serves to resolve all ambiguity and doubt. The deliberate representation of petitioners' publications as erotically arousing, for example, stimulated the reader to accept them as prurient; he looks for titillation, not for saving intellectual content. Similarly, such representation would tend to force public confrontation with the potentially offensive aspects of the work; the brazenness of such an appeal heightens the offensiveness of the publications to those who are offended by such material.

And the circumstances of presentation and dissemination of material are equally relevant to determining whether social importance claimed for material in the courtroom was, in the circumstances, pretense or reality—whether it was the basis upon which it was traded in the marketplace or a spurious claim for litigation purposes. Where the purveyor's sole emphasis is on the sexually provocative aspects of his publications, that fact may be decisive in the determination of obscenity. Certainly in a prosecution which, as here, does not necessarily imply suppression of the materials involved, the fact that they originate or are used as a subject of pandering is relevant to the application of the *Roth* test.

A proposition argued as to *Eros,* for example, is that the trial judge improperly found the magazine to be obscene as a whole, since he concluded that only four of the fifteen articles predominantly appealed to prurient interest and substantially exceeded community standards of candor, while the other articles were admittedly nonoffensive. But the trial judge found that "[t]he deliberate and studied arrangement of *Eros* is editorialized for the purpose of appealing predominantly to prurient interest and to insulate through the inclusion of nonoffensive material." . . . However erroneous such a conclusion might be if unsupported by the evidence of pandering, the record here supports it.

Eros was created, represented and sold solely as a claimed instrument of the sexual stimulation it would bring. Like the other publications, its pervasive treatment of sex and sexual matters rendered it available to exploitation by those who would make a business of pandering to "the widespread weakness for titillation by pornography." Petitioners' own expert agreed, correctly we think, that "[i]f the object [of a work] is material gain for the creator through an appeal to the sexual curiosity and appetite," the work is pornographic. In other words, by animating sensual detail to give the publication a salacious cast, petitioners reinforced what is conceded by the Government to be an otherwise debatable conclusion.

A similar analysis applies to the judgment regarding the *Handbook.* The bulk of the proofs directed to social importance concerned this publication. Before selling publication rights to petitioners, its author had printed it privately; she sent circulars to persons whose names appeared on membership lists of medical and psychiatric associations, asserting its value as an adjunct in therapy. Over twelve thousand sales resulted from this solicitation, and a number of witnesses testified that they found the work useful in their professional practice. The Government does not seriously contest the claim that the book has worth in such a controlled, or even neutral, environment. Petitioners, however, did not sell the book to such a limited audience, or focus their claims for it on its supposed therapeutic or educational value; rather, they deliberately emphasized the sexually provocative aspects of the work, in order to catch the salaciously disposed. They proclaimed its obscenity; and we cannot conclude that the court below erred in taking their own evaluation at its face value and declaring the book as a whole obscene despite the other evidence.

The decision in *Rebhuhn v. United States* . . . is persuasive authority for our conclusion. That was a prosecution . . . brought in the context of pandering of publications assumed useful to scholars and members of learned professions. The books involved were written by authors proved in many instances to have been men of scientific standing, as anthropologists or psychiatrists. The Court of Appeals for the Second Circuit therefore assumed that many of the books were entitled to the protection of the First Amendment, and "could lawfully have passed through the mails, if directed to those who would be likely to use them for the purposes for which they were written . . ." . . . But the evidence, as here, was that the defendants had not disseminated them for their "proper use, but . . . woefully misused them, and it was that misuse which constituted the gravamen of the crime." . . . Speaking for the Court in affirming the conviction, Judge Learned Hand said:

> . . . [T]he works themselves had a place, though a limited one, in anthropology and in psychotherapy. They might also have been lawfully sold to laymen who wished seriously to study the sexual practices of savage or barbarous peoples, or sexual aberrations; in other words most of them were not obscene per se. In several decisions we have held that the statute does not in all circumstances forbid the dissemination of such publications. . . . However, in the case at bar, the prosecution succeeded . . . when it showed that the defendants had indiscriminately flooded the mails with advertisements, plainly designed merely to catch the prurient, though under the guise of distributing works of scientific or literary merit. We do not mean that the distributor of such works is charged with a duty to insure that they shall reach only proper hands, nor need we say what care he must use, for these defendants exceeded any possible limit; the circulars were no more than appeals to the salaciously disposed, and no [fact finder] could have failed to pierce the fragile screen, set up to cover that purpose. . . .

We perceive no threat to First Amendment guarantees in thus holding that in close cases evidence of pandering may be probative with respect to the nature of the material in question and thus satisfy the *Roth* test. No weight is ascribed to the fact that petitioners have profited from the sale of publications which we have assumed but do not hold cannot themselves be adjudged obscene in the abstract; to sanction consideration of this fact might indeed induce self-censorship, and offend the frequently stated principle that commercial activity, in itself, is no justification for narrowing the protection of expression secured by the First Amendment. Rather, the fact that each of these publications was created or exploited entirely on the basis of its appeal to prurient interests strengthens the conclusion that the transactions here were sales of illicit merchandise, not sales of constitutionally protected matter. A conviction for mailing obscene publications, but explained in part by the presence of this element, does not necessarily suppress the materials in question, nor chill their proper distribution for a proper use. Nor should it inhibit the enterprise of others seeking through serious endeavor to advance human knowledge or understanding in science, literature, or art. All that will have been determined is that questionable publications are obscene in a context which brands them as obscene as that term is defined in *Roth*—a use inconsistent with any claim to the shelter of the First Amendment. "The nature of the materials is, of course, relevant as an attribute of the defendant's conduct, but the materials are thus placed in context from which they draw color and character. A wholly different result might be reached in a different setting." *Roth v. United States,* 354 U.S., at 495 (WARREN, C. J., concurring).

It is important to stress that this analysis simply elaborates the test by which the obscenity *vel non* [or not] of the material must be judged. Where an exploitation of interests in titillation by pornography is shown with respect to material lending itself to such exploitation through pervasive treatment or description of sexual matters, such evidence may support the determination that the material is obscene even though in other contexts the material would escape such condemnation. . . . *Affirmed.*

TWO DISSENTS IN THE GINZBURG CASE [3]

MR. JUSTICE BLACK, dissenting.

Only one stark fact emerges with clarity out of the confusing welter of opinions and thousands of words written in this and two other cases today. That fact is that Ginzburg, petitioner here, is now finally and authoritatively condemned to serve five years in prison for distributing printed matter about sex which neither Ginzburg nor anyone else could possibly have known to be criminal. Since, as I have said many times, I believe the Federal Government is without any power whatever under the Constitution to put any type of burden on speech and expression of ideas of any kind (as distinguished from conduct), I agree with Part II of the dissent of my Brother Douglas in this case, and I would reverse Ginzburg's conviction on this ground alone. Even assuming, however, that the Court is correct in holding today that Congress does have power to clamp official censorship on some subjects selected by the Court in some ways approved by it, I believe that the Federal obscenity statute as enacted by Congress and as enforced by the Court against Ginzburg in this case should be held invalid on two other grounds.

I

Criminal punishment by government, although universally recognized as a necessity in limited areas of conduct, is an exercise of one of government's most awesome and dangerous powers. Consequently, wise and good governments make all possible efforts to hedge this dangerous power by restricting it within easily identifiable boundaries. Experience, and wisdom flowing out of that experience, long ago led to the belief that agents of government should not be vested with power and discretion to define and punish as criminal past conduct which had not been clearly defined as a crime in advance. To this end, at least in part, written laws came into being marking the boundaries of conduct for which public agents could thereafter impose punishment upon people. . . . It seems to me that these harsh expedients used by bad governments to punish

[3] From the dissenting opinions of Justice Hugo L. Black and Justice William O. Douglas, in *Ralph Ginzburg et al, Petitioners, v. United States. United States Reports.* 383 U.S. 463 (1966). Supt. of Docs. Washington, D.C. 20402. '67.

people for conduct not previously clearly marked as criminal are being used here to put Mr. Ginzburg in prison for five years.

I agree with my Brother Harlan that the Court has in effect rewritten the Federal obscenity statute and thereby imposed on Ginzburg standards and criteria that Congress never thought about, or if it did think about them certainly did not adopt them. Consequently, Ginzburg is, as I see it, having his conviction and sentence affirmed upon the basis of a statute amended by this Court for violation of which amended statute he was not charged in the courts below. Such an affirmance we have said violates due process. . . .

I shall separately discuss the three elements which a majority of the Court seems to consider material in proving obscenity.

(a) The first element considered necessary for determining obscenity is that the dominant theme of the material taken as a whole must appeal to the prurient interest in sex. It seems quite apparent to me that human beings, serving either as judges or jurors, could not be expected to give any sort of decision on this element which would even remotely promise any kind of uniformity in the enforcement of this law. What conclusion an individual, be he judge or juror, would reach about whether the material appeals to "prurient interest in sex" would depend largely in the long run not upon testimony of witnesses such as can be given in ordinary criminal cases where conduct is under scrutiny, but would depend to a large extent upon the judge's or juror's personality, habits, inclinations, attitudes and other individual characteristics. . . .

(b) The second element for determining obscenity as it is described by my Brother Brennan is that the material must be "patently offensive because it affronts contemporary community standards relating to the description or representation of sexual matters. . . ." Nothing that I see in any position adopted by a majority of the Court today and nothing that has been said in previous opinions for the Court leaves me with any kind of certainty as to whether the "community standards" referred to are world-wide, nation-wide, section-wide, state-wide, county-wide, precinct- or township-wide. But even if some definite areas were mentioned, who is capable of assessing "community standards" on such a subject? Could one expect the same application of standards by jurors in Mississippi as in New York City, in Vermont as in California? So here again the guilt or innocence of a defendant charged with obscenity must depend in the final analysis upon the personal judgment and attitudes of particular individuals and the place where the trial is held. And one must remember that the Federal Government has the power to try a man for mailing obscene matter in a court three thousand miles from his home.

(c) A third element which three of my Brethren think is required to establish obscenity is that the material must be "utterly without redeeming social value." This element seems to me to be as uncertain, if not even more uncertain, than is the unknown substance of the Milky Way. If we are to have a free society as contemplated by the Bill of Rights, then I can find little defense for leaving the liberty of American individuals subject to the judgment of a judge or jury as to whether material that provokes thought or stimulates desire is "utterly without redeeming social value. . . ." Whether a particular treatment of a particular subject is with or without social value in this evolving, dynamic society of ours is a question upon which no uniform agreement could possibly be reached among politicians, statesmen, professors, philosophers, scientists, religious groups or any other type of group. A case-by-case assessment of social values by individual judges and jurors is, I think, a dangerous technique for government to utilize in determining whether a man stays in or out of the penitentiary.

My conclusion is that certainly after the fourteen separate opinions handed down in . . . three cases today no person, not even the most learned judge much less a layman, is capable of knowing in advance of an ultimate decision in his particular case by this Court whether certain material comes within the area of "obscenity" as that term is confused by the Court today. For this reason even if, as appears from the result of the three cases today, this country is far along the way to a censorship of the subjects about which the people can talk or write, we need not commit further constitutional transgressions by leaving people in the dark as to what literature or what words or what symbols if distributed through the mails make a man a criminal. As bad and obnoxious as I believe governmental censorship is in a nation that has accepted the First Amendment as its basic ideal for freedom, I am compelled to say that censorship that would stamp certain books and literature as illegal in advance of publication or conviction would in some ways be preferable to the unpredictable book-by-book censorship into which we have now drifted.

I close this part of my dissent by saying once again that I think the First Amendment forbids any kind or type or nature of governmental censorship over views as distinguished from conduct.

II

It is obvious that the effect of the Court's decisions in the three obscenity cases handed down today is to make it exceedingly dangerous for people to discuss either orally or in writing anything about sex. Sex is a fact of life. Its pervasive influence is felt throughout the world and it cannot be ignored. Like all other facts of life it can lead to difficulty and trouble and sorrow and pain. But while it may lead to abuses, and has in many instances, no words need be spoken in order for people to know that the subject is one pleasantly interwoven in all human activities and involves the very substance of the creation of life itself. It is a subject which people are bound to consider and discuss whatever laws are passed by any government to try to suppress it. Though I do not suggest any way to solve the problems that may arise from sex or discussions about sex, of one thing I am confident, and that is that Federal censorship is not the answer to these problems. I find it difficult to see how talk about sex can be placed under the kind of censorship the Court here approves without subjecting our society to more dangers than we can anticipate at the moment. It was to avoid exactly such dangers that the First Amendment was written and adopted. For myself I would follow the course which I believe is required by the First Amendment, that is recognize that sex at least as much as any other aspect of life is so much a part of our society that its discussions should not be made a crime.

I would reverse this case.

MR. JUSTICE DOUGLAS, dissenting [two brief excerpts].

The use of sex symbols to sell literature, today condemned by the Court, engrafts another exception on First Amendment rights that is as unwarranted as the judge-made exception concerning obscenity. This new exception condemns an advertising technique as old as history. The advertisements of our best magazines are chock-full of thighs, ankles, calves, bosoms, eyes, and hair, to draw the potential buyers' attention to lotions, tires, food, liquor, clothing, autos, and even insurance policies. The sexy advertisement neither adds to nor detracts from the quality of the merchandise being offered for sale. And I do not see how it adds to or detracts one whit from the legality of the book being distributed. A book should stand on its own, irrespective of the reasons why it was written or the wiles used in selling it. I cannot imagine any promotional effort that would make chapters 7 and 8 of the Song of Solomon any the less or any more worthy of First Amendment protection than does its unostentatious inclusion in the average edition of the Bible. . . .

[It is my conclusion] that the First Amendment allows all ideas to be expressed—whether orthodox, popular, off-beat, or repulsive. I do not think it permissible to draw lines between the "good" and the "bad" and be true to the constitutional mandate to let all ideas alone. If our Constitution permitted "reasonable" regulations of freedom of expression, as do the constitutions of some nations, we would be in a field where the legislative and the judiciary would have much leeway. But under our charter all regulation or control of expression is barred. Government does not sit to reveal where the "truth" is. People are left to pick and choose between competing offerings. There is no compulsion to take and read what is repulsive any more than there is to spend one's time poring over government bulletins, political tracts, or theological treatises. The theory is that people are mature enough to pick and choose, to recognize trash when they see it, to be attracted to the literature that satisfies their deepest need, and hopefully, to move from plateau to plateau and finally reach the world of enduring ideas.

I think this is the ideal of the Free Society written into our Constitution. We have no business acting as censors or endowing any group with censorship powers. It is shocking to me for us to send to prison anyone for publishing anything, especially tracts so distant from any incitement to action as the ones before us.

A PROTESTANT VIEW OF THE GINZBURG DECISION [4]

During its long and sometimes hectic history the United States Supreme Court has seldom grappled with an issue so thorny yet so slippery as the one on which it handed down multiple decisions on March 21 [1966]—the issue of obscenity. Specifically the court issued three split decisions. It upheld five to four the obscenity conviction of Ralph Ginzburg, publisher of *Eros* and other erotic literature. In this decision . . . the Court went beyond the standard of obscenity it set in the 1957 *Roth v. United States* case. In that case, which has until now been normative in obscenity rulings, the Court established as a test of obscenity "Whether to the average persons, applying contemporary community standards, the dominant theme of the material taken as a whole appeals to prurient interest." In the Ginzburg case the Court declared that the situation as well as the material has to be taken into consideration and that a piece of material which might not in itself be obscene could become obscene because of "the context of the circumstances of production, sale and publicity."

The introduction of advertising and promotion as factors in the testing of obscenity clouds rather than clarifies the problem; for by this test the Bible, a Sears Roebuck catalogue and *Little Women* could be made obscene even though not obscene per se. Few people will quarrel with the argument that advertising and promotion can in themselves be pornographic, but that they can confer obscenity on a particular piece of material is an unwarranted conclusion. Justice Douglas correctly pointed out in his dissent that "sexy advertisement neither adds to nor detracts from the quality of the merchandise being offered for sale. And I do not see how it adds or detracts one whit from the legality of the book being distributed. A book should stand on its own, irrespective of the reasons why it was written or the wiles used in selling it." Whatever the other demerits or merits of this decision it is unlikely that this aspect of the Ginzburg decision will survive rethinking by the justices.

In the second decision the Court upheld by a six to three vote the conviction of Edward Mishkin of Yonkers, New York, for selling

[4] From an editorial, "Court Stirs a Hornet's Nest." *Christian Century*. 83:451-2. Ap. 13, '66. Copyright 1966 Christian Century Foundation. Reprinted by permission from the April 13, 1966 issue of *The Christian Century*.

materials which the publisher—Mishkin—admitted to be "sadistic and masochistic." . . . Mishkin claimed that his materials, though sadistic and masochistic, appealed only to the prurient interests of perverted people and therefore passed the Roth test since they did not appeal to the prurient interest of average persons. The Court held that material designed for perverted people is obscene if it appeals to the prurient interest of those people. Even in this case the justices found no unanimous position, but their ruling on Mishkin will probably have more durability than their ruling on Ginzburg.

In the third obscenity case the Supreme Court reversed a Massachusetts ruling that *Fanny Hill*—John Cleland's 1750 *Memoirs of a Woman of Pleasure*—"is not entitled to the protection of the First and Fourteenth amendments to the Constitution of the United States." The high court held that *Fanny Hill* passed the *Roth* test in that the three elements which constitute prohibitable obscenity do not coalesce in the book. That is, *Fanny Hill* does not in the Court's opinion appeal as a whole to prurient interest in sex, offend contemporary community standards and wholly lack redeeming social value. Whether this is a correct and salutary decision or not, it will be difficult for the average American citizen to harmonize this ruling with the others issued on the same day. Nor will it be easy for anyone examining these cases to reconcile the Court's No to Ginzburg's *Eros* and to the *Housewife's Handbook on Selective Promiscuity* with its Yes to a book which in Justice Clark's words "is nothing more than a series of minutely and vividly described sexual episodes . . . from a lesbian encounter with a sister prostitute to all sorts and types of sexual debauchery."

The thorny side of this issue has its origin in the increasing number of Americans who find wanton public descriptions of man's sexual nature and behavior repugnant and dangerous and who demand that the courts legally restrict such expressions. Many Americans have watched with understandable alarm the increasing torrents of pornography flooding newsstands, drug stores, candy and tobacco shops and the mails. They are angered by the ease with which young people in major cities can purchase photographs which depict male and female genitals in exaggerated and titillating postures and magazines and books which describe in minute and lurid detail every form of hetero- and homosexual aberration and which encourage the expression of latent sadism and masochism in sexual relations. No doubt this rebellion is in some cases motivated by prudery and by neurotic views of man's sexual life, but to dismiss the revolt against libertinism in public expression as nothing more than this would be a grievous mistake. Many responsible, intelligent and sophisticated people are genuinely disturbed by what appears to them an inordinate public craving for lewdness, by the increasing number of panderers who for selfish purposes cultivate this craving and by the panderers' concentration of their sales campaign on youth. Moreover, some of the objectors are wise enough to see that erotic pictures and literature, rather than being aphrodisiac, are actually sexual sedatives which substitute for and lessen the capacity for normal sexual love.

But when the justices grasp this side of the issue of obscenity—as in two of these cases they tried to do—their judicial responsibility is pricked by another and more serious issue: the right of free speech and expression and the right of the people to every kind of information. In the Ginzburg case four of the justices—Douglas, Black, Harlan and Stewart—found the competing issue so paramount that they could not concur in the majority opinion. Since Justices Black and Douglas are categorically opposed to all forms of censorship, Stewart's dissenting opinion may be more enlightening. In part he said:

> Censorship reflects a society's lack of confidence in itself. It is a hallmark of an authoritarian regime. Long ago those who wrote our First Amendment charted a different course. They believed a society can be truly strong only when it is truly free. In the realm of expression they put their faith, for better or for worse, in the enlightened choice of the people, free from the interference of a policeman's intrusive thumb or a judge's heavy hand. So it is that the Constitution protects coarse expression as well as refined and vulgarity no less than elegance.

To the extent that the national mood is preoccupied with lasciviousness and perversion in all forms of public media we have a problem, but that problem cannot be corrected by the enactment of a law—certainly not by a bad law. And if the Supreme Court empowers Federal censorship we invite into the national body demons far more perilous than sexual wantonness. The difficulty is to correct the one problem—admittedly grave—without generating a host of others.

The slippery side of the issue has its origin in our proved inability to define the word "obscenity." To be sure, there are many people who cannot spell the word but who are positive that they can define what is and what is not obscene. They know. But nine of the wisest men in the United States do not know. The ignorance of the latter is much more to be trusted than the arrogance of the former. A pound or a meter or a boiling point can be precisely defined, but obscenity lies in a wholly different realm and has thus far resisted definition.

In the Ginzburg and Mishkin cases the majorities of the Court ignored what they know they do not know: they did not have and they will not have an inflexible standard by which to test obscenity. Therefore the Court in its three split decisions conceived arbitrary lines of legitimate literary traffic and painted those lines on the shifting sands of "contemporary community standards," the motivations of publishers, "the leer of the sensualist"—strange language for a justice—, "redeeming social value," obscenity by context. Subjective analysis, the probing of people's motives, the sampling of public taste—these are not solid foundations on which to erect the nation's laws. The Court will be back at this stand again and, we predict, soon. In these cases the Court started something, ended nothing.

Meanwhile the churches are complaining that the Supreme Court will not give them laws to change the public climate. The Court could complain in reply that the churches are not helping provide a climate which will make authoritarian, police state laws unnecessary.

CONFUSION ON OBSCENITY: A CATHOLIC VIEW [5]

The United States Supreme Court has decided three important cases involving obscene publications and has left the law on obscenity more confused, if anything than it was before.

[5] From editorial. *America*. 114:430. Ap. 2, '66. Reprinted with permission from *America,* The National Catholic Weekly Review. 106 W. 56th St. New York 10019.

The heart of the matter appears in the *Fanny Hill* case. There, Justice William J. Brennan Jr., speaking for the majority, repeated the definition of obscenity that he himself had written in *Roth v. United States* (354 U.S. 476) in 1957: "Whether to the average person, applying contemporary community standards, the dominant theme of the material taken as a whole appeals to prurient interest." By this definition, *Fanny Hill* is surely an obscene book, as Justice Tom C. Clark pointed out in his dissenting opinion. But Justice Brennan has added another element to the legal definition of obscenity: "A book cannot be proscribed unless it is found to be utterly without redeeming social value."

The lack of redeeming social value was originally stated in *Roth v. United States,* not as an element of the definition of obscenity, but as the reason why obscene publications do not enjoy the protection of the First Amendment. Justice Byron R. White, therefore, was right in saying in his dissenting opinion: "To say that material within the Roth definition of obscenity is nevertheless not obscene if it has some redeeming social value is to reject one of the basic propositions of the Roth case. . . . In my view, 'social importance' is not an independent test of obscenity but is relevant only to determining the predominant prurient interest of the material." In another dissenting opinion, Justice John H. Harlan argued wisely for leaving some discretionary power to the states in this area.

In upholding Ralph Ginzburg's conviction for sending obscene material through the mails, the Court noted that the way a book is advertised and promoted can help judges in deciding whether it is meant to appeal to prurient interest. That makes good sense. But for coherent and viable constitutional law on obscenity, one must turn, not to the majority opinions in these cases, but to the dissenting opinions written by Justices White and Harlan.

A CONSERVATIVE VIEW [6]

The fight against pornography is at least for the time being a losing fight. The majority decision ordained that in order to be

[6] From editorial, "Ginzburg & Pornography: Supreme Court's Ruling." *National Review.* 18:346. Ap. 19, '66. Reprinted by permission of *National Review.* 150 E. 35th St. New York 10016.

classed as a work of obscenity, a publication must be lacking in even "a shred" of redeeming social significance. That word, we warrant, will prove to be of critical importance in future litigation. What the pornographers will now do is to take especial care to insert, in the unrefreshing pauses between sexual bouts, a paragraph or two calling attention to the beauty of the Sermon on the Mount, say, or the necessity of the rule of law: which passages will be highlighted in future defensive actions as precisely constituting that "shred" which the Supreme Court has insisted upon.

The previous understanding, in the *Roth* decision, was more difficult to circumvent, since it talked not of isolated shreds, but of the meaning of books read whole. . . .

Not that we envy the Supreme Court's role. We have previously remarked the insurmountable difficulties of enforcing antiobscenity laws which tread the line surely between literary expression, which includes even psychopathic literary expression, and pure pandering. The effort, nevertheless, should continue to be made, however elusive the criteria. And the effort should continue to be made irrespective of the foreknowledge that standards do in fact change. It may be perfectly correct that *Lady Chatterley's Lover* should be generally available today, while still being correct that it ought not to have been generally available thirty years ago. The point is not to give up: to retain the intellectual and moral self-assurance sufficient to look the hypocrite Ginzburg in the face and call him what he is, a pornographer-for-profit. Mr. Ginzburg's next view of erotica may be much more unhurried than this last one.

A LIBERAL VIEW [7]

Mr. Ginzburg's sentence is an outrage. Justice Brennan, writing for a majority of five, allowed that he could not be quite sure that Ginzburg's wares were really obscene. He experienced not a little difficulty, moreover, as he has before now, in articulating a meaningful definition of obscenity. So he helped himself to his conclusion by finding that Ginzburg's advertising, even if, perhaps,

[7] From an editorial, "Obscenity and the Law." *New Republic*. 154:5-6. Ap. 2, '66. Reprinted by permission of *The New Republic*.

not his material "stimulated the reader to accept [the material] as prurient; he looks for titillation, not for saving intellectual content." That is a passage to be pondered!

There is little if anything to be said for Justice Brennan's opinion, or for the majority decision in the Ginzburg case. But this judgment is the beginning of the problem, not the end. The Ginzburg case should have been disposed of by holding that the First Amendment imposes on the Federal Government a more restricted definition of obscenity than it does on the states, and that Ginzburg's dubious product or his merchandising of that product does not meet that restricted definition. For as Justice Harlan said in dissent, "the dangers of national censorship" are much greater and more pervasive than the menace and inconvenience of various local "bannings-in-Boston," or Grand Rapids. For one thing, the Federal Government is apt to impose the standards of Grand Rapids on Greenwich Village, whereas Grand Rapids will impose them only on Grand Rapids.

In both the Ginzburg and the New York fetishism, etc., cases, the Court might also have said that obscenity is much too vague a term to form an allowable part of the criminal law. However else obscenity might be controlled, it should not be punished criminally, so that a man must hazard his very freedom on the guess that a profitable publication will not be found obscene. Even the concept of "hard-core" obscenity, which is all that Justice Stewart would forbid, is probably too vague. Justice Stewart admitted a couple of years ago that he could not quite define it, although he knew it when he saw it. And Justice Harlan's attempt at a definition is no less slippery—"that prurient material that is patently offensive or whose indecency is self-demonstrating." That makes hard-core obscenity a more subjective standard than is customary in the criminal law.

Censorship by civil process and criminal sanctions are very different things. There is first the harshness of the criminal penalty, as shown in the Ginzburg sentence. Secondly, where criminal penalties are involved, one conducts his business at his peril, whereas censorship by civil process can be brought to bear administratively, with full prior notice of the alleged wrongdoing in each individual case; a chance is given to an offender to desist, to take corrective action.

All this is not to say the Court should have gone along with dissenting Justice Douglas, who believes that the First Amendment renders all publications and utterances immune to all forms of Federal and state regulation or control, civil as well as criminal. Justice Douglas would tolerate "no exceptions . . . not even for obscenity." It would be nice if we could have a society in which nothing that others sold or displayed made anyone fear for the future of his children. But we are not that society, and it is hard to protect Mishkin's freedom to make a profit any way he likes, when his particular way is a stench in the nostrils of his community, even though the community would perhaps be better advised to ignore him. What should be protected is the right of adults, consenting sado-masochists, let us say, to write and read—and do—what they like, in private. The states—not the Federal Government and not through use of the criminal sanctions—should be permitted to regulate and control the Mishkins of this world, but in more sophisticated, more limited ways. Mishkin should be allowed to cater to those who seek out his wares. Beyond that, careful lines need to be drawn. Neither he nor they should be allowed to flaunt these wares in public, or create or enlarge the market for them. That could be discouraged—as is the dumping of one's garbage on the street and a great variety of other nuisances and obnoxious acts—by administrative inspection and regulation. A man should be entitled to have dirty pictures in his inside coat pocket, but they should stay there, and it is not beyond lawmaking ingenuity to see to that, and only to that.

MORE FREEDOM OR LESS? [8]

The Court decided the Ginzburg case, appropriately on the first day of spring, and as everyone knows, confirmed the barbaric five-year sentence imposed by Judge Body of the Eastern District of Pennsylvania, the ribald implications of whose name hardly suggest the bleak piety with which he viewed Ginzburg's transgressions.

[8] From "The Obscenity Business," by Jason Epstein, vice president of Random House. *Atlantic Monthly*. 218:56-60. Ag. '66.

Judge Body ruled that Ginzburg had used the mails to distribute obscene publications in violation of a Federal statute, and he based his verdict partly on an argument by the Federal prosecutor that no matter how hard it might be to define obscenity in the light of recent Supreme Court decisions, Ginzburg had considerably simplified matters in his own case by admitting in advance, through his five million or so direct-mail circulars, that his goods were, as Justice Brennan was later to write in upholding Judge Body's verdict, "created, represented and sold solely as a claimed instrument of the sexual stimulation [they] would bring." In other words, Ginzburg had convicted himself long before his case had come to court. Whether his publications were intrinsically obscene or not, Ginzburg sold them as if they were and thus, according to the Supreme Court, left himself without a defense.

For Ginzburg and his lawyers, as indeed for many others who followed the case, this reading of the law came as a surprise and has since become a source of consternation, especially among publishers who feel themselves at a loss to understand the Court's position. From lawyers too there has been much criticism of the Court's decision, and Justice Black in his dissent argued that Ginzburg had been unfairly trapped by the unusual line of attack which the Court was pursuing. In his decision for the majority, however, Justice Brennan anticipated this objection by pointing out that "the trial transcript clearly reveals that at several points the Government announced its theory that made the mode of distribution relevant to the determination of obscenity and the trial court admitted evidence otherwise irrelevant toward that end."

The fact is that the Court, and especially the Chief Justice, seem to have had some such theory in mind for at least a decade. At any rate, it was in 1957 in a concurring opinion in the Roth decision, from which much of our legal theory of pornography now derives, that Chief Justice Warren suggested that the mode of distribution was in fact relevant to the question of obscenity, that it is not a book that is on trial, it is a person. Had Ginzburg and his lawyers heeded this warning—had they sensed that while the Court was in the process of abandoning the idea of intrinsic obscenity it would nevertheless substitute for it an evaluation of the publisher's motives . . . [the outcome might have been different].

Ginzburg was correct, of course, in assuming that the Court was hopelessly entangled in the complex problem of establishing a definition of obscenity which could be reconciled with the First Amendment and that it was thus forced to extricate itself by taking an increasingly liberal position, whose outcome could only be the gradual abandonment of any attempt to define literary pornography. By the time Ginzburg put his circulars in the mail the Court seemed to have made it all but impossible to sustain a conviction in a literary obscenity case except perhaps where so-called hard-core pornography was concerned; and even here no one seemed to know what hard-core pornography, as opposed presumably to soft or peripheral pornography, was supposed to be. For a work to be considered obscene, the prosecution had to prove first that it was patently offensive, that it was without social value, and that to the average reader, applying the standards of the community, the work as a whole was addressed to the prurient interest of its readers. And, as the Court was to affirm in its decision on *Fanny Hill,* which was rendered on the same day as the Ginzburg decision, each of these criteria had to be met simultaneously.

A patently offensive work, which an average reader might feel was in fact addressed to prurient interest—which, as the Court has also made clear, is indescribably nastier than merely sexual interest—might still be protected under the First Amendment if it could be found to have the slightest redeeming social importance. As Justice Brennan wrote in reversing the judgment against *Fanny Hill,* a work, no matter how offensive, must be *utterly* (his italics) without redeeming social importance before it can be proscribed. In these circumstances, no wonder Ginzburg protested his innocence, for even Justice Brennan in upholding Judge Body's verdict specifically refused to grant the contention of the lower court that what Ginzburg published was, in itself, obscene. "The conviction," Justice Brennan wrote, "does not necessarily suppress the materials in question nor chill their proper distribution for a proper use."

In thus becoming the unhappy instrument by which the three criteria that the Court has established for the determination of obscenity are now amplified by or enclosed within a fourth, Ginzburg, it seems to me, is not, as he insists, a martyr to the cause of free expression so much as to the Court's anguished and complex efforts to preserve free expression while still suppressing those publishers who, in their zeal or greed or foolishness, might exploit this freedom excessively, if not clearly to the detriment of the body politic, at least to the embarrassment of the Court itself. In the Ginzburg and *Fanny Hill* decisions, the Court has said, in effect, that we are indeed free at last under the First and Fourteenth Amendments to express ourselves, in print at least, as we please, but we are warned that this is also a dangerous freedom and not to be used irresponsibly. Above all, we must not give the Court cause to regret its increasingly liberal stand.

The Court's present position was argued at length some five years earlier in an article published in the *Utah Law Review* for spring, 1961, written by Dean Lockhart of the University of Utah Law School and Robert C. McClure, professor of law at the University of Minnesota. In this article, which severely criticizes the Court's position on obscenity as of that time for its many obscurities and especially for its dependence upon a definition of pornography which no court could possibly establish, the authors proposed as an alternative "that censorship should not depend upon the intrinsic nature of the material independent of its audience and method of marketing. Instead it should depend upon the manner in which it is marketed and the primary audience to which it is sold." Presumably one of the aims of Lockhart and MClure was to amplify the argument which Chief Justice Warren had suggested in 1957. Thus, while *Lady Chatterley's Lover* is clearly not obscene in itself, it would become obscene according to these authors if it were sold, for example, to high school students for its sexual interest alone. . . .

If the *Fanny Hill* decision finally disposes of the idea of intrinsic obscenity, the Ginzburg decision . . . raises still other questions to which the Court so far has supplied no answers. It is, for example, only by the most whimsical logic that *Lady Chatterley's Lover* becomes obscene in one context while in another it is unobjectionable, or that Ginzburg's publications become obscene because Ginzburg publishes them, while if a more respectable or circumspect merchant sells them, they remain pure.

Conversely, would the Book of Job, under the present ruling, become obscene if it were sold for its sadomasochistic interest alone? Could the Court legitimately punish a bookseller for exploiting this aspect of such an ordinarily innocent work? Or will the *Autobiography of a Flea* become a legitimate publication if only the Harvard University Press brings it out? As absurd as it may appear, this is approximately how the Court seems to have left matters.

It is as if the Court had now asked us to return to the standards of the last century when pornography was allowed to circulate more or less freely among upper-class males in the privacy of their clubs or studies but was forbidden to women, children, servants, and the working class generally, who were presumed not to be sexual beings at all. The question now is whether, in having restricted pornography to a privileged class of presumably mature and therefore immune readers, the Court has in fact simplified matters for itself—as well as for writers, publishers, librarians, and booksellers—or whether it has merely translated the problem into another language as obscure and dangerous as the first.

In the Ginzburg decision, at any rate, one senses far beneath the legal surface of the case an argument which appears to stem, however remotely, from something like class bias. In its choice of such prejudicial epithets as "pandering" and "the leer of the sensualist" to describe Ginzburg's activities, the Court seems to be saying that Ginzburg's crime was no more than a function of his personality or character: that he was a vulgarian, and that therefore he had no right to trade in a market whose delicate and dangerous products must be limited only to gentlemen and scholars. Such an *ad hominem* judgment can hardly have been what the Court intended, no matter how the obscurity and occasional passion of Justice Brennan's language may seem to support such an interpretation.

From the point of view of serious literature it can only be beneficial that the Court has now rejected the idea of intrinsic obscenity and has thus moved closer than Justices Black and Douglas seem willing, in their dissents, to admit to the view that the First Amendment should be interpreted without restriction where literary expression is concerned. From the narrower interests of publishers and booksellers, however, the new ruling is bound to be troublesome until the Court provides clarification. For this reason, as well as for whatever personal sympathy one may have for Ginzburg and his family, one wishes that Ginzburg had been granted the new trial which he and his lawyers had requested. If Justice Brennan's decision has opened the door even a crack to the prosecution of any publisher or bookseller who happens also to be a vulgarian, then for the sake of us all that door must be shut immediately.

Meanwhile, for whatever small comfort one may take from the fact, one notices with pleasure that the Court has agreed to consider the case of a New York newsstand clerk who was arrested for selling obscene magazines so as to determine whether a salesman can be convicted under the new ruling without clear proof that he knew that what he was selling was obscene. One assumes that if the Court itself no longer knows how to define obscenity, it can hardly expect the clerk to do any better. Perhaps it will be on these epistemological rocks that the law will finally have to admit defeat and accept the views of Justices Black and Douglas, if only to extricate itself from an impossible problem of definition. Until such time we shall have to live with the ambiguities that remain, and that will remain in whatever measure, no matter what the Court decides, as long as sexuality retains its terrifying power.

Even so, the Court, it seems to me, has so far acted reasonably, though perhaps without that God-like intelligence and mercy which some of its critics expect of it. Though one's sympathies are with Justices Black and Douglas, one still recognizes that such sympathies seldom coincide with political reality. It is enough, perhaps, for now that the Court has come as far as it has and that in having come this far it is within sight, though it may still be facing in somewhat the wrong direction, of that brave land where so far Justices Black and Douglas have been the only inhabitants.

Whether the majority of the Court will ever join these two heroic voyagers is, of course, impossible to predict, and the accidents of life and death compound the puzzle. Even so, the days of literary censorship seem to me to be substantially over, and the burden on publishers and booksellers to maintain a certain minimum decorum, at least until the public accustoms itself to this new freedom, seems hardly too much to ask.

I should not, however, like to conclude on such an agreeable note, for it would be misleading to suggest that what the Court decides the people will necessarily accept. There are those among us who will continue to claim more freedom than the Court has so far allowed, and there are others who, despite the freedom so far granted, will insist on restrictions which the Court has now disapproved.

Within each of us too there is bound to remain a private version of the same conflict. We cannot have been born into a civilization such as ours, which for so many centuries has labored under such sexual dread and mystery, without finding ourselves implicated in our culture's general distortion of instincts and values. None of us is yet prepared to walk naked on the streets, as the Etruscans once did or as the Greeks did in their games, no matter what encouragement such writers as Blake and Lawrence, or Henry Miller, and Norman Mailer, or the fashion magazines, may provide. The world is still full of sheriffs whose grasp of the law, in its endless subtlety, will always be imperfect, and within the head of each of us, even within the heads of our most radical friends, there sits a tiny Madame de Gaulle saying no to this or that.

Yet the pressure within our culture toward greater sexual freedom, and its reflection in the Court's decision to trust us now not to debauch ourselves even within the embrace of Fanny Hill, may prophesy a change. Or it may not. We shall know better when the films—a more likely medium than books—begin to assert such freedom as up to now only literature has dared risk.

At any rate, we know from Marx as well as from Freud, and from our reading of the Calvinists and the interpretation of their motives in the work of Max Weber, that there is a historic connection between sexual regulation and economic necessity, a connection which is evident even now in such a society as China's, where the demand for rapid capital formation requires severe restrictions upon sexual behavior, so that work takes precedence over marriage and even within marriage the demands of the state override the preferences of its individual members.

In America and Europe we are beyond some of that necessity, as reluctant as most of us, still trapped in the habits and illusions generated by centuries of privation, may be to admit it. Such freedom is also terrifying, and in our terror we may arrange things so that none of us will survive to enjoy it. Even so, the prospect is there, no matter how obscure and uncertain the path to it may be. One regrets that Ralph Ginzburg must now go to prison for having done no more than try to sell a merely vulgar imitation of this future paradise. But such regrets are for Ginzburg personally and not for our society as a whole. The Court, in having acquiesced in such unprecedented freedom for literature, seems to me to have foreshadowed a time in which that obsessive sexuality, so distorted by so many years of privation and the prior claims of the struggle to survive, which has so permeated not only our literature but our lives, may eventually recede—as some of our other devils have—into a more manageable and less maddening perspective. At any rate, the choice hereafter is more nearly up to us as individuals than it has ever been before, which is to say that our responsibilities have never been greater.

2. *Fair Trial Versus a Free Press*

A RECENT SUPREME COURT DECISION [9]

On June 7, 1965, the Supreme Court of the United States ruled, in a 5 to 4 decision, that financier Billie Sol Estes had not received a fair trial in a Texas district court on charges of swindling, because of extensive television coverage in the trial courtroom (*Estes v. Texas,* 381 U.S. 532). The Court held that such use of television encourages an atmosphere which is likely to result in prejudice to the defendant and his rights.

The *Estes* case and its ramifications provide an excellent vehicle for illustrating one of the major dilemmas of government: the necessity of choice between two conflicting values, both of which are desirable. A fair trial, with full regard for due process of law, is basic to the American system of government. On the other hand, a

[9] From "Fair Trial vs. Free Press." (*Judgment.* Case Study no 6) *Social Education.* 30: 633-44. D. '66. Reprinted by permission.

free press with the ability to inform the public is one of the major pillars supporting our democracy. In the trial of Billie Sol Estes, these values were in conflict....

Majority Opinion

In a 5 to 4 decision, the Supreme Court reversed Estes' state conviction for swindling and ordered a new trial. The Court held that the televising and broadcasting of Estes' trial had deprived him of his Fourteenth Amendment right to due process of law.

Justice Tom C. Clark wrote the opinion of the Court, while Chief Justice Earl Warren and Justice John M. Harlan wrote separate concurring opinions.

Justice Clark said:

"It is contended that the two-day pretrial hearing cannot be considered in determining the question before us. We cannot agree. Pretrial can create a major problem for the defendant in a criminal case. Indeed, it may be more harmful than publicity during the trial for it may well set the community opinion as to guilt or innocence.... All of this two-day affair was highly publicized and could only have impressed those present, and also the community at large, with the notorious character of the petitioner as well as the proceeding. The trial witnesses present at the hearing, as well as the original jury panel, were undoubtedly made aware of the peculiar public importance of the case by the press and television coverage being provided, and by the fact that they themselves were televised live and their pictures rebroadcast on the evening show....

"It is said, however, that the freedoms granted in the First Amendment extend a right to the news media to televise from the courtroom, and that to refuse to honor this privilege is to discriminate between the newspapers and television. This is a misconception of the rights of the press....

"While *maximum* freedom must be allowed the press in carrying on its important function in a democratic society its exercise must necessarily be subject to the maintenance of *absolute* fairness in the judicial process.... The life or liberty of any individual in this land should not be put in jeopardy because of actions of any news media....

"Court proceedings are held for the solemn purpose of endeavoring to ascertain the truth. . . . Over the centuries Anglo-American courts have devised careful safeguards by rule and otherwise to protect and facilitate the performance of this high function. As a result, at this time those safeguards do not permit the televising and photographing of a criminal trial, save in two states and there only under restrictions. . . . It is true that the public has the right to be informed as to what occurs in its courts, but reporters of all media, including television, are always present if they wish to be and are plainly free to report whatever occurs in open court through their respective media.

"The state, however, says that the use of television in the instant case was without injustice to the person immediately concerned, basing its position on the fact that the petitioner has established no isolatable prejudice and that this must be shown in order to invalidate a conviction in these circumstances. . . . At times a procedure employed by the state involves such a probability that prejudice will result that it is deemed inherently lacking in due process. . . . Television in its present state and by its very nature, reaches into a variety of areas in which it may cause prejudice to an accused. Still one cannot put his finger on its specific mischief and prove with particularity wherein he was prejudiced. . . .

"As has been said, the chief function of our judicial machinery is to ascertain the truth. The use of television, however, cannot be said to contribute materially to this objective. Rather its use amounts to the injection of an irrelevant factor into court proceedings. In addition experience teaches that there are numerous situations in which it might cause actual unfairness. . . .

"1. The potential impact of television on the jurors is perhaps the greatest significance. They are the nerve center of the fact-finding process. . . . From the moment the trial judge announces that a case will be televised it becomes a *cause célèbre.* The whole community, including prospective jurors, becomes interested in all the morbid details surrounding it. . . . And we must remember that realistically it is only the notorious trial which will be broadcast, because of the necessity for paid sponsorship. The conscious or unconscious effect that this may have on the juror's judgment cannot be evaluated, but experience indicates that it is not only possible but highly probable that it will have a direct bearing on his vote as to guilt or innocence. Where pretrial publicity of all kinds has created intense public feeling which is aggravated by the telecasting or picturing of the trial the televised jurors cannot help but feel the pressures of knowing that friends and neighbors have their eyes upon them....

"2. The quality of the testimony in criminal trials will often be impaired. The impact upon a witness of the knowledge that he is being viewed by a vast audience is simply incalculable. Some may be demoralized and frightened, some cocky and given to overstatement; memories may falter, as with anyone speaking publicly, and accuracy of statement may be severely undermined. . . .

"In addition, witnesses . . . could view and hear the testimony of preceding witnesses, and so shape their own testimony as to make its impact crucial....

"3. A major aspect of the problem is the additional responsibilities the presence of television places on the trial judge. . . . Laying physical interruptions aside, there is the ever-present distraction that the mere awareness of television's presence prompts. Judges are human beings also and are subject to the same psychological reactions as laymen. Telecasting is particularly bad where the judge is elected, as is the case in all save a half dozen of our states. The telecasting of a trial becomes a political weapon, which along with other distractions inherent in broadcasting, diverts his attention from the task at hand—the fair trial of the accused. . . .

"4. Finally, we cannot ignore the impact of courtroom television on the defendant. Its presence is a form of mental—if not physical—harassment, resembling a police lineup or the third degree. . . . A defendant on trial for a specific crime is entitled to his day in court, not in a stadium, or a city- or nationwide arena. The heightened public clamor resulting from radio and television coverage will inevitably result in prejudice. Trial by television is, therefore, foreign to our system. Furthermore, telecasting may also deprive an accused of effective counsel. The distractions, intrusions into confidential attorney-client relationships and the temptation offered by television to play to the public audience might often have a direct effect not only upon the lawyers, but the judge, the jury, and the witnesses."

Dissenting Opinions

The major dissenting opinion was written by Justice Potter Stewart in support of his position that there was no constitutional basis for the majority's decision. He declared:

"Except for the closing arguments for the prosecution and the return of the jury's verdict, there was no 'live' telecasting of the trial. And, even for purposes of delayed telecasting on later news programs, no words or other sounds were permitted to be recorded while the members of the jury were being selected or while any witness was testifying. No witnesses and no jurors were televised or photographed over their objection.

"Finally, the members of the jury saw no telecasts and no pictures of anything that went on during the trial. In accord with Texas law, the jurors were sequestered, day and night, from the beginning of the trial until it ended....

"The members of the jury were *not* prejudiced by the widespread publicity which preceded the petitioner's trial. One ingredient of this pretrial publicity was the telecast of the September hearings. Despite the confusion in the courtroom during those hearings, all that a potential juror could have possibly learned from watching them on television was that the petitioner's case had been called for trial, and that motions had been made and acted upon for a continuance, and to exclude cameras and television. At those hearings, there was no discussion whatever of anything bearing on the petitioner's guilt or innocence. This was conceded by the petitioner's counsel at the trial....

"It is obvious that the introduction of television and news cameras into a criminal trial invites many serious constitutional hazards. . . . The plain fact of the matter, however, is that none of these things happened or could have happened in this case. The jurors themselves were prevented from seeing any telecasts of the trial, and completely insulated from association with any members of the public who did see such telecasts...

"In the courtroom itself, there is nothing to show that the trial proceeded in any way other than it would have proceeded if cameras and television had not been present. . . . There is no claim that the conduct of the judge, or that any deed or word of counsel, or of any witness, or of any juror, were influenced in any way by the presence of photographers or by television. . . ."

Justice Byron White agreed with Stewart, but wrote a separate dissent to declare: "There is, on the whole, a very limited amount of experience in this country with television coverage of trials. In my view, the currently available materials assessing the effect of cameras in the courtroom are too sparse and fragmentary to constitute the basis for a constitutional judgment permanently barring any and all forms of television coverage."

Justice William J. Brennan, while also agreeing with Stewart, wrote a separate one-page dissent to say the following:

"I write merely to emphasize that only four of the five Justices voting to reverse rest on the proposition that televised criminal trials are constitutionally infirm, whatever the circumstances. Although the opinion announced by my Brother Clark purports to be an 'opinion of the Court,' my Brother Harlan subscribes to a significantly less sweeping proposition. . . .

"Thus today's decision is *not* a blanket constitutional prohibition against the televising of state criminal trials."

AMERICAN BAR ASSOCIATION PROPOSALS [10]

A special panel of the American Bar Association . . . [has proposed] drastic new restrictions on the release and publication of information about persons accused of crimes.

The 226-page report by the Association's Advisory Committee on Free Press and Fair Trial emphasized recommendations for tough new curbs on statements by lawyers and the police.

However, the report also contained a recommendation that would authorize judges to punish journalists, among others, for

[10] From "Bar Report Urges Curbs on News About Suspects," by Fred P. Graham, member, New York *Times* Washington Bureau. New York *Times*. p 1+. O. 2, '66. © 1966 by The New York Times Company. Reprinted by permission.

disseminating prejudicial statements during a trial, a power not now recognized in American law.

Justice Paul C. Reardon of the Supreme Judicial Court of Massachusetts directed the study.

The proposed rules would also give defendants the power to exclude the press and public from pretrial hearings and from portions of the trial that take place outside the presence of the jury.

Although the report is still described as tentative, it is the result of a twenty-month study. . . . Thus, it could be expected to emerge essentially intact as the organized bar's answer to the conflict posed by the First Amendment's free press guarantee and the Sixth Amendment's assurance of fair trials.

If approved by the Bar Association's Board of Governors and House of Delegates at the annual meeting next August [1967], the restrictions on lawyers would be incorporated into the association's canons of ethics. These are usually adopted by the states, where they become grounds for disbarment if violated.

The Committee recommended that the restrictions on lawyers and similar curbs on police and law enforcement agencies be incorporated into the rules of all criminal courts. This would give criminal judges the power to punish violators for contempt of court.

Current Restrictions

At present, most states have no restrictions on information that police officials can divulge, and the vague limitations on lawyers' comments, contained in Canon 20 of the code of ethics, have never been enforced.

If the proposed rules are put into effect, lawyers and the police would be barred from disclosing the following matters concerning an arrested person:

His prior arrest record or statements as to his character or reputation.

The existence or contents of any confession or his refusal to make one.

The results of any test or his refusal to take one.

The identity, testimony or credibility of prospective witnesses.

The possibility of a guilty plea.

Other statements regarding the evidence or the merits of the case.

The proposed rules would permit only the release of the defendant's name, age, residence, occupation and family status, the facts and circumstances of the arrest, a brief description of the offense charged, and a factual statement describing evidence seized by authorities.

The police would also be forbidden to pose arrested persons for photographs or televising, or to permit press interviews with the accused before he consults a lawyer.

Defense attorneys, who now frequently open their defense in the press on the morning after the arrest, would be allowed to state only that their client denies the charge.

In the first response from an official news media source, D. Tennant Bryan, chairman of the American Newspaper Publishers Association's Committee on Free Press and Fair Trial, warned against steps that would "deprive the public of truthful information which our public needs."

Tone Is Conciliatory

The publisher of the Richmond *Times-Dispatch* and *News Leader* singled out the proposed ban on releasing an arrested person's criminal record. He said the bar committee gave "no adequate reasons" for this rule.

But the general tone of his statement was conciliatory and cautious. He asked the bar and press not to harden their attitudes until an upcoming study by the publishers' association is released. [See next selection.—Ed.]

If enforced, the restrictions would substantially modify the crime reporting of most newspapers, particularly when the story of the crime and arrest appear in the same article. These typically include many details about the crime and the suspect—for instance, his motive or his race—that the police would not be permitted to disclose.

During a trial, lawyers would be barred from saying anything outside the official record of the case, and even after the verdict the lawyers could not make comments that might affect the sentence.

Transfers of Trials

The Committee also suggested liberalizing existing rules for transferring trials to other communities or for importing jurors from nearby communities.

In what would be an important change from existing law, any prospective juror "who has been exposed to and remembers highly significant information" could be challenged off a jury. The effect of such a change is apparent, for example, from the Dallas trial of Jack Ruby, where a majority of the jurors were allowed to take their seats after conceding that they saw the killing of Lee Harvey Oswald on television.

The report specifically denounced the English system of direct judicial control of the press, "specifically during the pretrial or posttrial periods."

However, it stated that the period of the trial itself was on a different footing, and recommended that judges be allowed to punish "any person" who "disseminates by any means of public communication" a prejudicial statement that goes beyond the trial record.

Citing several extreme examples of press accounts that sought to arouse sentiment against the accused during a trial, including articles in the Cleveland *Press* about the 1954 murder trial of Dr. Samuel H. Sheppard, the report declared:

"The Committee does not believe that in the limited circumstances here described, a conviction for contempt would abridge freedom of speech or of the press."

It also recommended that if such an account were to cause a mistrial, the offending party should be made to pay the cost of a new trial, thus raising the specter of the heavy fines against journalists that are a byproduct of the English system.

VIEWS OF THE AMERICAN NEWSPAPER PUBLISHERS ASSOCIATION [11]

The American Newspaper Publishers Association . . . [in a report released January 4, 1967] strongly defended press coverage of crime stories, rejected any code of conduct for crime-news reporting and opposed "restriction or censorship at the source of news."

"The people's right to a free press, which inherently embodies the right of the people to know, is one of our most fundamental rights, and neither the press nor the bar has the right to sit down and bargain it away," the publishers said in a 143-page report of its special committee on free press and fair trial.

The report, which took two years to prepare, was sharply critical of "some segments of the American bar" for "indicting" and "convicting" the press on charges of prejudicial pretrial reporting "without clear evidence that such is true."

In fact, the report asserted, the cases tend to show "that pretrial and in-trial reporting in criminal matters have no real bearing on the outcome of such cases."

"The only thing pretrial news endangers is ignorance," the publishers said.

A number of state and local bar associations have established principles and guidelines for lawyers and newsmen regarding crime publicity.

Perhaps the most important proposal was made in October [1966] by a special panel of the American Bar Association. That proposal called for contempt punishment of police officials, court officers, prosecutors and defense lawyers who released prejudicial information in criminal cases to news media. [See preceding selection.—Ed.]

Curb on Lawyers Sought

In addition, the American Bar committee proposed a change in the Canon of Legal Ethics that would prohibit lawyers for either

[11] From "Publishers and City Bar Group Oppose Crime News Restrictions," by Sidney E. Zion, staff reporter. New York *Times*. p 1+. Ja. 5, '67. © 1967 by The New York Times Company. Reprinted by permission.

side, at the risk of suspension or disbarment, from making statements outside of court about matters involved in or likely to be involved in a criminal trial.

The proposal would also authorize judges to punish newsmen of all media through the contempt power for reporting prejudicial statements during a trial, under certain circumstances.

The publishers' report made no mention of the ABA committee's recommendations, but its position appeared to be substantially different from the bar group's.

This was particularly clear in regard to possible judicial restrictions on statements made by law enforcement officers.

"To this committee," the publishers said, "it is inconceivable that such drastic restrictions . . . [as] censorship at the source of news should be imposed upon the American democratic system because of possible prejudice in a rare case."

However, despite the strong language here and elsewhere in the report, spokesmen for the bar committee and the publishers were carefully conciliatory. . . .

"We are in agreement with a great deal of its content," Justice Paul C. Reardon of Massachusetts, the chairman of the bar committee, said of the publishers' report.

He said his committee "looks forward" to working with the publishers on the problem "prior to the promulgations of our final recommendations."

Stanford Smith, general manager of the publishers' association, said in an interview: "We get along well with the Reardon committee and we want to keep the lines of communications open to continue to discuss these things with them."

Area For Agreement

One likely area for conciliation, Mr. Smith said, is the proposal by the bar committee to expand the Canon of Legal Ethics to prevent lawyers on both sides from issuing prejudicial statements to the media.

The publishers appeared to concede this right to the bar in a paragraph in their report that said: "In respect to suggested restrictions by bar associations on their own members, this committee feels that this is a matter of decision for the bar itself."

While this might seem to contradict the publishers' basic principle that there are "grave inherent dangers to the public in the restriction or censorship at the source of news," Mr. Smith said that was not the intention of the paragraph.

"Some of the proposals by the bar," he said, "that would bottle up a defendant and prohibit his attorney from making any public statement would not be in the public interest or in the interest of the defendant. And the same thing goes for prosecutors."

The use of the Canons of Ethics to "clean up our own house" has been supported by many lawyers and judges. However, a growing number of defense lawyers are becoming wary of this method of enforcement, believing that it will almost invariably be used against them and not against prosecutors.

Justice Reardon . . . did not mention the Canon of Ethics point. In an interview, however, he indicated that he believed the publishers had agreed that the bar could police itself in that manner.

In his short statement, Justice Reardon said that the main difference between his committee and the publishers was in the pervasiveness of prejudicial crime publicity.

> We have found [he said] as they do now, no necessary incompatibility between the First and Sixth Amendments. We too are against secret arrests and secret trials and darkness where there should be light. Our labors have convinced us, however, that there has been and is now on the American scene a problem of prejudicial publicity infecting altogether too many criminal trials, and if we diverge from the views of the publishers it is mainly on that score.

The publishers took the position that the press was a "positive influence in assuring fair trial" and asserted that the "presumption of some members of the bar that pretrial news is intrinsically prejudicial is based on conjecture and not on fact."

In rejecting the recommendations made by bar groups for the adoption of a press code of conduct, the publishers said:

"From a practical standpoint any such codes would be without value because there is no way to enforce them."

VIEWS OF THE ASSOCIATION OF THE BAR OF THE CITY OF NEW YORK[12]

A special committee of the Association of the Bar of the City of New York advocated . . . [on February 23, 1967] a "drastic" tightening of the Canons of Legal Ethics to halt the flow of prejudicial publicity by lawyers in criminal and civil cases.

The bar group said, however, that the courts were generally powerless to impose direct controls on the news media or the police. Therefore, it urged that strict voluntary codes be adopted by the press and the police in the reporting of crime news.

Aims of the Committee

"What we suggest is action that we hope may result in appropriate controls of the lawyers and the law enforcement officials, under the auspices of the lawyers and the police themselves, more positive and effective action by the courts and the judges, and a larger measure of self-restraint by the news media," Judge Harold R. Medina, chairman of the committee, wrote in a preface to the 70-page report. Judge Medina is a retired member of the United States Court of Appeals for the Second Circuit.

At a news conference at the Overseas Press Club, Judge Medina said that the report differed on "points of critical importance" from a proposal made in October by a committee of the American Bar Association [See "American Bar Association Proposals" in this section, above.]

He explained that under the ABA proposal newsmen could be held in contempt of court for publishing prejudicial stories during a trial, and police officers could be punished for contempt if they "leaked" prejudicial pretrial publicity.

Under the Medina committee's recommended voluntary code for police and law enforcement agencies, the release of information concerning a defendant would be limited to his name, age, occupation, marital status, and personal data not related to the crime or the character of the defendant.

[12] From "City Bar Advocates Tight Restriction on Trial Publicity," by Sidney E. Zion, staff reporter. New York *Times*. p 1+. F. 24, '67. © 1967 by The New York Times Company. Reprinted by permission.

Prosecutors and defense lawyers would be prevented from making virtually any statement regarding the case, at the risk of suspension or disbarment, under the Medina committee's recommended new canon of ethics.

Under the ABA proposal lawyers could be held in contempt of court as well as coming under the discipline of the bar association.

Editors Give Views

The report was both praised and criticized by officers of the American Society of Newspaper Editors in a statement issued ... [February 23, 1967].

The editors said that the Medina committee was "eminently correct" in holding that the courts lacked power to control the police and the press.

But they declared that "it is neither necessary nor proper to shut off virtually all communications between attorneys or public officers and the press before or during trial."

The police code proposed in the report was attacked by the editors as "unduly restrictive . . . a code of virtual silence [that] fails to recognize that the courts are conducting public business."

"The code of silence," the editors said, "would attempt to do indirectly what the Constitution expressly forbids—interdict a free flow of information on public affairs to the public."

The statement, signed by Robert C. Notson, president of the editors' society, and J. Edward Murray, chairman of the group's freedom of information committee, asserted that the "voluntary" code of silence "could, and almost certainly would cover up incompetence, venality and deliberate frustration of criminal procedures."

I. William Hill, president of the Associated Press Managing Editors Association, criticized the Medina report for "choking off news from the public."

The report did not detail a voluntary code for the press, as it did for the police. But it praised the guidelines adopted in August by the Toledo *Times* and the Toledo *Blade.*

Those guidelines would, in the absence of "very special circumstances," rule out the publication of such things as confessions, prior criminal records and arguments made when the jury was not present.

Ethics Canon Stressed

Judge Medina . . . placed principal emphasis on the proposed new Canon of Ethics that would drastically revise both the American Bar Association's code on publicity and the New York State Bar Association's canon. Both are known as Canon 20. The New York canon is more detailed.

"We need a new Canon 20 right now," Judge Medina declared. "The one we have has too many loopholes and escape hatches." . . .

The "loopholes" referred to by Mr. Medina are that under the ABA canon newspaper discussion of pending litigation is held to be "generally" condemned with publicity allowed in "extreme circumstances." The New York Canon's "escape hatch" permits lawyers to "reply to any public statement which adversely affects the interest of his client."

Bar Curbs Detailed

The proposed Canon 20 would read, in part, as follows:

"It is unprofessional for a lawyer to make, or sanction the publication or broadcast of an out-of-court statement or disclosure of fact or opinion regarding a pending or anticipated civil action or proceeding or criminal prosecution."

A number of specifics are mentioned in connection with this ban, including any comments on guilt or innocence, whether there had been a confession, and the rulings of the court during litigation.

A catchall paragraph bars any statements by lawyers that "may tend to interfere with a fair trial, or may otherwise tend to prejudice the due administration of justice."

A prosecutor would be limited to a statement identifying a defendant, naming the charges against him and the time and place of arrest.

Defense lawyers would be restricted to a "brief statement" concerning their clients' intention to plead not guilty. Moreover, the new canon would make it the "duty" of a lawyer to restrain his client and witnesses from making any out-of-court statement or disclosure of fact or opinion that the lawyer himself could not make.

The restrictions on defense counsel are similar to those advocated by the ABA committee. But prosecutors could give out more information under the latter proposal, such as the evidence seized from the defendant.

Under both proposals indictments could be printed in full.

Judge Medina conceded that under his committee's proposals "overbalancing exists" in favor of the government and against defendants.

"For example," he said, "you can produce a 262-page indictment with every little detail known to man or beast and it can come out like a regular press conference. I don't know how you're going to curb that."

He said that instances were "rare" in which defense counsel tried criminal cases in the news media.

"Most of 'em don't know how to do it," he said, "but those few who sure do know how to do it are a real menace."

The judge said that "80 per cent" of the publicity abuses would be laid to prosecutors.

"But the only way we can do it," he declared, "is to have an absolute prohibition against any lawyer trying a case in the newspapers.

"It's a disgrace to the bar because the place to try a case is in the courtroom."

Hopeful About Police

Asked what a defense lawyer should do if the police in a community did not accept a voluntary code and "flooded" the media with prejudicial material, Judge Medina said: "We believe we've provided means to deal with the police through the voluntary codes and we're only hopeful."

The judge said that the issue of prejudicial publicity in criminal cases "has been exaggerated."

> But it exists [he asserted] and sometimes it is extremely serious. Let's not tear down the whole edifice, though, because we think it can be cured and we think our report helps in that direction.

We see a very perceptible improvement in the press and among lawyers and policemen in recent months.

The Sheppard case made a tremendous difference . . . it brought in a new era.

He was referring to the ruling . . . [in 1966] by the United States Supreme Court reversing the 1954 conviction of Dr. Samuel H. Sheppard because of "virulent" publicity surrounding his trial for the murder of his wife.

Dr. Sheppard was acquitted last fall on a retrial.

A growing number of defense lawyers have objected to the canon of ethics proposed by the ABA committee. They say that the sanctions will be used against them almost exclusively, since bar associations have seldom disciplined prosecutors for more serious offenses than leaking a news story, such as suppression of evidence.

Southern civil-rights lawyers are reported to be particularly concerned that the new canon would give segregationist bar associations a powerful hammer against them without any substantial offsetting benefits.

The city bar report called the ABA committee's proposals "a major contribution" and said that "the differences between us are not nearly so significant as our basic agreements."

AMERICAN CIVIL LIBERTIES UNION'S VIEW[13]

No problem within the scope of its interest has proved more difficult for the American Civil Liberties Union than that raised by the publicizing of pending criminal trials. On the one hand, the Union has steadfastly held as its core principle the inviolability of First Amendment freedoms, including freedom of the newspapers and electronic media to report all matters which they hold to be newsworthy. On the other, we have consistently urged throughout our history ever more rigorous standards of due process in criminal proceedings, including methods of insuring impartial judges and juries.

[13] From "Statement, Board of Directors, Fair Trial and Free Press." Mimeo. American Civil Liberties Union. 156 Fifth Ave. New York 10010. D. '66. p 1-9. Reprinted by permission.

We have no doubt that any attempt to suggest proper guidelines in this area may offend what many regard as a virtually absolute right to report events which qualify as news. We are even more certain that the release or reporting of all information relating to a criminal prosecution, no matter how unreliable, irrelevant, or prejudicial, can, in a significant number of instances, effectively destroy the right of an individual to a fair trial. For, in a case which has been widely publicized, the defendant must either take his chances with a jury whose members he knows have been exposed on numerous occasions to the press version of the crime, or forgo the constitutional right and protection of a jury trial, trusting to the supposedly greater objectivity of a judge. . . .

II

In attempting to resolve the dilemma posed by conflicting civil liberties values in this area, the ACLU has sought to isolate the traditional arguments in the controversy.

A. The Arguments for Not Restricting Information Relating to Trials

The First and Fourteenth Amendments forbid governmental censorship of the press. It is at the very least within the spirit of those provisions to allow the press a free hand in reporting information relating to our judicial institutions, including criminal trials. The positive advantages of permitting thorough press coverage of our judicial institutions may be a heightened public awareness of and interest in our legal system, our crime problem and the need for improvements in criminal trial procedures. Equally important, journalistic probing may serve as a vital barrier to kangaroo courts and a prop for the innocent, witness the recent Whitmore case in New York. Last, in light of the fact that not much is really known about the secret deliberations of jurors and the effect of newspaper publicity on the minds of jurors or judges, we should not make haste to impose far-reaching limitations on the public's access to information [in] the interest of influencing an uncertain mental state.

B. The Arguments in Favor of Limitation

The Sixth and Fourteenth Amendments give every person accused of crime the right to a fair trial. This right includes, along with other procedural protections, the right to be tried by an impartial jury or judge responsive to the evidence, not to public opinion generated by inflammatory publicity, nor, most important, to preconceived notions of the guilt of the accused. Enough is known of the workings of juries to support the judgment that juries are particularly subject to bias stemming from publicity about a pending case. And it has been also noted that,

> [T]o deny that bludgeoning or poisonous comment has power to influence or at least to disturb, the task of judging is to play make believe and to assume that men in gowns are angels. The psychological aspects of this problem become particularly pertinent in the case of elected judges with short tenure. (328 U.S. 331, 359)

The argument that freedom of the press is absolute, even when it may adversely affect the functioning of the courts or destroy the right to a fair trial, has been seriously questioned by several members of the Supreme Court. Concurring in *Irvin v. Dowd, supra* Mr. Justice Frankfurter stated:

> [A]gain and again, such disregard of fundamental fairness is so flagrant that the Court is compelled . . . to reverse a conviction in which prejudicial newspaper intrusion has poisoned the outcome. . . . This Court has not yet decided that the fair administration of criminal justice must be subordinated to another safeguard of our constitutional system—freedom of the press, properly conceived. The Court has not yet decided that, while convictions must be reversed and miscarriages of justice result because the minds of the jurors are poisoned, the poisoner is constitutionally protected in plying his trade. (366 U.S. 730)

In addition, while the power of the courts to hold the press in contempt has been severely restricted in the interests of free discussion, some residue of that power undoubtedly still exists. However, whether or not contempt actions are proper where massive newspaper publicity threatens the impartial functioning of the courts, it can be argued that where there exists a clear and present danger of an unfair criminal trial, appropriate measures other than contempt citations may be taken to limit the effect of such publicity. In the ACLU's view, these measures need not directly touch media of communication, but should be aimed in the first instance at law enforcement officials, members of the bar, and the courts themselves. The advantages of this approach are that it avoids a direct collision between two rights deeply embedded in our constitutional fabric and that it narrows the application of sanctions to those persons most intimately concerned with the administration of justice.

III

In 1958, after consideration of this issue by the ACLU's Free Speech and Due Process Committees, the Board of Directors adopted a statement urging local ACLU units to criticize media and law enforcement officials where it was evident that they failed to exercise self-restraint in publicizing criminal cases prior to trial. The ACLU at that time also asked the press, the bar and the courts to cooperate in formulating acceptable standards for the reporting of criminal trials. However, in the years that have passed, there have been few meaningful efforts in this direction by responsible officials and little visible improvement in the abuses stemming from the publicizing of criminal cases. Upon reexamination of the entire question, the ACLU has concluded that specific changes in our laws are necessary to preserve the historic right to a free trial without unduly limiting public discussion and public understanding of the machinery of justice. We feel first, that specific standards should be adopted by the courts, legislators, bar associations and mass media governing the information which is to be made available in connection with criminal trials, and second, that more effective sanctions must be brought to bear to eliminate the effects of prejudicial publicity.

A. Information Standards

The American Civil Liberties Union recommends that all officials involved in the enforcement of law and prosecution of criminals on the local, state and Federal levels abide by these guidelines applying to the release of information to news media from the time a person is arrested or is charged with a criminal offense until the proceeding has been terminated by trial or otherwise.

1. At no time shall any official furnish any statement of information for the purpose of influencing the outcome of a defendant's trial.

2. Officials, subject to specific limitations imposed by law or court rule or order, may make public the following information:

   a. The defendant's name, age, residence, employment, marital status, and similar background information
   b. The substance or text of the charge, such as a complaint, indictment, or information
   c. The identity of the investigating and arresting agency and the length of the investigation
   d. The time and place of arrest

3. No judicial, prosecutorial, or police official or employee shall reveal any information about any individual's criminal or arrest record of or about a confession of a person accused of a crime. Under no circumstance shall such information be given out for the purpose of publicity.

4. The release of certain types of information generally tends to create dangers of prejudice without serving a significant law enforcement function. Therefore, officials should refrain from making available the following:

   a. Observations about a defendant's character
   b. Statements, admissions, confessions, or alibis attributable to a defendant
   c. References to investigative procedures, such as fingerprints, polygraph examinations, ballistic tests, or laboratory tests
   d. Statements concerning the identity, credibility, or testimony of prospective witnesses
   e. Statements concerning evidence or argument in the case, whether or not it is anticipated that such evidence or argument will be used at trial

f. The circumstances immediately surrounding an arrest, including resistance, pursuit, possession and use of weapons, and a description of items seized at the time of arrest

5. The officials in charge of the custody of an arrested person have a duty to protect him from being photographed or televised while in the custody of the police. Moreover, photographs of a defendant should never be released unless they serve a proper investigatory function.

6. This statement of policy is not intended to restrict the release of information concerning a defendant who is accused of a crime when such release is deemed necessary to apprehend him.

B. Appropriate Sanctions

The ACLU favors directing sanctions initially against law enforcement officers and prosecution and defense attorneys responsible for presenting a case to the press instead of to the court. One of the simplest methods of controlling the release of prejudicial information prior to trial is to insure that police departments and prosecuting attorneys adopt specific administrative measures and policy statements designed to guide the conduct of all employees in this area as the United States Department of Justice has recently done. Thus, improper release of such information as prior arrest records, which could make a fair trial impossible for the defendant or the state, would be grounds for disciplinary action.

In order to control improper actions by attorneys seeking to influence the course of a trial by publicity, and in order to guard against the failure of the administrative checks proposed above, the ACLU urges that a procedure be adopted by rule or statute in all courts allowing judges to publicly admonish prosecution and defense attorneys and law enforcement officers responsible for aiding or creating prejudicial publicity. A judge could be empowered to summon the offending attorney before him, either on his own motion, or at the request of the opposing counsel, administer a rebuke in open court, and permit the opposing counsel upon request to publicize a statement answering the damaging information previously publicized. In addition, the court could refer the matter to the appropriate bar association committee on ethics, if warranted. Aside from the advantages of its deterrent effect, ACLU feels that this proposal would enable a judge to apply curative measures immediately after the release of prejudicial publicity by labeling the release as wrongful and by permitting an "equalizing" statement to be made under controlled conditions. Currently, whatever ability a court may have to counteract publicity, such as the limited power to instruct a jury to disregard newspaper comment, can be exercised only at trial, when it is generally too late to dissipate the effects of prejudicial reporting.

The major and traditional means of insuring that jurors who are influenced by pretrial publicity do not sit in judgment on criminal cases is the *voir dire* examination, during which prospective jurors are questioned by counsel and by the court to ascertain their fitness to serve. If the questioning shows that a juror has read or seen a great deal of publicity about a case, no matter how lurid or erroneous, he may still be allowed to sit in the jury box if he states that he can put to one side what he has learned and render an impartial verdict. Thus, it is generally only those jurors who admit that the publicity has influenced their opinion and that they no longer can have an open mind, who may be challenged for cause.

ACLU proposes that this narrow scope of the traditional challenge for cause be expanded to permit the challenge of any juror who has gained a substantial degree of knowledge about a case from pretrial publicity, because the present system simply does not insure an objective jury. A juror knows he is expected to say that he is impartial, and there is simply no way to verify a juror's subjective judgment that he can ignore inflammatory publicity to which he has been exposed, any more than he could ignore personal observation of facts which could disqualify him as a juror. This change in the nature of the challenge for cause should accomplish two important results. First, it should prevent persons from sitting as jurors who have not accurately gauged the extent of their own bias flowing from newspaper publicity. Second, it should remove the incentive for police and prosecuting authorities to instigate prejudicial publicity in the hope of making convictions easier to obtain. Since the release or publication of any substantial information about a pending criminal case will disqualify many prospective jurors, thus delaying the trial, police and prosecutors will have to choose between encouraging pretrial publicity and disposing of cases promptly and effectively.

We recognize that such a change in the scope of the challenge for cause may make it difficult to secure a jury in those sensational cases if (despite the precautions previously recommended) pretrial publicity reaches virtually all members of the community. However, in such cases a change of venue to another community is usually possible, as is a substantial pretrial delay to enable the effects of the publicity to dissipate. In any event, the difficulty in securing an impartial jury is a reasonable price to pay for insuring that the basic right to a fair trial will not be destroyed by intentional efforts to sway the community through publicity. Delay caused by undue publicity should be a ground for reduction of bail.

Our suggestions and discussion have focused on the need to take specific measures to eliminate the possibility of biased jurors in criminal cases. However, in the general discussion of this problem the potential bias that inflammatory publicity may create in judges is too often ignored, as if, in Justice Frankfurter's words, "men in gowns are angels." The ACLU suggests that the Judicial Conference of the United States explore this problem with a view to adopting standards governing the conduct of judges in sensational, well-publicized cases. We submit that the Conference should attempt to answer such questions as: Should a judge be free to see any media report or comment on a case he is about to try? If so, should he be required to state for the record what he has read or seen, and when?

It is the hope of the ACLU that these measures—administrative directives, judicial admonishment, bar association censure, expanded challenge for cause—will contribute significantly to meeting the extremely difficult problems posed by the desire of the press to report and the basic requirements of an impartial trial. We feel at this time that it would be a mistake to enact sanctions directly against the press. We urge the press, the bar, the bench, and all law enforcement agencies to cooperate in working out effective measures, including those we have suggested, as guarantees that neither of the great institutions of our society—the free press and the fair trial—will be sacrificed to the other.

3. *Extending Freedom of Speech*

THE JULIAN BOND CASE [14]

The Supreme Court's decision in the case of Julian Bond, the twice-barred Georgia legislator, was a vigorous affirmation of the rights of free speech of all citizens as well as members of state legislatures.

It also was the first time an American court had overruled a state legislature's decision on the qualifications of its own members. This is an important extension of Federal power which admittedly raises new questions involving both the Federal-state relationship and the line of separation between legislative, judicial and executive branches of the Government.

The Court based its decision on Mr. Bond's rights of free speech under the First Amendment to the Constitution. These rights it upheld unanimously. In the words of Chief Justice Warren, the Court wrote a new chapter in the constant battle for man's right to think and to speak as his conscience dictates:

"Just as erroneous statements must be protected to give freedom of expression the breathing space it needs to survive, so statements criticizing public policy and the implementation of it must be similarly protected."

Up to now, there had been no court decisions interpreting the power of a legislative body to bar or expel a member. The usual method of resisting legislative ouster was to get reelected. Mr. Bond tried this—he had been elected three times and rejected twice by the Georgia House of Representatives because of his expressed views on the Vietnam war—but he also went to court, and the new ruling is the result.

It struck down the Georgia legislature's contention that it had the power to test the sincerity of a legislator to swear to uphold the

[14] From "The Court Speaks for Freedom," an editorial. New York *Times*. p 46. D. 6, '66. © 1966 by The New York Times Company. Reprinted by permission.

Constitution. "Such a power could be utilized to restrict the right of legislators to dissent from the national or state policy, or that of a majority of their colleagues under the guise of judging their loyalty to the Constitution," the Court said.

In a time when many Government policies are being debated and when the American effort in Vietnam particularly is open to constant questioning, this decision is a refreshing reminder of the necessary vitality of dissent. The policing of thoughts cannot be tolerated, especially by legislators seeking conformity and advance agreement among their own membership.

The Court has spoken for freedom, both for legislators and for those whom the legislators represent.

III. CENSORSHIP AND POLITICS

EDITOR'S INTRODUCTION

The citizen's never-ending "need to know" in a democracy often collides with the withholding of information by the Government or the issuance of misleading reports by its officials. In this section the problem is raised in terms of a new law on Government information policy and the Federal Government's influence on publishing which results from subsidizing the publication of certain books.

The new information law's guidelines are set forth by a New York *Times* staff member, John D. Pomfret. The Government as publisher is discussed by Geoffrey Wolff, book editor of the Washington *Post.* His concern is mainly with the book-subsidy program undertaken by the United States Information Agency which is responsible for America's information programs addressed to foreign countries.

Early in 1967 it was revealed that the Central Intelligence Agency (CIA) had also subsidized private book publishing. Frederick A. Praeger (president of the publishing firm of the same name) here defends his actions in accepting such subsidies.

The critical issue of free press versus national security is discussed by two members of the editorial staff of the New York *Times* —James Reston and Clifton Daniel. The latter reveals the inside story of how the reporting of the Bay of Pigs affair was handled by the press and President John F. Kennedy. A New York *Times* editorial follows, giving the newspaper's general position on the freedom of the press.

A NEW LAW [1]

[The new law on Government information policy, signed by President Lyndon B. Johnson on July 4, 1966] establishes the right

[1] From "Johnson Supports Greater Access to U.S. Data," by John D. Pomfret, member, New York *Times* Washington Bureau. New York *Times*. p 25. Jl. 5, '66. © 1966 by The New York Times Company. Reprinted by permission.

of judicial review of Government decisions to withhold records. The law, which becomes effective . . . [July 4, 1967], puts on the Government the burden of proving that it has the right to withhold records.

The law provides exceptions to the kinds of information that Federal agencies are required to give inquiring citizens or reporters. The exemptions include:

National security secrets, foreign policy information required by executive order to be kept secret, trade secrets and other commercial information the Government may have acquired through questionnaires or through mediation of labor-management disputes, personnel files and medical reports on Government employees.

Also, documents solely related to personnel regulations, reports submitted by banks and other financial institutions in compliance with laws, and memorandums and correspondence between agency officials that would not be available by law to a private party engaged in litigation with the Government.

In a statement, President Johnson said:

> Democracy works best when the people have all the information that the security of the nation permits. No one should be able to pull curtains of secrecy around decisions which can be revealed without injury to the public interest.

One section of Mr. Johnson's statement seemed to imply that he had reservations about the inclusiveness of the new law. It said:

> Officials within Government must be able to communicate with one another fully and frankly without publicity. They cannot operate effectively if required to disclose information prematurely or to make public investigative files and internal instructions that guide them in arriving at their decisions.
>
> I know that the sponsors of this bill recognize these important interests and intend to provide for both the need of the public for access to information and the need of the Government to protect certain categories of information.

The President's statement also said that the bill "in no way impairs the President's power under our Constitution to provide for confidentiality when the national interest so requires."

This appeared to be a reference to executive privilege under which Presidents at times have withheld information from Congress. The new law is not intended to deal with executive privilege. It applies only to the executive branch of Government, not to Congress or the judiciary.

The bill, it is believed, may make it easier to find out how members of regulatory bodies vote and to get access to the manuals of administrative procedures of Federal agencies.

It may also make it easier in some cases to ascertain the contents of Government contracts.

The new law resulted from a ten-year fight by Representative John E. Moss, Democrat of California. Mr. Moss is chairman of the Freedom of Information subcommittee of the House Committee on Government Operations. . . .

> I have always believed [the President's statement continued] that freedom of information is so vital that only the national security, not the desire of public officials or private citizens, should determine when it must be restricted. . . .
>
> I signed this measure with a deep sense of pride that the United States is an open society in which the people's right to know is cherished and guarded.

A JOURNALISTIC REACTION [2]

The passage of the Federal open records law was the major achievement in the Freedom of Information fight in 1966. . . . Even this gain must be viewed as only a potential bright spot until the press has had time to examine how it is administered by the Johnson Administration. An atmosphere of censorship and secrecy has characterized the Administration's policies, particularly at the White House and the Pentagon.

The activities and attitudes expressed by high officials of the Johnson Administration on information policies should serve as a warning that there could be efforts to twist the open records law into a closed records law. The Pentagon continues in force the Sylvester Directive of October 1962 that requires all Pentagon em-

[2] From "Report of the 1966 Sigma Delta Chi Advancement of Freedom of Information Committee." Sigma Delta Chi, professional journalistic society. 35 E. Wacker Dr. Chicago 60601. Fall '66. p 5+. Reprinted by permission.

ployees, civilian and military, to report all press contacts before the end of the working day. The use of grossly inflated claims of "savings" of $14 billion through the Defense Department cost-reduction program is an example of the Big Lie technique that the Administration uses in connection with big and complicated programs to mislead the press and the public. Certainly, the experienced White House reporters do not find this to be an era of open government and open discussion on government operations. The President is recognized for his angry reaction over "leaks" of information on appointments or on the views of dissenters. . . .

The provisions of the new law, a major goal for Sigma Delta Chi and other journalistic groups for many years, do not take effect until next July 4 [1967], giving the vast Federal establishment time to adjust to the new rules.

In the meantime, newsmen can start familiarizing themselves with the law. The measure provides that "any person" shall have access to the records of all executive branch agencies. There are nine categories of records that are exempted from coverage including items involving national defense and foreign policy. Also protected are matters involving personnel policies and information that might reveal trade or financial secrets.

In general, the new statute follows the recommendations of Sigma Delta Chi for this kind of legislation. The main thrust of such laws should be to put the burden of proof on government that information sought by newsmen should not be disclosed. All government information should be public information, unless it can be proved that a higher public interest can be served by secrecy.

The proof of the law, of course, will come over time as newsmen probe and explore to see how it is being enforced. Two different bureaucrats can use the same law in two different ways. And the same bureaucrat can use the same law differently on different days of the week, depending on the issues involved. There will still be plenty of room left for the use of that all-too-rare journalistic talent—enterprise.

THE GOVERNMENT AS PUBLISHER: THE USIA [3]

"Words are loaded pistols," says Sartre, and official voices in this country have come to fully acknowledge this dictum. In the months before the 1964 election, for example, 18 of our 50 Senators were working on one or more books, most of which would be ghost-written and published under their names. The publish or perish syndrome is even more prevalent in the executive branch: we have had platoons of books and nonbooks about the Peace Corps, introduced by Sargent Shriver; the Defense Department has been endlessly chronicled, as have NASA, the diplomatic corps, the Internal Revenue Service, and the rest of the Establishment's interests.

A story often heard in Washington has President Kennedy looking ahead to the 1964 election and huddling with his lieutenants to come up with a campaign issue. In one of the meetings, the story goes, he asked if there was anything of substance in Michael Harrington's study of poverty, *The Other America.* Assured that there was, Kennedy called for memorandums, documents, and ideas. Shortly thereafter, poverty books came forth by the dozens—many written by persons who were part of or close to the Administration. Magazine articles followed; silence and ignorance gave way to public clamor; an issue was born, and the War on Poverty began.

In principle, there is nothing alarming about public officials generating books to further their political ideals and careers. In practice, however, political expediency has made many writers so arrogant that they scorn facts and ignore their duty to learn and the reader's right to know. There is much evidence that books are used increasingly as engines of propaganda, that highly placed persons are precensoring books they find repellent or embarrassing, and that they are commissioning and controlling the writing of books without disclosing the facts of such control. If we believe that truth has a more exclusive claim to our attention than partial truth or falsehood, and if we believe that openness and disclosure of the circumstances surrounding the writing, publishing, and marketing of a book are requisites of a free access to ideas, then we must

[3] From "Government Book Control," by Geoffrey Wolff, book editor. Washington *Post Book Week.* p2+. F. 5, '67. Reprinted by permission.

be alarmed at the sham, illegality, and indirection that have infected much of what is sold as objective reality.

Recently, for example, Mr. George Carver wrote for the highly respected periodical *Foreign Affairs* an article supporting our official policy toward North and South Vietnam. Mr. Carver is with the CIA but this crucial information was not related by *Foreign Affairs*. Worse, it is possible it was not given to the magazine. It is illegal for the CIA to operate as an intelligence-gathering or intelligence-disseminating organization in the United States. The same restrictions apply to USIA, which is bound to confine itself to propaganda activities abroad. Yet its officers admitted several months ago in hearings before a subcommittee of the House Committee on Appropriations that part of the activity of its "Book Development Program" has been the *secret* production of manuscripts, published by private companies which the USIA subsidizes, and sold in this country without any government *imprimatur* or other acknowledgment of the circumstances of their origin.

Reed Harris, appearing before the subcommittee in his capacity as director of the USIA Information Center Service, said of these books: "We control the things from the very idea down to the final edited manuscript." Perhaps the books are accurate and valuable, perhaps they are self-serving or meretricious; what is certain is that they do not tell the reader what he surely wants to know: that they are works which the USIA admits would never have been written without Government support and would not have been released by a commercial publishing house without subsidization—either because they were unworthy of publication or they were unmarketable.

Leonard Marks, director of USIA, and Ben Posner, assistant director, were questioned about the Book Development Program by Congressman Glenard Lipscomb (Republican, California). Portions of the exchange follow:

MR. LIPSCOMB: What were the books that were developed in the 1966 [sic] fiscal year Book Development Program?

MR. POSNER: In fiscal year 1965 there were four books that were developed. *The Ladder Dictionary* by John R. Shaw, *The Sword and the Plow* by Ralph Slater, *President Kennedy in Africa* by Robert Marshall, *The Truth*

About the Dominican Republic by Jay Mallin. . . . We will be pleased to make this information available to the committee. Because it has not been our policy to make our support known in connection with these items, the material that I have is not for the record, Mr. Chairman.

MR. LIPSCOMB: Do I understand that this list is considered as classified?

MR. POSNER: In the sense that we have not in the past divulged the Government's connection with it, yes sir.

MR. LIPSCOMB: Are any of these books on this classified list distributed and sold within the United States?

MR. POSNER: I believe that they are; yes.

MR. MARKS: In other words, we assist.

At this juncture Mr. Marks agreed to put in the record the titles of the books and the cost, $90,258, of commissioning manuscripts and supporting the publication of books commissioned by private publishers. The taxpayer who buys one of these books pays for it three times: he pays to have it written; he pays to have it published, and he pays its retail price at the bookstore. He also pays to support a Government Printing Office which could publish and sell the book at a fraction of its cost as produced privately and secretly. But Mr. Marks, in later testimony, explained why books under Government *imprimatur* are not useful to the purposes of USIA.

MR. LIPSCOMB: Why is it wrong to let the American people know when they buy and read the book that it was developed under Government sponsorship?

MR. MARKS: It minimizes their [sic] value.

MR. LIPSCOMB: Why is it not a good policy to maintain the same ground rules that you maintain with motion pictures, with newspaper stories, and do your work just for overseas and make it a policy that these books that are prepared under your supervision and prepared with taxpayers' money are not for distribution within the United States?

MR. MARKS: . . . Where an audience overseas reads a book with the label of the United States Government they look upon it in a particular manner. Where they read a book that is published in the United States and we distribute it, they look upon it differently, as the expression of the author. It is the expression of the author, it is not our expression. We did not write that book. We merely bought copies and helped to distribute it. But if we say this is our book, then the author is a Government employee, in effect.

Of course the author *is* a Government employee—in fact, not in effect. He does a chore at the order and to the requirements of the Government. Further, his work is then published under the copyright of a private publisher even though Section 8 of the Copyright Laws says that any work produced by a Government employee within the scope of his employment is not copyrightable, even though produced by a private publisher. Thus the taxpayer pays again: he pays royalties on each copy of a book that the USIA buys for distribution—a book which is already their property. Mr. Lipscomb was very gentle with Mr. Marks on this point:

MR. LIPSCOMB: I am for the Book Development Program for distribution overseas. I believe you can do lots of good with it. But why not limit your activities for overseas? You are making a subsidy to the author and publisher. The taxpayer is not complaining about it, but there is a principle involved in my mind that when an American citizen who subsidizes a book reads it, he should know.

MR. MARKS: That is a point of view which I understand.

MR. LIPSCOMB: I assume you are distributing them overseas, for lack of a better word, for propaganda purposes.

MR. MARKS: Yes, definitely; to tell a story.

MR. LIPSCOMB: Is it being sold in the United States for propaganda purposes?

MR. MARKS: No.

In other words, what is meant to manipulate a foreign reader is believed by Mr. Marks to be a fair and objective account to an American reader. But the truth is that a student writing a paper about our intervention in the Dominican Republic has before him in Mallin's account of *The Truth About the Dominican Republic* a controlled package which is not truly labeled. If he is misled before he gets past the dust jacket and title page, what can he expect of the book itself? The CIA also has had for years a great respect for the power of books to influence opinion. The names of Frederick A. Praeger and the M.I.T. Press (The Center for International Studies at M.I.T. was set up with CIA money fifteen years ago) are only two of many that crop up again and again in the company of the USIA and the CIA. One welcomes the written views of men connected with such agencies as well as those of scholars working without such support, but the taxpayer has the right to know what he is paying for and the reader has the right to know the basic beliefs and qualifications and sources of the man whose book he buys.

And the evil is compounded by the fact that the reader is often guided to a book by the good reputation of its publisher. Praeger, who is one of the chief contractors of books purchased by USIA, and whose company was recently purchased by the Encyclopaedia Britannica (think of the potential *there!*), is no Government stooge. Praeger books on politics, foreign affairs, and history have an excellent reputation for accuracy and timeliness. But we have no way of knowing *which* Praeger books were supported by the Government. For example, Praeger is the publisher for Bernard Fall, whose books about Vietnam are indictments of Administration policy. Praeger also published Philip Geyelin's *Lyndon B. Johnson and the World,* an objective study of the President's foreign policy that was not purchased by USIA for foreign distribution because it did not answer the Agency's propaganda needs. But Praeger is also named as the publisher of five of the sixteen titles USIA supported or generated in 1965....

A typical case of book control works this way: a Government agency keeps information essential to the writing of a given book under a security classification. The agency then contacts a writer and agrees to lift the classification in exchange for the right to edit the entire book—not just the portions that touch on the previously classified material. Whether such censorship is in the interest of national security or in the interest of political expediency is a moot question: the effect of such an agreement is to grant enormous leverage to the Establishment, whose editorial judgments are neither disclosed nor subject to review.

When one considers the tens of millions of dollars spent by the Government on books, the economic leverage that results must be enormous. Books by, about, and for the Government claim a massive share of the book selling and writing business and any publisher who . . . [flouts] the power structure does so at his peril. Recently, a free-lance writer, Ralph Schoenstein, revealed that a book he wrote in 1965 about President Johnson and his three dogs, Blanco, Her, and the late Him, was submitted by his publisher, Doubleday, for review by Elizabeth Carpenter, Mrs. Johnson's press secretary. Mrs.

Carpenter was furious: she fancied the 65-page manuscript to be repellent to the dignity of the President's high office and made it clear that for Doubleday to print the book would be to sacrifice the cooperation of the White House with its future writers. It never appeared.

We should not lament the loss of the doggy book were it not that such *sub rosa* censorship sets extremely dangerous precedents. The writing of a book and the reading of one are private enterprises that constitute a crucial defense against the tyranny of the majority. The cornerstone of such a defense is the frank disclosure of the manner in which the book came to be written or controlled. . . .

It is not Government money or Government interest itself that sullies books. All one wants is that Government acknowledge its involvement and keep its hands off the writer's work. To ask this is to ask for no more than the Government demands of charitable foundations. But now there is a double activity, the secret suppression and creation of history, which reinforces the fears of American writers that their Government cannot be trusted and that it is not mature or brave enough to subsidize the open dissemination of ideas.

THE GOVERNMENT AS PUBLISHER: A REPLY [4]

The article entitled "Government Book Control" [see previous selection] by your *Book Review* editor Geoffrey Wolff does a disservice to all authors and publishers to imply that all books are suspect because three or four were commissioned each year for the past several years. The reputable book publishers of the United States are as jealous of their independence as are the newspaper publishers. When they accept a commissioned manuscript they subject it to the same objective editorial scrutiny they apply to any manuscript to whose publication they are willing to assign their imprints. And to charge, as Mr. Wolff has, that the Government's expenditures for books is large enough to control the output of the book publishing industry (a $2 billion industry) strikes me as being ridiculous.

[4] From a letter to the editor of the Washington *Post* by Reed Harris, assistant director (Information Centers) United States Information Agency, Washington, D.C. Washington *Post*. p A 20. F. 9, '67. Reprinted by permission.

GOVERNMENT SUBSIDIES TO PUBLISHERS [5]

Frederick A. Praeger, in telling how his firm was connected with the CIA, said:

Less than "1 per cent of all book projects we've ever published or been engaged in have any CIA connection."

The CIA never actually prepared or ordered printed any book itself.

Praeger retained the ultimate decision as to whether or not his firm would publish any given book, based upon academic quality and truth.

The firm actually lost money in handling the CIA books.

The Praeger firm has offices at 111 Fourth Avenue [New York City], as well as in Washington and London. Last April, it was purchased by Encyclopaedia Britannica, but under that arrangement Praeger remained in charge of the book house with complete control of the books he publishes.

Praeger, a native of Vienna, is a naturalized citizen who has been in the United States since 1938 and served in United States Army intelligence during World War II. He says he regards as his mission in life the preservation of American democratic institutions.

> I have friends in the CIA as well as in other Government organizations —USIA, the Pentagon, the State Department [he said]. And if I considered that it furthered the interests of the country, I did not refuse my help. We have a way of life worth preserving. We have an obligation to help anti-totalitarian organizations throughout the world.
>
> I have knowledge of CIA projects involving facts, data, information and interpretation of events and conditions in the Communist world. And I have helped to publish books on these fields, limiting the volumes to truth, content and over-all quality of the literary product.

While admitting his CIA connections, Praeger declined to identify any particular books or authors involved in these projects or to say how his "1 per cent" figure was arrived at.

"What specific books or projects? This I will not say." But Praeger insisted he was not bound by any CIA-imposed secrecy. "I have never signed any secrecy agreement, nor am I bound by any oath," he said.

[5] From "Book Firm Spells Out CIA Ties," by Arthur Greenspan, correspondent. New York *Post*. p 5+. F. 23, '67. Reprinted by permission of New York *Post*. Copyright 1967, N. Y. Post Corp.

A look at the Praeger catalog shows a heavy concentration of books about international affairs, particularly with Russian and Chinese economic and ideological problems. It has often been thought by many in publishing that such books might have originated, in some way, through the CIA.

Praeger would not confirm nor deny this, but gave the following example of how such books came to be printed by his firm:

> Let us say someone in an organization is developing a book, and I suspect or know that he is in the CIA. Well, this material has been prepared by a responsible writer, and I evaluate it. I, and I alone, will decide whether I publish it, after I have sent the manuscript to several of the author's peers for their assessment.
>
> I did not say I have knowledge of any case, or even any suspicion, of any instance in which the agency itself has prepared such a book.
>
> In all cases, any discussion of the issues concerns the possibilities of the use of truth in psychological warfare.
>
> These are my guiding principles: facts, balance, fairness, scholarship, the highest kind of scholarship available . . . the absolute minimum we have to provide are facts and truth.

Who writes these books?

> There are a number of people who have had jobs at CIA who are publishing the most knowledgeable academic works. Some may still be with the Agency.
>
> It is my duty as a publisher to get the best possible book on a subject. If the writer happens to be a CIA man expert in the field, it makes no difference.
>
> My assumption is that if a man has had access to material such as the CIA files, he probably will use it. But if a man leaves the CIA and goes to a university, this doesn't make him a nonscholar.

Praeger insists "the posture of this publishing house has been antitotalitarianism and libertarian since the day it was founded. Part of my purpose in life is to provide the truth." . . .

In this light, Praeger was asked about the company's profits from such work. He said there were none:

> In terms of income to the company, whatever assistance I was able to give to various agencies was extremely costly. And in terms of economics, it could only be that I regard this as an obligation, a duty to my country. . . .
>
> Insofar as is possible, I try to give my friends at the various agencies my professional advice on my fields of interest, which happen to be international affairs and communism.

He deplored the recent attacks on the CIA which have been filling newspaper columns:

> I deplore the self-righteous hounding of this agency, the witch-hunt. I'm sure they did many things horribly wrong. But fundamentally, they're honest men trying to do the best job they can, as honestly and as decently as they can.
>
> I think the United States Government has an obligation to assist in the dissemination of truth and fact. I do not think it is wrong to assist one's government. I take a certain amount of pride in being asked to undertake such work, if the work is useful.

THE PRESS, THE PRESIDENT AND FOREIGN POLICY [6]

The conflict between the men who make and the men who report the news is as old as time. News may be true, but it is not truth, and they never see it the same way....

The first constitutional principle is that the success of any group of people in dealing with their common problems rests on their knowledge and understanding of the problems to be solved, and on their intelligence, judgment and character in meeting those problems. The conclusion drawn from this is that the intelligence, judgment and character of a majority of the people, if well-informed, will probably produce more satisfactory solutions than any leader or small band of geniuses is likely to produce.

This is undoubtedly sound doctrine for sinking a sewer or building a bridge or a school in a local community, but is it a practical way to conduct foreign policy? Are the people getting adequate information to enable them to reach sound judgments on what to do about South Asia, or the Atlantic, or the balance of payments, or China, or outer space? Is there any such information and any such people? And would enough of them pay attention to sustain a commercial newspaper or radio or television station that concentrated on these fundamental questions? These questions raise the old problem of the people's right to be informed and the government's obligation to govern effectively, which sometimes means governing secretly.

[6] Abridgment of "The Press, the President and Foreign Policy," based on material in *The Artillery of the Press* by James Reston, associate editor, New York *Times*. Originally appeared in *Foreign Affairs*, July 1966, and reprinted by permission of Harper & Row, Publishers. Copyright © 1966, 1967 by Council on Foreign Relations.

Two contemporary situations illustrate the dilemma. Over 300,000 Americans, many of them conscripts, are now fighting a war in Vietnam. Most of them do not know how it started, and even many officials are extremely vague about how we got so deeply involved. It cannot be said that the people were well informed before their commitment to the battle, or even that their representatives in the Congress really debated the decision to wage this kind of war. On the other hand, the President is now conducting that war as commander-in-chief with television cameras on the battlefield recording daily for vast television audiences the most brutal and agonizing scenes of the struggle.

In the first case, there was so little information and so much executive authority that the President could do about what he pleased; and in the second case, the people have so much information about the violent incidents of the war that it is questionable whether the President of a democratic country can really sustain his policy over a long period of time while the public is being invited to tune in on the eleven o'clock news and see Johnny killed. Something is obviously out of balance. . . .

The natural and historical differences between the American diplomat and the American reporter are still the main cause of their present trouble. The American diplomat before the Second World War was trained in the days of our isolation to be a silent observer of world affairs. He was as discreet as a priest; he was supposed to know everything and to tell nothing. . . .

The American reporter of my generation was brought up to believe in the cocky frontier tradition of "publish and be damned," but the American diplomat of the same age quickly came to believe that if he helped you to publish the facts, *he* was likely to be damned, and this was only one of the conflicts that soon developed between the government and the press.

The conduct of foreign policy is a process that never ends; the production of a newspaper or a television news program is a miracle that has to be accomplished somehow on the split second. The secretary of state must think in generations and continents, but the reporter thinks in "stories," in "minutes" and often in "fragments."

One profession is quiet, the other noisy; one slow, the other fast; one precise, the other imprecise. What makes their relationship even more difficult is that they are stuck with one another. . . .

The conflict between journalists and diplomats is getting worse instead of better for a variety of reasons. The press corps in the major capitals is getting so large that it is often smothering the news rather than covering it. When I started covering the State Department for the New York *Times* in 1941, Secretary of State Hull saw the "regulars" every weekday in his office. He could explain his policies, often in the most vivid Tennessee mountain language, read from the diplomatic cables if he felt like it, and indicate, with full assurance that his confidence would be respected, what was on the record and what had to be off the record. A generation later, the secretary of state has to meet the reporters in an auditorium where everybody is wired for sound.

The change in the nature of war has also complicated the problem of reconciling the traditions of press and government. The nation is engaged in an underground war, an economic war, an intelligence war, in every continent of the earth. This requires a vast American secret service operation in the armed services and the Central Intelligence Agency. What it costs and all that it does are not disclosed, and this is not only necessary, but it is something comparatively new in American life, at least on the present scale. The old tradition of the American press is that anything a government hides, except in open and declared war, is wrong and should be exposed, but a press demanding unlimited freedom for this principle could in some cases risk the nation's freedom. Yet the problem cannot be solved simply by saying that the operations of the intelligence services of the government are none of the public's business. I knew for over a year that the United States was flying high-altitude planes (the U-2) over the Soviet Union from a base in Pakistan to photograph military and particularly missile activities and bases, but the New York *Times* did not publish this fact until one of the planes was shot down in 1960. Was this a correct judgment? I think it was, but in other circumstances, the press is criticized for not printing intelligence and even military information. . . .

The obvious conclusion to be drawn from all this is that neither the press, nor the Congress, nor the executive branch has yet adjusted effectively to the new demands of the age. We are all following the procedures that were no doubt adequate when foreign policy was a secondary consideration. At the State Department, the men who are available to most reporters are not informed, and the men who are informed are usually too busy with the crisis to be available. On Capitol Hill, each committee is sovereign and assumes that Cabinet officers have nothing else to do but to repeat the same testimony three or four times to three or four different committees. And in the news-gathering agencies we go on doing more or less what we did a generation ago.

Personally, I do not believe that the constitutional assumption that "the people know best" is a very reliable guide to the conduct of American foreign policy today. Similarly even the modern techniques for reporting foreign news are not yet adequate to the subject or to the need, but we should be careful about reaching the conclusion that the remedy lies with a less assertive press. It is not the press that is extending its power to the detriment of a sound balance between public opinion and foreign policy, but the President, whose power in this field is greater than that of any head of government in the modern world.

The question we have to ask is not about the President's interests, but about the public interest. No doubt both President and press will abuse their power from time to time, but where is the greater danger to the public interest—in the present power of the press or in the present power of the President?

I believe the power of the presidency has been increasing steadily since the Second World War, particularly since the introduction of nuclear weapons, and that the power of the press and even of the Congress to restrain him has declined proportionately during this same period.

The presidential power in the foreign field is in direct proportion to the size of the issue. The press can still embarrass him by premature disclosure of his plans, and the Congress can still oppose and even defy him on peripheral issues, but on the great acts of foreign policy, especially those involving the risk or even the act of war, he is more powerful in this age than in any other, freer to follow his own bent than any other single political leader in the world—and the larger and more fateful the issue, the greater is his authority to follow his own will. . . .

The press may report the news but the President makes it. If senators are dominating the front pages with their protests against his foreign policy, and editors and professors are creating newsworthy disturbances on the university campuses and on the editorial pages, the President has a convenient remedy. He can divert public attention to himself. He can arrange a conference on an island in the Pacific, for example. Within seventy-two hours, he can bring the leaders of the nations on his side to a meeting that will arrest the interest of the world. Reporters and photographers will converge from all the capitals and fill the front pages with accounts of the proceedings, thereby overwhelming the less dramatic senatorial mutterings.

This gives the President quite an edge. The reporters and commentators on the scene may see all this as an elaborate camouflage of realities and write their waspish critiques of the proceedings at his conference, but unless the great man is incorrigibly clumsy, which with the help of an experienced civil service he usually is not, the big front-page headlines will have much more effect than the witty chatter on page 32. . . .

The power of the President to use the free press against itself is very great. If, for example, an influential columnist or commentator criticizes him for landing 25,000 marines in the Dominican Republic to put down a rebellion, it is very easy for him to call in several other carefully selected commentators and give them the detailed argument for landing the marines. He has all the vivid facts of the situation, and if he wants to put them out, he does not have to announce them himself. Other reporters will be perfectly willing to accommodate him, even though they know they are being used to knock down the story of another colleague.

The function of criticism itself has changed in an odd way during President Johnson's Administration. In the past, there has been a reasonable expectation among people writing political criticism that if they identified a problem, checked it out thoroughly, and proposed a reasonable remedy, publication of these things would be read within the government in good faith and maybe even considered worthy of executive action.

This is still true today on questions of policy, but if the topic deals with individuals in the Administration, the chances are that the criticism will perpetuate the situation criticized. For example, if you write today that a particular Cabinet member has been exhausted by overwork, and should be liberated for his own and the nation's good, you can be fairly sure that you have condemned that man to stay at his grindstone until everybody has forgotten that you ever mentioned him.

Also, if you learn that the President is going to do something on Friday and print it on Tuesday, this is likely to be regarded as an impertinence and a presumption which the President will punish by changing his plans. I once saw the speech President Johnson was going to make at the twentieth anniversary celebration of the founding of the United Nations and printed his plans for ending the financial crisis that was going on in the UN at that time. He was furious. He called in the Secretary of State the very night of publication, ordered the speech rewritten to eliminate the reported plans and made a different speech.

This is fair enough, but behind it there is a philosophic idea that has some disturbing possibilities. Bill Moyers, the [former] White House press secretary, explained the President's view in these terms: "It is very important for a President to maintain up until the moment of decision his options, and for someone to speculate days or weeks in advance that he's going to do thus and thus is to deny to the President the latitude he needs in order to make, in the light of existing circumstances, the best possible decision."

No doubt this is true in many circumstances, but not in all. Is absolutely nothing to be printed about clandestine plans by the President to mount an illegal invasion at the Bay of Pigs in Cuba for fear of interfering with the President's option to humiliate the country? Are the people to be denied information about presidential options that will involve them in a war they have to finance and fight? If all presidential options are to be protected from speculation "until the very last minute," what redress will there be the next day after the President has opted to dispatch the marines or bomb Hanoi, or publish a request to wage war as "he" deems necessary all over Southeast Asia?

These are hard questions, and the answers are not that the Commander-in-Chief must telegraph all his punches in advance. But at the same time, the doctrine of "no speculation" before action, even on nonmilitary matters, is something new in the catalog of presidential privilege.

In such a world, no doubt he needs all the advantages and privileges he can get. He has to take responsibility for his actions and we do not. He is the principal actor on the stage, but he did not write the script and may not even like the role. Therefore, he tries constantly to use whatever devices he can to ease the agony. He manages the news, as the heads of all institutions do, by emphasizing his successes and minimizing his losses. He has his own photographers constantly taking his picture and releases those that convey the impression of strong leadership or compassion or whatever other mood he wants to convey at the moment. All this is understandable, but we should not be fooled: the trend of power is running with the President, the danger of excessive use of power lies not in the newspapers but in the White House, and even the most casual look at the influence of reporters and commentators today makes this fairly obvious. . . .

Some improvements are desirable and even possible. The attitude of the President toward the reporters is vital. If he regards them primarily as a problem and therefore tries to manipulate them, they eventually convey their suspicion and even hostility to the people. If, on the other hand, he regards them as an opportunity and tries to explain his problems to them, they can be a valuable educational force. It is the President, however, who has the initiative and the capacity to define the rules and set the tone of public discussion. A revival of the calm philosophic talk or the quiet "conversation," as typified by Roosevelt's fireside chat, could help keep the public mind on the larger questions and minimize the capacity of others to divert attention onto narrow personal issues.

There has been a decline, too, in recent years in the relations between the experts in the State Department and the reporters. The reason for this is that the experts know the President likes to dominate public announcements and are afraid that they might disclose something that would detonate his temper. And since the most useful information comes, not from the top leaders, but from the men who brief the leaders, this chokes down a very valuable stream of information.

No government in history ever received such a torrent of information from abroad as the United States Government does at present. Washington is inundated every day with reports on every imaginable problem. A good deal of this information is interesting and unclassified and could help nourish the flow of knowledge into the newspapers and periodicals of the nation, but it is not made available mainly because nobody thinks of making it available or because the idea has grown up that all this "belongs" to the Government.

It should be possible for officials and reporters to do much better than they have done in discussing these problems and opportunities together. There is a great deal of chatter about it with the White House Press Secretary on the presidential press plane flying between Washington and Texas, but all suggestions for more formal committees to analyze and correct obvious shortcomings, or alternatively for the press to establish some way of correcting itself, have usually ended in useless vapor.

"If there is ever to be an amelioration of the condition of mankind," John Adams wrote in 1815, "philosophers, theologians, legislators, politicians and moralists will find that the regulation of the press is the most difficult, dangerous and important problem they have to resolve. Mankind cannot now be governed without it, nor at present with it."

I am more hopeful. There is some reason to believe that the old conflict will diminish in time. Powerful forces are working for coexistence. In his own interest, the reporter is having to become an educator, and the more he concentrates upon explaining the news instead of being first with the news, the more the official will want to cooperate with him.

A FOOTNOTE TO HISTORY [7]

I am going to tell you a story—one that has never been told before—the inside story of the New York *Times* and the Bay of Pigs, something of a mystery story.

In its issue of November 19, 1960, *The Nation* published an editorial under the heading, "Are We Training Cuban Guerrillas?"

I had never seen this editorial and had never heard it mentioned until a reader of the New York *Times* sent in a letter to the editor. He asked whether the allegations in the editorial were true, and, if so, why hadn't they been reported by the New York *Times*, whose resources for gathering information were much greater than those of a little magazine like *The Nation*.

The Nation said:

> Fidel Castro may have a sounder basis for his expressed fears of a United States-financed "Guatemala-type" invasion than most of us realize. On a recent visit to Guatemala, Dr. Ronald Hilton, Director of the Institute of Hispanic-American Studies at Stanford University, was told:
>
> 1. The United States Central Intelligence Agency has acquired a large tract of land, at an outlay in excess of $1 million, which is stoutly fenced and heavily guarded. . . . It is "common knowledge" in Guatemala that the tract is being used as a training ground for Cuban counterrevolutionaries, who are preparing for an eventual landing in Cuba. . . . United States personnel and equipment are being used at the base. . . .
>
> 2. Substantially all of the above was reported by a well-known Guatemalan journalist . . . in *La Hora*, a Guatemalan newspaper. . . .
>
> 3. More recently, the President of Guatemala, forced to take cognizance of the persistent reports concerning the base, went on TV and admitted its existence, but refused to discuss its purpose or any other facts about it.
>
> . . . We believe the reports merit publication: they can, and should, be checked immediately by all U.S. news media with correspondents in Guatemala.

Off to Guatemala

With that last paragraph, the New York *Times* readily agreed. Paul Kennedy, our correspondent in Central America, was soon on his way to Guatemala. He reported that intensive daily air training

[7] From "Excerpts from Speech on Coverage of Bay of Pigs Buildup," by Clifton Daniel, managing editor. New York *Times*. p 14. Je. 2, '66. © 1966 by The New York Times Company. Reprinted by permission. The address, "A Footnote to History; the Press and National Security," was delivered at the World Press Institute, Macalester College, St. Paul, Minnesota, June 1, 1966.

was taking place there on a partly hidden airfield. In the mountains, commandolike forces were being drilled in guerrilla warfare tactics by foreign personnel, mostly from the United States.

Guatemalan authorities insisted that the training operation was designed to meet an assault from Cuba. Opponents of the government said the preparations were for an offensive against the Cuban regime of Premier Fidel Castro. Mr. Kennedy actually penetrated two miles into the training area.

His article was published in the New York *Times* on January 10, 1961.

The Nation also printed another article in its issue of January 7, 1961, by Don Dwiggins, aviation editor of the Los Angeles *Mirror*.

And now Arthur M. Schlesinger, Jr., takes up the story in *A Thousand Days*, his account of John F. Kennedy's years in the White House.

> On March 31 [Mr. Schlesinger says] Howard Handleman of *U.S. News and World Report*, returning from ten days in Florida, said to me that the exiles were telling everyone that they would receive United States recognition as soon as they landed in Cuba, to be followed by the overt provision of arms and supplies.
>
> A few days later Gilbert Harrison of the *New Republic* sent over the galleys of a pseudonymous piece called "Our Men in Miami," asking whether there was any reason why it should not be published. It was a careful, accurate and devastating account of CIA activities among the refugees, written, I learned later, by Karl Meyer. Obviously its publication in a responsible magazine would cause trouble, but could the Government properly ask an editor to suppress the truth? Defeated by the moral issue, I handed the article to the President, who instantly read it and expressed the hope that it could be stopped. Harrison accepted the suggestion and without questions—a patriotic act which left me oddly uncomfortable.
>
> About the same time Tad Szulc filed a story to the New York *Times* from Miami describing the recruitment drive and reporting that a landing on Cuba was imminent. Turner Catledge, the managing editor, called James Reston, who was in his weekend retreat in Virginia, to ask his advice. Reston counseled against publication: either the story would alert Castro, in which case the *Times* would be responsible for casualties on the beach, or else the expedition would be canceled, in which case the *Times* would be responsible for grave interference with national policy. This was another patriotic act; but in retrospect I have wondered whether, if the press had behaved irresponsibly, it would not have spared the country a disaster.

Article Was Not Suppressed

As recently as last November, Mr. Schlesinger was still telling the same story. In an appearance on "Meet the Press," he was asked about the article in the New York *Times* in which he was quoted as saying that he had lied to the *Times* in April 1961 about the nature and size of the landing in the Bay of Pigs.

Mr. Schlesinger replied that, a few days before he misinformed the *Times*, the newspaper had suppressed a story by Tad Szulc from Miami, giving a fairly accurate account of the invasion plans.

> If [he said] I was reprehensible in misleading the Times by repeating the official cover story, the *Times* conceivably was just as reprehensible in misleading the American people by suppressing the Tad Szulc story from Miami. I, at least, had the excuse that I was working for the Government.
>
> I prefer to think [he said] that both the *Times* and I were actuated by the same motives: that is, a sense, mistaken or not, that [it] was in the national interest to do so.

Mr. Schlesinger was mistaken, both in his book and in his appearance on "Meet the Press." The *Times* did not suppress the Tad Szulc article. We printed it . . . on page 1 (under a one-column headline) of the issue of Friday, April 7, 1961.

What actually happened is, at this date, somewhat difficult to say.

None of those who took part in the incident described in Mr. Schlesinger's book kept records of what was said and done. That is unfortunate, and it should teach us a lesson. The Bay of Pigs was not only important in the history of United States relations with Latin America, the Soviet Union and world communism; it was also important in the history of relations between the American press and the United States Government.

We owe a debt to history. We should try to reconstruct the event, and that is what I am attempting to do today.

Late in March and early in April 1961, we were hearing rumors that the anti-Castro forces were organizing for an invasion. For example, the editor of the Miami *Herald,* Don Shoemaker, told me at lunch in New York one day, "They're drilling on the beaches all over southern Florida."

Tad Szulc, a veteran correspondent in Latin America with a well-deserved reputation for sniffing out plots and revolutions, came upon the Miami story quite accidentally. He was being transferred from Rio de Janeiro to Washington and happened to stop in Miami to visit friends on his way north. He quickly discovered that an invasion force was indeed forming and that it was very largely financed and directed by the CIA. He asked for permission to come to New York to discuss the situation and was promptly assigned to cover the story.

His first article from Miami . . . began as follows:

> For nearly nine months Cuban exile military forces dedicated to the overthrow of Premier Fidel Castro have been in training in the United States as well as in Central America.
>
> An army of 5,000 to 6,000 men constitutes the external fighting arm of the anti-Castro Revolutionary Council, which was formed in the United States last month. Its purpose is the liberation of Cuba from what it describes as the Communist rule of the Castro regime.

His article, which was more than two columns long and very detailed, was scheduled to appear in the paper of Friday, April 7, 1961. It was dummied for page 1 under a four-column head, leading the paper.

While the front-page dummy was being drawn up by the assistant managing editor, the news editor and the assistant news editor, Orvil Dryfoos, then the publisher of the New York *Times*, came down from the fourteenth floor to the office of Turner Catledge, the managing editor. He was gravely troubled by the security implications of Szulc's story. He could envision failure for the invasion, and he could see the New York *Times* being blamed for a bloody fiasco.

He and the managing editor solicited the advice of Scotty Reston, who was then the Washington correspondent of the New York *Times* and is now an associate editor. . . .

Mr. Reston was asked what should be done with the dispatch.

"I told them not to run it," Mr. Reston says.

He did not advise against printing information about the forces gathering in Florida; that was already well known. He merely cautioned against printing any dispatch that would pinpoint the time of the landing. Others agree that Szulc's dispatch did contain some phraseology to the effect that an invasion was imminent, and those words were eliminated.

Tad Szulc's own recollection, cabled to me from Madrid . . . , is that "in several instances the stories were considerably toned down, including the elimination of statements about the "imminence" of an invasion.

> Specifically [Mr. Szulc said] a decision was made in New York not to mention the CIA's part in the invasion preparations, not to use the date of the invasion, and, on April 15, not to give away in detail the fact that the first air strike on Cuba was carried out from Guatemala.

After the dummy for the front page of the *Times* for Friday, April 7, 1961, was changed, Ted Bernstein, who was the assistant managing editor on night duty at the *Times,* and Lew Jordan, the news editor, sat in Mr. Bernstein's office fretting about it. They believed a colossal mistake was being made, and together they went into Mr. Catledge's office to appeal for reconsideration.

Mr. Catledge recalls that Mr. Jordan's face was dead white, and he was quivering with emotion. He and Mr. Bernstein told the managing editor that never before had the front-page play in the New York *Times* been changed for reasons of policy. They said they would like to hear from the publisher himself the reasons for the change.

Lew Jordan later recalled that Mr. Catledge was "flaming mad" at this intervention. However, he turned around in his big swivel chair, picked up the telephone, and asked Mr. Dryfoos to come downstairs. By the time he arrived, Mr. Bernstein had gone to dinner, but Mr. Dryfoos spent ten minutes patiently explaining to Mr. Jordan his reasons for wanting the story played down.

His reasons were those of national security, national interest and, above all, concern for the safety of the men who were preparing to offer their lives on the beaches of Cuba. He repeated the explanation in somewhat greater length to Mr. Bernstein the next day.

I describe the mood and behavior of the publisher and editors of the New York *Times* only to show how seriously and with what intensity of emotion they made their fateful decisions.

Mr. Bernstein and Mr. Jordan now say, five years later, that the change in play, not eliminating the reference to the imminence of the invasion, was the important thing done that night.

"It was important because a multicolumn head in this paper means so much," Mr. Jordan told me the other day.

Mr. Reston, however, felt that the basic issue was the elimination of the statement that an invasion was imminent.

Ironically, although that fact was eliminated from our own dispatch, virtually the same information was printed in a shirttail on Tad's Szulc's report. That was a report from the Columbia Broadcasting System. It said that plans for the invasion of Cuba were in their final stages. Ships and planes were carrying invasion units from Florida to their staging bases in preparation for the assault.

When the invasion actually took place ten days later, the American Society of Newspaper Editors [ASNE] happened to be in session in Washington, and President Kennedy addressed the society. He devoted his speech entirely to the Cuban crisis. He said nothing at that time about press disclosures of invasion plans.

Appeal by President

However, a week later in New York, appearing before the Bureau of Advertising of the American Newspaper Publishers Association, the President asked members of the newspaper profession "to reexamine their own responsibilities."

He suggested that the circumstances of the cold war required newspapermen to show some of the same restraint they would exercise in a shooting war.

He went on to say, "Every newspaper now asks itself with respect to every story, 'Is it news?' All I suggest is that you add the question: 'Is it in the interest of national security?' "

If the press should recommend voluntary measures to prevent the publication of material endangering the national security in peacetime, the President said, "the Government would cooperate wholeheartedly."

Turner Catledge, who was the retiring president of the ASNE, Felix McKnight of the Dallas *Times-Herald,* the incoming president, and Lee Hills, executive editor of the Knight newspapers, took the President's statement as an invitation to talk.

Within two weeks, a delegation of editors, publishers and news agency executives was at the White House. They told President Kennedy they saw no need at that time for machinery to help prevent the disclosure of vital security information. They agreed that there should be another meeting in a few months. However, no further meeting was ever held.

That day in the White House, President Kennedy ran down a list of what he called premature disclosures of security information. His examples were mainly drawn from the New York *Times.* He mentioned, for example, Paul Kennedy's story about the training of anti-Castro forces in Guatemala. Mr. Catledge pointed out that this information had been published in *La Hora* in Guatemala and in *The Nation* in this country before it was ever published in the New York *Times.*

"But it was not news until it appeared in the *Times,*" the President replied.

While he scolded the New York *Times,* the President said in an aside to Mr. Catledge, "If you had printed more about the operation you would have saved us from a colossal mistake."

"Sorry You Didn't Tell It"

More than a year later, President Kennedy was still talking the same way. In a conversation with Orvil Dryfoos in the White House on September 13, 1962, he said, "I wish you had run everything on Cuba. . . . I am sorry you didn't tell it at the time."

Those words were echoed by Arthur Schlesinger when he wrote, "I have wondered whether, if the press had behaved irresponsibly, it would not have spared the country a disaster."

They are still echoing down the corridors of history. Just the other day in Washington, Senator Russell of Georgia confessed that, although he was chairman of the Senate Armed Forces Committee, he didn't know the timing of the Bay of Pigs operation.

"I only wish I had been consulted," he said in a speech to the Senate, "because I would have strongly advised against this kind of operation if I had been."

It is not so easy, it seems, even for Presidents, their most intimate advisers and distinguished United States senators to know always what is really in the national interest. One is tempted to say that sometimes—sometimes—even a mere newspaperman knows better.

My own view is that the Bay of Pigs operation might well have been canceled and the country would have been saved enormous embarrassment if the New York *Times* and other newspapers had been more diligent in the performance of their duty—their duty to keep the public informed on matters vitally affecting our national honor and prestige, not to mention our national security.

Perhaps, as Mr. Reston believes, it was too late to stop the operation by the time we printed Tad Szulc's story on April 7.

> If I had it to do over, I would do exactly what we did at the time [Mr. Reston says]. It's ridiculous to think that publishing the fact that the invasion was imminent would have avoided this disaster. I am quite sure the operation would have gone forward.
>
> The thing had been cranked up too far. The CIA would have had to disarm the anti-Castro forces physically. Jack Kennedy was in no mood to do anything like that.

Prelude to Graver Crisis

The Bay of Pigs, as it turned out, was the prelude to an even graver crisis—the Cuban missile crisis of 1962. In Arthur Schlesinger's opinion, failure in 1961 contributed to success in 1962. President Kennedy had learned from experience, and once again the New York *Times* was involved....

In the Cuban missile crisis, things were handled somewhat differently than in the previous year. The President telephoned directly to the publisher [then Orvil Dryfoos] of the New York *Times*. He had virtually been invited to do so in their conversation in the White House barely a month before.

That conversation had been on the subject of security leaks in the press and how to prevent them, and Mr. Dryfoos had told the President that what was needed was prior information and prior consultation. He said that, when there was danger of security information getting into print, the thing to do was to call in the publishers and explain matters to them.

In the missile crisis, President Kennedy did exactly that.

Ten minutes before I was due on this platform this morning Mr. Reston telephoned me from Washington to give me further details of what happened that day.

> The President called me [Mr. Reston said]. He understood that I had been talking to Mac [McGeorge] Bundy and he knew from the line of questioning that we knew the critical fact—that Russian missiles had indeed been emplaced in Cuba.
>
> The President told me [Mr. Reston continued] that he was going on television on Monday evening to report to the American people. He said that if we published the news about the missiles Khrushchev could actually give him an ultimatum before he went on the air. Those were Kennedy's exact words.
>
> I told him I understood [Mr. Reston said this morning], but I also told him I could not do anything about it. And this is an important thought that you should convey to those young reporters in your audience.
>
> I told the President I would report to my office in New York and if my advice were asked I would recommend that we not publish. It was not my duty to decide. My job was the same as that of an ambassador—to report to my superiors. I recommended to the President that he call New York. He did so.

That was the sequence of events as Mr. Reston recalled them. . . . The President telephoned the publisher of the New York *Times;* Mr. Dryfoos in turn put the issue up to Mr. Reston and his staff.

And the news that the Soviet Union had atomic missiles in Cuba only ninety miles from the cost of Florida was withheld until the Government announced it.

What conclusion do I reach from all these facts? What moral do I draw from my story?

My conclusion is this: Information is essential to people who propose to govern themselves. It is the responsibility of serious journalists to supply that information—whether in this country or in the countries from which our foreign colleagues come.

Still, the primary responsibility for safeguarding our national interest must rest always with our Government, as it did with President Kennedy in the two Cuban crises.

Up until the time we are actually at war or on the verge of war, it is not only permissible—it is our duty as journalists and citizens to be constantly questioning our leaders and our policy, and to be constantly informing the people, who are the masters of us all—both the press and the politicians.

FREEDOM AND THE PRESS[8]

Our news columns . . . [in the first week of June 1966] carried reports on the role that the New York Times *played prior to the Bay of Pigs operation in 1961 and during the Cuban missile crisis of 1962. We reprint in its entirety, and reaffirm as the policy of the* Times *today, the following editorial that appeared on this page under the above title on Friday, April 28, 1961:*

An issue fundamental to the security and to the freedom of the American people was raised last night by the President of the United States in his speech to the Bureau of Advertising of the American Newspaper Publishers Association. It is an issue that most immediately and directly affects the press in our free democratic society; and it is an issue that, especially since American participation in the fiasco of the Cuban landings became publicly known, has been deeply troubling thoughtful newspapermen throughout the country.

It is the question of how to reconcile, in the context of cold war and of the Communist technique of fighting that war, the basic American principle of the public's right to know with the basic necessity of maintaining the national security. In time of open and declared war the question is regularly posed, but the solution is relatively simple. Under such circumstances the need for censorship, even if it is self-censorship, as it was in this country during the last war, is universally recognized and generally observed.

But cold war is different, and we are living in a period of cold war. It is a kind of war, and yet it is not war. For the preservation of our democratic society in this time of "clear and

[8] Editorial. New York *Times*. p 12 E. Je. 5, '66. © 1966 by The New York Times Company. Reprinted by permission.

present danger" it is more essential than ever that the people be fully informed of the problems and of the perils confronting them. This is a responsibility as much of the press as of the President. But it is equally essential that the secrets of military technique and—as the President said—of "covert preparations to counter the enemy's covert operations"—be kept inviolate. On matters affecting policy the people must know so that the people in the last analysis can decide; but the terrible difficulty arises in that twilight zone where the revelation of military secrets might affect immediately and adversely the security of the country, and yet where the withholding of information might involve deception of the public. This is a problem that no society but our kind of open democracy faces; and it is because the maintenance of our kind of open society is so precious that the dilemma is so terrible.

Naturally, when "secret" activities become matters of general knowledge in the community, there is no longer a secret—as to a large extent was the case in connection with the Cuban landings. But to dismiss the problem with that observation is to beg the question. For there are often real secrets, and they are often discovered. The President did not attempt to solve the problem, but he did ask American journalists to apply something more than the mere test of "is it news?" He asked that we also apply the test of "is it in the national interest?"—an unsatisfactory test because it is so subjective, and yet one that in the context of the present day must also be applied.

No formula can be entirely satisfactory. Certainly censorship is not, and complete license is not, either. The best for the moment is to take seriously the President's request for self-restraint. Along with this ought to go greater accessibility of officials, so that newspapermen may have frank and informed advice on the harm that might come from revelation of a discovered secret. No responsible newspaper would knowingly damage the national interest; and the greater candor in Government promised by the President will materially help protect that interest.

IV. CENSORSHIP AND INTELLECTUAL FREEDOM

EDITOR'S INTRODUCTION

The growing body of opinion favoring more liberal views about censorship is nowhere more evident than in the reexamination of sexual mores and ethics that has taken place in our churches, Catholic and Protestant alike. The winds of change that flowed from Vatican Council II have caused the discontinuance of the historic Index of Forbidden Books (noted in the first selection) and have set in motion other liberal tendencies. An article in the Catholic magazine *Commonweal* by Elizabeth Bartelme, an editor, suggests that other censorship regulations in the Catholic church should be lifted.

A new film production code for the American motion picture industry, considerably more liberal than the previous one, was adopted in 1966. Its provisions are set forth by a New York *Times* staff writer, Vincent Canby.

The censorship of history took a different turn, at least in 1966. Two much-publicized cases were those of the attempts by Miss Helen Clay Frick and Mrs. John F. Kennedy to prevent publication of certain portions of books to which they took exception. The former is dealt with in a bulletin of the Freedom of Information Center, the latter by Irwin Karp, legal representative of the Authors League of America. Mr. Karp is concerned mainly with author-patron contracts in which the latter has the right to review the work to be published—the heart of the dispute over the book about President Kennedy's assassination.

This section closes with a consideration of censorship as it affects the purchase and display of books in libraries. The editor of the *Wilson Library Bulletin*, Kathleen Molz, places the problem in its historic setting; and David Dempsey covers a conference of the Intellectual Freedom Committee of the American

Library Association at which librarians and others discussed at length the librarian's task in the face of current censorship efforts directed at them and their collections.

THE PASSING OF THE INDEX OF FORBIDDEN BOOKS [1]

[In early May 1966] Alfredo Cardinal Ottaviani told Vatican City's weekly newspaper, *L'Osservatore della Domenica,* that the Roman Catholic Index of Forbidden Books now remains not as an applicable and enforceable instrument of censorship but solely as a "historic document." The cardinal explained that the last edition of the Index was published in 1948 and that the Sacred Congregation for the Doctrine of the Faith—that part of the Curia responsible for the Index—is no longer competent to judge the flood of literature published today. The responsibility for evaluating literature to be read—and not to be read—by Roman Catholics now passes from the Curia to the Church's various national episcopal conferences. For this elimination of a central censorship in the Catholic Church thanks are due to several converging forces. The practical problems of maintaining a centrally governed Index of Forbidden Books have been made insuperable by the sheer bulk of printed material in our time. In addition the Roman Catholic Church tried earnestly in Vatican Council II to come abreast of the modern world in an openness to all knowledge and in its recognition of the increasing maturity and sophistication of Roman Catholic laymen. Censorship will of course continue in a few of the Church's national episcopal conferences and, according to Cardinal Ottaviani, Communist publications are automatically proscribed by canon law. This leaves Roman Catholics who want complete freedom to know much to rejoice about and much to hope for.

[1] From "The 'Index' Becomes an Appendix," editorial. *Christian Century.* 83:608-9. My. 11, '66. Copyright 1966 Christian Century Foundation. Reprinted by permission from the May 11, 1966 issue of *The Christian Century.*

LET IT BE PRINTED [2]

The *imprimatur,* like the Index of Forbidden Books, is an offshoot of the Reformation, and, like the latter, was originally meant to keep heretical printed matter out of the hands of the faithful. As the Latin makes clear, it was simply "permission to print." Systematized and codified under Pope Leo XIII, the *imprimatur* is now an indication that a book has been examined by a qualified censor who has declared it free from doctrinal or moral error by giving the book his *nihil obstat* [nothing prevents (publication)], and that the bishop of the diocese in which the book is either written, published or printed, basing his judgment on the censor's report, has given permission to publish. It is interesting to observe the shift in the original meaning: books privately printed and distributed do not now need an *imprimatur.*

One of the most common misunderstandings about this permission is that its appearance in a book constitutes the seal of the approval of the bishop who grants it. This has never been true. . . .

Another misconception, this one common to anxious writers, is that every Catholic who puts a line on paper must have it censored. The results are headaches for the censors, and certain literary works carrying tiny six-point lines of type that are quite unnecessary. Novels, poetry, literary essays, biographies and similar works do not fall within the censor's competence. But quite a few other books do, specifically, any work, written by a Catholic, on theology, Sacred Scripture, religion, natural theology and ethics, Church history, an *ex professo* [expert] treatment of a moral or religious topic, or a subject involving religious discipline, one dealing with politics (more common in Europe than in this country) or with economics (Federal aid to education might illustrate the latter), or books on secular or profane matters which because of the treatment of the subject might come within the competence of the censor.

Who must obtain an *imprimatur?* All Catholics, lay or religious, writing on any of the above subjects. Only bishops are

[2] From article by Elizabeth Bartelme, a member of the editorial staff of a New York publishing house. *Commonweal.* 81:701-3. F. 26, '65. Reprinted by permission.

exempt from this regulation, and, I have been told, most of those who write will submit their work to a censor even though they are not required to do so. And the obligation of the censor? He must give a competent, unbiased report, leaving aside his own point of view on any matter which he is judging, and taking into account only the moral and doctrinal elements involved.

Searching for "Soft" Censors

What, in fact, actually happens in the censorship of books? Frequently, nothing at all. An author or a publisher may submit galleys to the diocesan censor and have them returned completely unmarked or with only a few minor corrections. This is the norm rather than the exception. It is the exceptions, however, that raise questions about the validity of prepublication censorship. How valid, for example, is censorship when a *nihil obstat* is refused by one censor and granted by another? Which is the more competent theologian—the one who passes the book or the one who refuses to? How should a writer or an editor react to a censor who indulges a passion for copy-editing?—a niggling question, but it involves a niggling passion and an affront to the writer.

Again, how valid is this kind of censorship when publishers shop around for an "easy" censor? It is common knowledge that certain dioceses are notably lenient about book censorship while others make a point of being difficult. . . .

Another problem may arise. Delays! The publisher's nightmare! Will the censor return the book in three weeks? He might. Will the printer keep the presses open if the publisher is late in returning page proofs? Most certainly he won't. Will the author be amenable when he discovers that his book has been postponed from fall until spring? No, he will depart to the haven of another, more sympathetic publisher who will soothe him with optimistic promises until once again the stormy waves of censorship move his book from fall to spring. . . .

Catholic publishers, who represent themselves as such, are bound to obtain the *imprimatur* on any book which canon law indicates requires such a permission. General publishers, however, are not bound by any such requirement since they do not fall under the jurisdiction of the Church. A Catholic author, of course, must obey the law of the Church and the dictates of his conscience, but the general publisher may love God and do as he pleases. If this sounds frivolous, it is not meant to be. Those who have actively put themselves at the service of the Church are often penalized; those who publish for purely commercial reasons cannot be.

This, however, can work in reverse. In many dioceses a translation from a foreign language, unless the translator is a Catholic, will not be given an *imprimatur*. The translation may be accurate, beautiful and completely in accord with the original, but unless the translator professes the faith, his translation cannot be published with permission. Here again it is a matter of jurisdiction. No one who is not a Catholic is bound by the laws of the Church. *Ipso*, a bishop may not (although it has been known to happen) give permission to publish to one who is not of his flock. And this, despite the anguished cries of editors and salesmen, seems completely reasonable. (But a word of advice to the intrepid author or editor: one *can* get around this by applying to the Ordinary of the diocese in which the book was first published and given an *imprimatur*, and ask to have authority delegated to the Ordinary of the diocese in which the translation is being published or printed.)

It is tempting to illustrate the various problems connected with obtaining an *imprimatur* with case histories—"the case of the censor who locked up an office filled with galleys and went off for the summer," "the case of the censor who . . . ," etc., etc.—but this is not an exposé.

It is more important and more to the point to examine the purpose of the *imprimatur*, and to try to make a judgment as to whether it is being fulfilled. The purpose of prepublication censorship, I have been told, is to protect the reader. The reader, however, does not wish to be protected. If he is interested in a particular work he will read it, and if he is an intelligent man (and he is likely to be if he is browsing in theology, Scripture studies and natural law) he is rarely concerned with whether or not the writer has asked permission to publish. The most obvious example of this lack of concern is the wide circulation of the works of Teilhard de Chardin, none of which bears an *imprimatur*. (One might note here the censorious attitude that was taken toward the private circulation of some of Teilhard's papers before publication when an *imprimatur* was not needed.) One could cite other works in the areas of Church history or books which deal, at least incidentally, with theological or moral matters, in which the *imprimatur* has not appeared and which have nevertheless found a wide readership even among subscribers to Catholic book clubs.

Further, I think it would be astonishing to most Catholics to discover that a work dealing with certain areas of politics or economics requires the approval of a *censor librorum*. It is difficult to imagine a trained economist or political theorist submitting his work to the scrutiny of a theologian, and even harder to imagine that a reader would shun such a work because the author has not requested permission to publish. And as for those secular and profane matters—well, at best the wording is vague.

None of this proves, of course, that the *imprimatur* has no value. What it does indicate, however, is that those whom it was designed to protect feel no need for it; are truly unaware of it. It would therefore seem to follow that the *imprimatur* has lost its usefulness.

There is a larger issue, however, than usefulness. The past decade has seen what can only be described as a revolution in the Church. *Aggiornamento* [the modernizing movement initiated by Pope John XXIII] has brought together men of differing beliefs, and freedom of inquiry has become the basis for understanding between them. Censorship, no matter how carefully or discreetly exercised, has overtones of repression, and when it is badly handled it becomes a scandal and a reproach. Then, too, censorship does not exist in a vacuum. It springs from fear and expresses a defensive mentality. It indicates that alarums are being sounded from every bell tower and that the enemy is at the gates. But are we at war? Must we be so defensive, so circumspect, so frightened of ideas? Does it really advance truth to let the work of seminal scholars be mutilated or left to gather dust on a shelf because a censor does not approve a man's ideas or feels that his thinking is too avant garde? It has happened, although in fairness it should be pointed out that censors appointed by religious orders are greater culprits in this respect than are diocesan censors.

What is really called for, or so it seems to me, is the freedom to make a mistake. A mistake is not a catastrophe, and even censors have been known to stumble. When one considers *imprimaturs* that have been granted and later withdrawn, or the granting of an *imprimatur* here when it has been refused there, one can hardly be blamed for developing certain skeptical attitudes. (Germany, I am told, has a more efficient system. If one bishop refuses his *imprimatur*, by agreement no other German bishop will grant it. It appears that Americans, in the midst of their confusion, are freer.) If a censor makes an error in judgment he is protected both by his position and by his anonymity (prior to publication). The writer does not know who is judging his work, whether the critic is competent, sympathetic or hypercritical. If the writer were allowed to publish without prepublication censorship, any criticism of his work would be aired publicly, and the writer himself would be better able to judge its fairness.

As it is, prepublication censorship develops a psychology of fear, particularly in priests. It is not an atmosphere in which ideas flourish, and I don't think we can afford to cultivate atmospheres or attitudes that discourage freedom of thought. And, although the *imprimatur* is designed primarily to protect the reader, its chief effect is on the writer. In short it is not effective in its initial function. I take my stand with a theologian who remarked, "If a man is competent in his field, his competence should be the only *imprimatur* needed."

A NEW MOVIE CODE [3]

The board of directors of the Motion Picture Association of America [MPAA] voted unanimously . . . [September 20, 1966] to adopt a new production code. The code is the set of regulations by which the major American film companies attempt to control the content and the treatment of their films.

The new code replaces the one originally adopted in 1930, which, although revised several times since then, contained specific prohibitions against such things as "lustful kissing" and passion that "stimulates the baser emotions."

By eliminating many specific taboos, the new code gives the office of the Production Code Administration, situated in Hollywood, considerably more leeway in deciding what is or is not "acceptable." It also, for the first time, provides the code office with the authority to label certain approved films "recommended for mature audiences."

The action of the MPAA board was announced . . . at a press conference held by Jack J. Valenti, the Association's president, in company with Louis Nizer, the Association's general counsel, and Geoffrey Shurlock, the administrator of the code.

The move was not unexpected. The code authorities have been the target of increasing criticism in recent years on the ground that they have not been following the letter of their own laws by approving films of obviously "adult" themes. . . .

According to Mr. Valenti, the new code has two principal objectives:

> (1) To encourage artistic expression by expanding creative freedom, and (2) to assure that the freedom that encourages the artist remains responsible and sensitive to the standards of the larger society.
>
> This is still self-restraint, self-regulation and self-discipline [Mr. Valenti declared]. We want to make clear that expansion of the artist's freedom doesn't mean tolerance of license.

The adoption of the new code is to be accompanied by Association campaigns to persuade more producers to submit their

[3] From "A New Movie Code Ends Some Taboos," by Vincent Canby, staff writer. New York *Times*. p 1+. S. 21, '66. © 1966 by The New York Times Company. Reprinted by permission.

films for code approval and to publicize the meaning of the code seal in the general press.

Although Mr. Valenti stressed that the Association, as it has in the past, remains opposed to censorship and to statutory film classification, it was apparent from the questions put to him . . . that some members of the press regard the "mature audiences" recommendation as a form of classification.

"Call it anything you want," said Mr. Valenti. "It's really a question of semantics. What we are saying is: 'Look, Mr. Parent, this may not be a picture you want your child to see.' "

Ten Standards Approved

The Association also hopes to have the code seal itself displayed prominently in all film advertising and to be given a prominent spot in the onscreen credits of films.

The new code contains the following standards by which films will be judged:

(1) "The basic dignity and value of human life shall be respected and upheld. Restraint shall be exercised in portraying the taking of life." (In contrast, the old code contained four paragraphs dealing specifically with the treatment of murder, i.e. "Brutal killings are not to be shown in detail.")

(2) "Evil, sin, crime and wrongdoing shall not be justified." (In contrast, the old code contained ten lengthy paragraphs dealing with the treatment of crime, ranging from suicide ["It shall never be justified"] to mercy killing and drug addiction.)

(3) "Special restraint shall be exercised in portraying criminal or antisocial activities in which minors participate or are involved."

(4) "Detailed and protracted acts of brutality, cruelty, physical violence, torture and abuse shall not be presented."

(5) "Indecent or undue exposure of the human body shall not be presented." (The old code specified that "complete nudity, in fact or in silhouette, is never permitted, nor shall there be any licentious notice by characters in the film of suggested nudity.")

(6) "Illicit sex relationships shall not be justified. Intimate sex scenes violating common standards of decency shall not be portrayed. Restraint and care shall be exercised in presentations dealing with sex aberrations."

(The comparable section in the old code contained eight paragraphs specifically prohibiting, among other things, any treatment of abortion, the use of seduction or rape as material for comedy and "sex perversion or any inference of it.")

(7) "Obscene speech, gestures or movements shall not be presented. Undue profanity should not be permitted."

(8) "Religion shall not be demeaned."

(9) "Words or symbols contemptuous of racial, religious or national groups, shall not be used so as to incite hatred."

(10) "Excessive cruelty to animals shall not be portrayed and animals shall not be treated inhumanely."

Both Mr. Valenti and Mr. Nizer expressed the opinion that these new standards are so worded as to allow the code authorities a good deal of interpretation. Despite the prohibition against "indecent or undue exposure of the human body," Mr. Valenti said he felt Mr. Shurlock today would be able to pass a film like *The Pawnbroker,* which contained two scenes showing a woman's bare breasts, and which was originally denied a seal.

Room for Flexibility

"In other words," Mr. Valenti was asked, "could bare breasts be deemed indecent in one film and decent in another?"

"Yes," said the MPAA president.

He was similarly questioned as to the meaning of Paragraph 6 of the new code, dealing with "illicit sex relationships."

Mr. Shurlock commented cheerfully that "we've been struggling with the meaning of 'illicit' for thirty years."

Said Mr. Nizer: "The standards of reasonable men will be applied to the interpretation of the new code."

Mr. Valenti's comment was: "As they come down the shoot, we'll label them."

The new code provides for the establishment of a Motion Picture Code Board, which will hear the appeal from a producer when his film is denied a seal or when the producer does not feel that his film deserves a "mature audiences" rating. The board will also advise the Code Administration, if requested, on interpretation of the code standards.

The Board will consist of the president of the Association, nine other directors of the Association, six exhibitors nominated by the National Association of Theater Owners and four producers nominated by the Screen Producers Guild.

"There will be no exemptions from the new code," Mr. Valenti stressed. This was in reference to *Who's Afraid of Virginia Woolf?* and *Alfie,* two recent films that obtained code seals only after being specifically exempted from code provisions.

SELF-CENSORSHIP OF TV [4]

Back in the days of "live-live" television, the medium was frequently jolted by blue jokes and *double entendres*. Now that almost all shows are taped (live-on-tape is the euphemism), the only untoward sound is that of the bloop—the noise made when the erase head of the tape recorder censors out the audio portion of the TV picture.

On NBC's "Tonight" show with Johnny Carson, for instance the words "God," "damn" and "hell" are automaticallyblooped out of all conversations, as are any remarks deemed "suggestive." . . . On Gypsy Rose Lee's syndicated afternoon talk show, Gypsy mentioned LeRoi Jones's play, *The Toilet*. Or, rather, tried to mention it. As it came out, Jones had written *The Bloop*. "Darling," recalls Miss Lee, "it was ridiculous."

Blooping is only the latest electronic manifestation of television's self-censorious attitude. At a time when books, movies and the theater are relaxing restrictions and expanding their fields of coverage, TV still kills shows because of subject matter and story line. Homosexuality is taboo, as is any violence considered "exces-

[4] From "Time of the Bloop." *Newsweek*. 67:54-5. Ja. 24, '66. Copyright, Newsweek, Inc., January, 1966. Reprinted by permission.

sive." And each network has its own guardians of the public morality, called, variously, reviewers, supervisors of broadcast standards and practices, or continuity acceptance men.

Though their titles vary, their arguments for cutting are usually the same. Television, the defense goes, must guard children against corrupting influences. At NBC, Ernest Lee Jahncke, Jr., killed a show which tried to explain venereal disease to teen-agers—because it was on at a time when teen-agers would be watching. "I have three sons, and we talk about sex freely," he told *Newsweek's* Willa Beattie last week, "but not in the living room when their mother is present." Indeed, time plays a key part in the decisions of censors. Subjects of "controversy" are reserved for the after-nine time slots when children presumably are in bed. "What can be allowed on 'Kildare,'" said Richard Eastland, NBC's West Coast S and P [Standards and Practices] man, "might not be allowed on 'Camp Runamuck'—say, an unexpected pregnancy."

The standards and practices men will often see a show in four or five different forms—story line, outline, shooting script, rough-cut film—before giving it a final OK. Even the scripts of "Bonanza," the most wholesome horse opera on the air are sometimes revised because of too much blood. On the other hand, ABC's Grace Johnsen, whose job as director of ABC continuity acceptance since 1949 makes her the top female censor, found "Peyton Place" acceptable. "It is a morality type of play," she says. "There really isn't any action; it's all talk."

Sponsors still have some say about what can and can't be shown, though their authority is less than in the days when more shows were fully sponsored by one company. When "Route 66," was big, said NBC's Eastland, Chevrolet made sure no one was seen drinking liquor before hopping into a Chevy. More recently, the sponsor of NBC's "Run for Your Life," the Brown & Williamson Tobacco Company, asked the producer to make it clear on the air that Ben Gazzara's incurable disease was not cancer.

In addition to the networks' men, two other groups have a say in what goes on the air. The National Association of Broadcasters can withdraw its seal of approval from a station, as it did this month to five stations that aired commercials for a hemorrhoid cure.

And the FCC can take a station's license away, but only for violating the Federal laws governing obscenity, false statements and the promotion of lotteries.

FCC Commissioner Robert E. Lee is concerned that TV stations are running out of program material so fast that they will have to turn to more movies, including those now rejected as being too risqué. "But I don't think some movies should be shown to a television audience," he said last week. "Think about those James Bond movies!" For the censor, in fact, films present an entirely new challenge. Recently, NBC canceled Alfred Hitchcock's *Psycho* because it was "an intentional shocker."

Lee has also assailed the "Tonight" show for being blue. "Carson puts some beauties on there once in a while," he said. "Some of this late-night stuff borders on trouble." The late-night talk shows, the FCC feels, provoke frank talk for titillation's sake rather than honestly attacking subjects of substance.

Carson brushes off the complaints. "What are you supposed to say—go to heck?" he asks. "There are some people who object to the words *naked* and *pregnant*. Should you say, 'Hey, I hear you're with child'?"

When a person himself is denied work on TV, censorship becomes more savage than restrictive. Actress Jean Muir was dropped from NBC-TV's "The Aldrich Family" in 1950 because the sponsors, General Foods, considered her a "controversial person." Miss Muir had been mentioned in the notorious blacklist Red Channels. For fifteen years she has tried to make a comeback. . . . [In 1965] her appearance on ABC's "Girl Talk" was canceled. An ABC lawyer said: "There is some mention of names that might expose the station to defamation-of-character suits."

"When I was asked to do the show," Miss Muir said, "they asked *me* to talk about the blacklist." The show was finally aired . . . but the tape was edited and all the "controversial" names were blooped.

Yet some people defend the medium's censorious ways. "We have traveled a million miles in the maturing of themes," said David Susskind, whose "Open End" has been blooped now and then. And CBS's new S and P man, William H. Tankersley, passes the buck to the audience. "We bend with the times and the changing mores," he said. "People expect television to be an island of serenity in a troubled sea."

AN ATTEMPT TO REWRITE HISTORY [5]

The New York *Times* article . . . [August 3, 1965] read:

In an air-conditioned courtroom with the slogan "There is nothing so powerful as the truth" on the wall, both the truth and the freedom of historians in Pennsylvania to write interpretive assessments of the dead are at stake in this unusual trial.

Miss Helen Clay Frick, the only living child of the nineteenth century "coke king," Henry Clay Frick, brought suit (January 19, 1965) to bar the sale of a book, *Pennsylvania: Birthplace of a Nation,* that calls her father "brusque" and "autocratic."

According to the book's publisher, Random House, nine thousand copies of the first edition, which went on sale in December 1964, had either been sold or were on dealers' shelves when the trial began. A spokesman for the company called it "a good sale," and said the book had been favorably reviewed.

Defendant in the suit is the book's author, Dr. Sylvester K. Stevens, executive director of the Pennsylvania Historical and Museum Commission and former president of the American Association for State and Local History.

The suit was tried (July-August 1965) before Common Pleas Judge Clinton R. Weidner in the courthouse of Cumberland County in Carlisle, Pennsylvania, Dr. Stevens' home town.

Random House apparently was not named in the suit because it is a New York corporation. New York courts have ruled that the dead cannot be defamed. But Pennsylvania courts have held that under state law statements "tending to blacken the memory" of the dead in a way which lowers living descendants "in the esteem of the community" are actionable.

Three sections of the book were mentioned in the suit. The first refers to a Pittsburgh church which the author says Frick attended

[5] From Freedom of Information Center. Publication no 172. The Center. School of Journalism. University of Missouri. Columbia. D. '66. p 5-6. Reprinted by permission.

with other industrialists whose wealth was "not all . . . amassed in exact accordance with what many regarded as Christian principles and practices." Without conceding any error, Dr. Stevens agreed to delete all or part of this paragraph in future editions of the book on grounds of "taste."

The second section says that Frick, who once controlled 80 per cent of the coke production in western Pennsylvania, "made extensive use of immigrant labor" in his mines, and "cut wages to an average of about $1.60 a day, while extracting the longest hours of work physically possible." Housing provided by the company consisted of "shoddy wooden shacks without sanitary facilities, which they rented at a high price to the workers."

In the third section Dr. Stevens, describing Frick's successful defeat of the organizing efforts of the Amalgamated Iron, Steel and Tin Workers Union, wrote that "the power of the union was broken in the bloody and disastrous Homestead strike in 1892 by stern, brusque, autocratic Henry Clay Frick."

The New York *Times* reported (July 25, 1966) that a number of historians thought Dr. Stevens "had been 'more generous than most of his colleagues' in describing Mr. Frick's role in the state's industrial history."

This was not so, said Miss Frick in her complaint. Dr. Stevens had merely accepted the judgments of earlier historians who had written about her father.

Her attorney, David B. Buerger, said that "while the conditions the book describes have been generally true, Frick was the exception." Continued Buerger:

> He did not cut wages, he actually raised them. He did not use immigrant labor. He did not charge excessive rents, and, in fact, by today's standards he would be regarded as an enlightened man.

Commenting on the case, the Washington *Post* wrote (July 1, 1965):

> Suits to enjoin publication amount to a form of private censorship. It is true, of course, that a book or a newspaper or a magazine article, or any other form of expression, if distributed to the general public, may do irreparable injury and injustice. But a court injunction which forbids expression does even graver injury and injustice, with far wider social im-

plications and repercussions. The only socially acceptable remedy for defamatory expression—and the only remedy which, in our judgment, can be said to comport with the United States Constitution—is a suit for libel or slander. . . . It strikes us that [historians] are the best judges of Dr. Stevens' scholarship. If his judgment of Mr. Frick's place in the history of Pennsylvania is warped or erroneous, they will, through critical reviews, condemn it to oblivion; if his judgment is a valid one, it deserves distribution however uncomfortable this may be for Mr. Frick's descendants. The suppression of history—which is to say the judgments of historians—is an incongruity in a free society.

When the trial ended in August 1965, it was expected that Judge Weidner's decision would not be handed down for a period ranging from weeks to months. Fifteen months later, it was still forthcoming.

Almost a year after the end of testimony in the Pennsylvania trial, Dr. Stevens appealed (July 26, 1966) to the United States District Court in New York, asking it to take the unusual step of intervening in a state court. Simon H. Rifkind, Dr. Stevens' attorney, said the Pennsylvania proceeding was an infringement of the right of free press guaranteed by the First and Fourteenth amendments and the Civil Rights Act.

A committee of fourteen historians, calling itself the Joint Committee for the Defense of the Rights of Historians Under the First Amendment, and representing the American Historical Association and *American Heritage* magazine, supported Dr. Stevens' suit.

The committee issued a statement on the case which deserves to be quoted at length:

At the heart of this suit lies the fundamental right of the public to be fully and well informed about any aspects of the past.

We believe that an historian is bound by the canons of his profession to present the truth about the past as honestly, as accurately, and as objectively as is humanly possible, even if that truth may be uncomplimentary. Obviously, the historian is accountable to his peers in the profession and we do not question the right of any living person who is damaged by a defamatory falsehood to sue for damages within the framework of the First Amendment and the law of libel. What we do question—and what concerns us vitally here—is the assault by Miss Frick which, if successful, would inhibit our right to speak freely about the past based upon scholarly research, and which would permit the descendants of long-dead historical figures to have serious books removed from circulation simply because something critical was said about their ancestors. Success in her suit would lead to direct censorship.

The historian has obligations to the public. He is, in a sense, custodian of the public conscience in everything touching the past. His professional obligation, as well as the public interest, require that none of his statements should be expressed merely because of their popularity or conformity to accepted orthodoxies. His purpose in exploring the past is to advance truth and to expose error. The rectification of his own errors can best be left to the process of mutual questioning and verification that goes on in the learned professions.

No historian can—or should—permit any orthodoxy or any authority to compel him to state what his conscience and the canons of his profession forbid him to state. "The public," as a distinguished historian has written, "is the historian's client, not his sovereign." There are often harsh and unpleasant truths that he must say to his client. This is the peculiar glory of historical writing in a democracy. The past may be manipulated in an authoritarian state, but this can never be permitted in a free society.

Dr. Stevens' case is unique. It is the first case we know of in which a serious work has been challenged in the courts, in which the court has been asked to ban a book, and in which the court has proceeded to hear the suit on the merits. But that makes its danger even greater, for a victory for Miss Frick would encourage others to take similar action and soon we would be spending all our time defending lawsuits instead of studying and writing. A victory for Miss Frick would be a crippling blow to scholarly study and would eventually shake the very foundations of our great democracy which depends so much on the free and unfettered flow and exchange of ideas.

Rifkind said the Pennsylvania case was not the usual kind brought against a writer, which is an action charging libel and claiming damages, but instead was an action in equity asserting that Miss Frick had suffered a loss of reputation from the book and asking that Dr. Stevens be prohibited from distributing the book (New York *Times*, July 26, 1966). A spokesman for Miss Frick said (August 2, 1965) she chose the latter action because "she does not need the money." Her fortune is estimated at $38 million.

Federal Judge Harold Tyler took under consideration (September 27, 1966) Dr. Stevens' request. In questioning attorneys for both sides, the judge appeared to narrow the case to two principal issues. He indicated he had a doubt about the right of a descendant of an historical figure to get an injunction against an historian for writing critically about that figure, which was the chief argument made by Dr. Stevens' lawyer.

But he also questioned the advisability of a Federal court acting on a matter which was before a state court when a trial had already been held and a decision might be forthcoming soon. This was the main contention of Miss Frick's attorney.

According to Random House, the book had sold about thirteen thousand copies by August 1966. It had also received a commendation from the Senate of Pennsylvania (*Publishers' Weekly,* August 15, 1966).

Judge Tyler handed down (October 17, 1966) a brief decision rejecting Dr. Stevens' request, saying that he believed it inappropriate for a Federal court to intervene in a state action. He noted that should Dr. Stevens lose in Pennsylvania, he would have the right to appeal to higher courts in that state, and to the United States Supreme Court if necessary. [On May 25, 1967, Judge Weidner dismissed Miss Frick's suit, holding, as reported by the New York *Times* (May 26, 1967), that Dr. Stevens' right "to make an unflattering assessment of Mr. Frick was fully protected by the Federal and state constitutions," and that Dr. Stevens' "allegedly defamatory statements were not only true in every respect, but were even milder than might have been warranted by the facts."—Ed.]

WRITING HISTORY ON APPROVAL [6]

The Kennedy-Manchester dispute raises a fundamental question that should concern authors, publishers, and the public: does the Constitution prohibit the courts from enforcing a right-of-approval contract when author and publisher move to issue the book without obtaining the required consent?

The question does not assume that William Manchester breached his agreement. But if the Constitution bars suits to enforce such a contract, a court would never decide whether a breach had occurred. It would have to dismiss the suit at the outset, breach or no breach. And if the Constitution bars this type of litigation everyone would be better off.

[6] Article, "The Author's Right to Write," by Irwin Karp, legal representative for the Authors League of America, here expressing only his personal opinion. *Saturday Review.* 50: 28-9. Ja. 21, '67. © 1967 by Saturday Review, Inc. Reprinted by permission.

Authors and publishers could not be compelled to suppress portions of their work. The "subjects" of future books, forewarned of the consequences, would not give authors intimate details they did not wish exposed to public view, thus effectively protecting their right of privacy. The press would be relieved of its present, painful duty of disclosing the very material a plaintiff sues to keep from being published. And the public's right to have freedom of speech and press kept untrammeled would be preserved.

It is likely that the Supreme Court, following a twenty-year-old precedent, would rule that the First and Fourteenth Amendments bar courts from restraining publication of a book which has not obtained the approval required by a contract and also bar them from awarding damages for violation of the right of approval.

The Court may not deal with the issue for years. But the possibility that the right of free speech may take precedence over private contract rights should be aired before the next suit; in fact, before the next contract is signed. Considering it prospectively, rather than during an emotional litigation, might dissipate the notion that there is something unfair about preserving freedom of speech and press. Some of the "let's have no First Amendment nonsense" editorials reflected that attitude: Mrs. Kennedy would not have disclosed the material she objected to had her legal advisor foreseen that the Constitution might nullify her right of approval; therefore, the First Amendment should not prevent her from enforcing that right.

Despite Mr. Manchester's harrowing experience, other authors will sign right-of-approval contracts; and there will be more suits. Mrs. Kennedy's success in compelling *Look* to make deletions will itself induce subjects or sources of future biographies or authorized histories to demand rights of approval. Further stimulus may come from comments by New York's Appellate Division in the suit brought by Warren Spahn, under the state's right of privacy law, against the author and publisher of an unauthorized biography. Affirming an injunction against the book, and an award of damages to Mr. Spahn, the court said: "If the publication . . . by intention, purport or format is neither factual nor historical, the [right of privacy] statute applies and if the subject is a living person his written consent must be obtained." It also said that "the consent . . . can be avoided by writing *strictly factual* biographies."

An unauthorized biography may not be "strictly factual." It may contain honest errors of fact, and there is no rule for determining how many are allowed before it ceases being "strictly factual." The court's comments may impel cautious publishers to seek consent for potentially controversial biographies. Obviously, the subject will demand the right of approval before giving his consent. (Equally obvious: if he doesn't like what he reads, he will sue to enforce that right.) Actually, the *Spahn* case involved considerably more than factual errors or distortions; the court found that the biography was larded with "dramatization, imagined dialogue, manipulated chronologies, and fictionalization of events." But until subsequent opinions make it clear that fictionalization (and not factual inaccuracy) is really what the court held to violate the privacy statute, a nervous publisher may take the court's *dicta* at face value and seek consent for any book that may not be "strictly factual."

Obviously, while it costs nothing to preach that an author should never grant the right of approval, it may be more difficult to follow this advice. Writing is a precarious profession. It is not easy for an author to turn down a book that may have the potential of financial success. The temptation will be harder to resist when it is suggested that the pitfalls of the Kennedy-Manchester memorandum could be avoided by more careful drafting. The memorandum leaves room for improvement, and more protection could be provided for an author.

But once an author signs such a contract, no matter how well drawn, he hands the other party a weapon that can be used to suppress his book. It makes no difference that he may have complied, or thought he had complied, with the agreement. If the subject wants material deleted he can commence a suit. Often this will be enough to compel the requested changes. Litigation may threaten costly delays in publication, entail heavy expenses for defense and (unless the First Amendment bars it) create some risk of an injunction or a judgment for damages. Any of these factors may bring sufficient pressure on the author to capitulate, even though he might ultimately win on the merits. As the Supreme Court emphasized in *New York Times Company v. Sullivan,* the fear of damage awards in private suits and the costs of defending against them "may be markedly more inhibiting" on free speech than the fear of prosecution under a criminal statute.

It may be asked, why should the First Amendment protect an author or publisher who voluntarily signs a contract giving others the right to determine whether the book should be published? If they choose to surrender their freedom to publish, why should the courts restore that freedom to them? The answer is that the First Amendment guaranties of free speech and free press are not personal privileges granted to an author or publisher for his private benefit. The First Amendment secures freedom of speech and press for the benefit of the community at large, to ensure that unfettered discussion of issues which is the fundamental condition of a democratic society. It is not in the public interest that authors and publishers be permitted to abdicate those freedoms by private contract.

A right-of-approval contract can be used as a potent instrument for private censorship. It can force deletion of historical or political opinions that are offensive or inconvenient to the subject. It can suppress material the author obtained from other sources, or his own opinions. And it can be used to suppress material that would not violate the subject's rights under state privacy statutes. As the New York Court of Appeals emphasized in the *Spahn* case, "in balance with the legitimate public interest, the law affords [a public person's] privacy little protection." Moreover, a contract-given right of approval is not necessary to enforce one's right under the privacy laws.

It seems clear that the public's interest in preserving freedom of speech and press, for its benefit, is inconsistent with the enforcement of a contract in which author and publisher surrender that right and submit themselves to private censorship. Refusal by the courts to enforce such contracts is the only effective way to prevent them. And such refusal is by no means unusual; courts frequently decline to enforce private and voluntary contracts if they run contrary to some aspect of public policy.

Moreover, once the dispute reaches a court and it is asked to issue an order enjoining publication of the book, a new problem is presented. The question now is whether the state, acting through the court, may suppress publication of the book. This is the nub of the constitutional issue under the First and Fourteenth Amendments.

In 1947 the Supreme Court set aside injunctions issued to prevent the breach of voluntary and lawful private agreements. The case was *Shelley v. Kraemer*. The agreements were restrictive covenants prohibiting the sale of property to Negroes, agreements which were then lawful. The Court said that "the restrictive covenants standing alone cannot be regarded as violative of any rights guaranteed to the petitioners by the Fourteenth Amendment. So long as the purposes of these agreements are effectuated by voluntary adherence to their terms, it would appear clear that there has been no action by the state and the provisions of the Amendment have not been violated."

But, said the Court, the Fourteenth Amendment prohibits the state from imposing such restrictions on the ownership of property. It ruled that an order of the court enforcing the agreements and enjoining their violation was an act of the state, prohibited by the Fourteenth Amendment. It said that such a court order, in a private suit, was as much forbidden by the Constitution as would be an act of the legislature barring the sale of property to Negroes. In 1952 the Supreme Court went one step further and held (in *Barrows v. Jackson*) that state courts were also barred by the Fourteenth Amendment from granting damages for the breach of such agreements.

The right to own property free from discriminatory restrictions is but one of the rights protected by the Fourteenth Amendment. It also prohibits the states from restricting the rights of free speech and press, guaranteed by the First Amendment. Applying the 1947 opinion, a court order enjoining publication of a book to prevent breach of a contractual right of approval (or granting damages for the breach) would constitute a state restraint on freedom of publication—a restraint the state, and its courts, are prohibited from imposing by the First and Fourteenth Amendments.

Furthermore, the Court cited as precedent for the decision prior opinions in which it reversed orders that enforced "common-law policy of the state" because they restricted the constitutional "guaranties of freedom of discussion."

In addition to the Supreme Court's opinion in *Shelley v. Kraemer,* there is the traditional refusal of courts to enjoin the publication of allegedly libelous works. For example, in a 1946 libel suit against *PM,* the New York Supreme Court said:

> The exercise of equitable jurisdiction to enjoin the publication of a libel is repugnant to the democratic tradition. The judicial restraint of the written or spoken word implies the concept of censorship, unprecedented in our jurisprudence. The constitutional guaranty of a free speech and a free press may not be thus circumscribed.

If courts will not enjoin publication to protect the right not to be libeled, will they do so to protect rights under a contract?

The ultimate paradox is that litigation can destroy the very protection a right-of-approval contract is supposed to provide. A constitutional barrier to these agreements would not only safeguard freedom of discussion; it would also lead the subjects of future biographies and authorized histories to use more effective means of preserving the privacy of material too intimate to be published now. The First Amendment does not compel anyone to disclose information to an author; it does not prevent anyone from making his own record of intimate information for future historians, without using authors as intermediaries.

THE ROLE OF THE PUBLIC LIBRARIAN [7]

[The public librarian, on the surface] would appear a most improbable candidate for involvement in questions of pornography. The pulp literature of the cheaper bookstalls has never found room on library shelves, nor is there much likelihood that it ever will. But the curious anomaly of the present traffic in erotica has been its aura of sudden respectability: many an old chestnut from the world's abundant literature of sex has been refurbished, put out

[7] From "The Public Custody of the High Pornography," by Kathleen Molz, editor of the *Wilson Library Bulletin. American Scholar.* 36:93-103. Winter '66-'67. Reprinted from *The American Scholar.* Copyright © 1967 by the United Chapters of Phi Beta Kappa. By permission of the publishers.

under the imprint of a respectable publishing house, decorously bound, subtly advertised, and almost invariably prefaced by the commentary of some reputable scholarly figure. Confronted by the appearance of a new edition of the very book that has languished for years in the stacks (because it had proved a problem child for the collection), the librarian may sometimes feel a little like the lad at the royal procession, who whispered to his father: "But the Emperor has nothing at all on." . . .

Charged with making decisions about various titles, with funds derived from the public treasury, the librarian holds rather a unique position among all those engaged in the writing, publication and dissemination of books. That is *not* to say that conscionable writers, publishers and booksellers exhibit no concern for their readers, but to emphasize that the *public custody* of books is the librarian's prime responsibility, one that leaves him accountable to every licit or illicit critic who finds fault with the presence (or absence) of certain books on library shelves.

The concept of the library collection as a public trust dates back to the origins of the public library itself. No better statement, descriptive of its high function as the means through which the general public could seek knowledge and enlightenment, exists than the 1852 report of the trustees of the Boston Public Library, the first such institution to be established in a major American city. Although the trustees specified no books by name, they were quite clear as to the type of collection required. In referring to the popular books of the times, they made note that "the more respectable" would be purchased; indeed, the trustees conceded that in the matter of book selection "the popular taste" could even be followed, "unless it should ask for something unhealthy."

With a residual puritanical distrust for light reading including, of course, fiction, the trustees envisioned a hierarchical structure of cultural improvement. At the lowest step of this Victorian *Gradus ad Parnassum,* the prospective patron would be expected to peruse only the "lighter publications"; next he would progress to the "older and more settled works in Biography, in History," finally reaching those titles comprised in "the graver departments of knowledge." If the trustees were less than explicit about what was comprised in the "lighter publications," their contemporary, Horace Mann, was not. In his *Common School Journal,* he had already looked askance at the holdings of early libraries, the stock of which he castigated as "novels, and all that class of books which is comprehended under the familiar designation of 'fictions,' 'light readings,' 'trashy works,' 'ephemeral' or 'bubble literature.' " By initiating their own version of "upward cultural mobility" the trustees hoped to achieve not only the improvement of individual taste, but also, and more important, the obviation of "a great deal of the mischievous poor reading now indulged in."

Ironically, their report was issued but a few months after the initial publication in book form of *Uncle Tom's Cabin.* Apart from its more pertinent political influences, the book, written by a minister's wife and devoted to so serious a theme, did much to establish in this country the benefits of the novel as an instrumentality of social good. Consequently, fiction, ephemeral or not, was to become a large part of the country's newly formed public libraries, and for many years the circulation of novels exceeded that of all other materials comprised within the library's total holdings.

Nonetheless, the reluctant encouragement of the novel (and its frequent associations with mischief and malaise) had so penetrated the roots of public librarianship that, from the nineteenth century on, libraries bifurcated all knowledge into two classes, maintaining statistical records for the circulation of what was termed fiction and nonfiction. . . .

The gnawing fear that the novel was basically a device to while away time, and by inference, a lesser form of art, died slowly. Even as late as 1908, Arthur Bostwick, then president of the American Library Association, singled out French fiction as a genre offensive to "canons of decency." "Mr. Wister has told librarians," he said, "that all subjects are 'fit for fiction.' This is interesting as an academic thesis, but when the French proceed to act upon it, the Anglo-Saxon catches his breath. . . . An American public library is justified in requiring its books to respect American prejudices." In an unhappy burst of rhetoric, Bostwick embraced the role of the librarian as "a censor of literature," thus casting the die for the continuing debate as to whether the rejection of controversial novels can be construed as the legitimate exercise of a responsible book selection policy or as the shabby exemplification of what Morris Ernst once called "the subterranean censorship" of the public library....

With a pall of community Grundyism forever over his head, the librarian was never the innovator in the selection of suspect items, and for the most part, copies of *Jurgen*, *Sister Carrie*, *The Well of Loneliness* or the Studs Lonigan trilogy found their way onto library shelves long after they had proved themselves part of the classic canon of fiction already represented there. As the number of such books grew, the increasing sexual candor of the novel no longer seemed a point of critical relevance, and by 1933, with the determination of the *Ulysses* case, the librarian found in the temperate wording of the decision a more proper and rational focus for his own book selection policies. Judge Woolsey's emphasis on the whole book (as opposed to the isolated passage) and the stress placed on the reader as an average person (in contrast to the immature, the deviant or the eccentric) afforded saner avenues for the examination of novels than the alarmist views of Arthur Bostwick.

Other factors contributed toward a more libertarian view: the book burnings of Hitler's Germany, the anti-intellectualism inherent in the work of the Gathings Committee, and the divesting of libraries during the McCarthy era, each in turn tended to convince the librarian that the dangers of governmental or private proscription were far worse than the palpable coarseness of any one book, however crude. During the early sixties, at the height of national concern over the outcome of the *Tropic of Cancer* case, the library profession came full circle, and through the action of its national organization, the American Library Association, even entered an *amicus curiae* brief in defense of the book. In addition, a number of individual librarians staunchly stood their ground, refusing to comply with extralegal community pressures to remove the book from their collections. Yet, it is not unfair to say that what librarians basically defended in the *Tropic* case was not so much the book itself, but rather the principle guaranteeing its free and open dissemination.

Far from resolving the issues in contemporary library book selection, the *Tropic* case was soon found only to have accentuated them. The book's exoneration before the Supreme Court held considerable promise to many publishers that works of equal, if not surpassing, frankness would be similarly protected, and the market was inevitably glutted with a veritable bordello school of fiction. Grounded in the nineteenth-century tradition of the novel, in which the theme of sexual misconduct was invariably associated with grief, the librarian was left to evaluate the easy virtues of a Candy and a Fanny Hill who, unlike Anna Karenina, Emma Bovary or Tess Durbeyfield, skip through the back streets of their fictional worlds with neither a thought of repentance nor a semblance of shame. Fearing that any criticism he might make of this widely advertised old/new fiction would label him forever as "a prurient prude," the librarian turned more and more to the opinions of others hoping to find some resolution of the issues he mentally raised when the salacious novel came up for review. Three in number, these questions are: How much of this sexually burdened literature will the local community traffic bear? Do such books possess qualities, either esthetically or philosophically, to warrant the expenditure of public funds for their purchase? And, what is the library's responsibility for the inclusion of such books, not only toward its mature readers, but also *in loco parentis* toward those users of the collection not yet legally of age?

On the first of these, at least prior to the recent rulings in the Ginzburg case, librarians had tended to rely upon the discrimination of the courts; that is, works proscribed by local magistrates or banned from importation into this country were not circulated by public libraries. This reliance on juridical discrimination may be, however, totally unfounded, since the law continues to ban a book as obscene without in any way showing a causative relationship between the reading of a book and the subsequent delinquent or antisocial actions that it presumably provokes. That such a causality is a matter of supposition, but never of proof, remains the essential weakness of our present obscenity laws.

Then, too, the law seeks a determination of the author's intent in writing a book, surely a most difficult factor to ascertain when the work in question is one of the imagination. Yet the crux of the *Ulysses* decision was, in essence, Joyce's motivation. ". . . In any case where a book is claimed to be obscene," Judge Woolsey wrote, "it must first be determined, whether the intent with which it was written was what is called, according to the usual phrase, pornographic,—that is, written for the purpose of exploiting obscenity. . . . But in *Ulysses,* in spite of its unusual frankness, I do not detect anywhere the leer of the sensualist. I hold, therefore, that it is not pornographic."

Destined to become a kind of legal shibboleth, the phrase "leer of the sensualist" was used again, in a totally different context when Judge Frederick vanPelt Bryan handed down his 1959 decision relating to *Lady Chatterley's Lover*. Here Judge Bryan subtly shifted the burden of proof as to the merits of the work away from the author and straight into the camp of his publishers and advertisers. "There is nothing of the 'leer of the sensualist,' " he commented, "in the promotion or methods of distribution of this book. There is no suggestion of any attempt to pander to the lewd and lascivious minded for profit. The facts are all to the contrary."

With such a precedent, it should not have been so very surprising that Mr. Justice Brennan based his findings of obscenity in the Ginzburg case primarily on the methods used to promote the works at issue. Even the language of his decision bears a marked similarity to that of Judge Bryan: "The 'leer of the sensualist' also permeates the advertising for the three publications. The circulars sent for *Eros* and *Liaison* stressed the sexual candor of the respective publications, and openly boasted that the publishers would take full advantage of what they regarded an [*sic*] unrestricted license allowed by law in the expression of sex and sexual matters." Conservative though the librarian may be, he was never so naïve as to believe that the packaging of a product could substantively alter its contents. That the Supreme Court could, on the one hand, absolve *Fanny Hill,* which for two hundred years has been considered a pornographic classic, and, on the other, convict a publisher for an advertising campaign, however meretricious, struck the librarian with as much a sense of dismay as it did the rest of the nation.

It may seem unfortunate that librarians have traditionally placed a greater reliance in these matters on the literature of jurisprudence than on the literature of criticism, for pornography is essentially an esthetic, not juridical, problem. Put another way, the advent of an under-the-counter book in an over-the-counter display becomes, surely in our time, not a question of morals, but of taste. By rights, the strongest opponents of the inherent tawdriness of much modern fiction should be the academic or literary critic. His analyses of this fiction, however, tend to read more and more like briefs for the defense. As one reviewer wrote of a recent novel: it fractures "the last rationale of censorship," thus begging the question as to the worth of a book whose sole merit seems to be comprised in its narrow escape from proscription.

The day in court of many a critic, called upon to testify as an expert witness in a local or state obscenity trial, has done the cause of letters little service. Respected voices from the scholarly community have been heard to deny solemnly that there are any obscenities in Henry Miller's books and to characterize *Fanny Hill* as "a minor work of art." . . . The rationale behind this testimony is, of course, understandable; under the aegis of our current obscenity statutes, no better solution can be afforded. The law requires that lubricious material be proved not obscene in order to be circulated; since art is presumably exempt from these rules, the best defense for this literature lies in proving that it is "art," an enormous tent of a word which now must accommodate the peculiar alliance of *Lady Chatterley's Lover* and *Fanny Hill*.

In an unfortunate reversal of roles, the literary critics have become our guarantors of intellectual freedom (surely the province of our jurists), and the nation's judges have become our literary critics, deciding what is art and therefore licit and what is nonart and therefore banned. It is the place of law, nevertheless, to secure for man his freedom to read, a freedom permitting him access to good books, bad books, indifferent ones. The critic's function is to remind the reading public that distinctions among such books still pertain. . . .

In this topsy-turvy scheme of things, in which the jurist adjudicates our national esthetic and the critic serves as the watchdog of our national ethic, it is small wonder that the nation's public libraries present so confused a policy in the handling of controversial books. . . .

Raised through critical and commercial exploitation to the level of a cultural phenomenon, the "high pornography" remains a subcultural literature. That is not to say that advertising and promotion can make a work pornographic (as the decisions of the Supreme Court would seem to imply), but rather to indicate that the criteria used to appraise such books can be so devalued that the only factors left relevant are those of shock or titillation. Pornography becomes "high" in precise proportion to the downgrading of the critical apparatus used to accommodate its inescapable limitations. Such a situation pertained, I believe, in the critical reviewing afforded *Candy* and *Story of O*, both of them books designed to meet the needs of the bibliovoyeur. That those desiring such entertainment should be left free to obtain it, there should be no question, but it does not lie within the responsibility of a public library to indulge every vagary of human taste. Nor should the rejection of these books or others of like ilk lead to any inference that the librarian is acting in this regard as a censor. Censorship is the formal interdiction of a book or other material by a government, and the exclusion of books by libraries in no way curtails their availability through other sources. To raise the hue and cry of intellectual freedom over every title rejected by a library becomes in the long run merely ridiculous, since, by its very nature, intellectual freedom protects the right of choice, whether it be wise or faulty.

At the same time, the librarian must face up to some defects of his own: traditionally, he has always demanded more of the novel than he has of any other genre. From the beginning of the public library movement, the novel has been tolerated as a concession to the public taste. It may be time to reexamine the remnants of this old prejudice, and admit fiction into the literature class of the library's collection. If this were achieved, the works of the Marquis de Sade would not be left swimming in an alphabetic sea, but would be juxtaposed with the evaluative studies that place his writings in their historic and critical context. The delimitation of the adult fiction collection to meet the requirements of the adolescent reader is also false, and librarians should exercise caution that the significant literature of their contemporaries is not rejected on the grounds of its unsuitability for the thirteen-year-old. Genet's style mandates the inclusion of his writings in the nation's libraries; poor the collection that would deny him access.

In defense of librarians, it should be said, however, that they stand dead center in the midst of muddle. Enjoined by a critical literature that wraps up every sex-obsessed book in a mantle of artistic "freedom," and beset by a conservative, if not reactionary, element of the public, which scents down the off-color words even in the *Dictionary of American Slang*, the librarian is not without rights to call down "a plague o' both your houses." With all its fallacies the statement of the Boston trustees still pertains: in their regard, the public library was intended as a mirror of the mind, casting back to man not only the reflection of his greatest accomplishments, but also the sorrier image of his mistakes. That such an institution should be supported by public funds was, admittedly, a grand design, and grand designs have seemingly gone out of fashion. Society, with its shorter view that the public should get what it pays for, has so chipped away at the concept of a public library that, in all too many communities, it has become little more than an informational hodgepodge, furnishing its staff and resources as a solver of riddles for the community's contestants, a reference arm for the burden of community homework, and a supplier of cheap best sellers for the titillation of the middle class. In this age of assets, people have every right to *buy* what they want to read, and the question of pornography, or smut literature or whatever other designation it goes under, will eventually boil down to nothing more than what is encompassed in the old phrase, "*chacun à son goût.*"

What is inane about our present situation is that the worst of advertisements, every frenzied line of which spells out *caveat emptor* to the discriminating and sensible reader, renders a man liable to conviction. As long as pornography is made a legal issue, purveyors of bad taste become martyrs and their cheap haberdashery comes off as shirts of silk. I would hope that the public library, conservative, square, or what you will, would resist the banalities of a literature squalid in style, poor in effect. The blandishments and soporifics of most of "the high pornography" will add little luster to those houses of high culture located around the corner from Elm Street.

ADVICE TO LIBRARIANS [8]

What this country needs is a good Right-wing folk singer, quipped a cabaret MC at Washington's Shoreham Hotel during a . . . [January 1965] conference sponsored by the Intellectual Freedom Committee of the American Library Association. Although he was not on the program, to a good many of the delegates who heard him (unofficially) the remark was appropriate and the timing apt. The conference had been called to deal with the growing pressures on our libraries, much of which comes from the "radical Right." And if there is anything that distinguishes the Right from the Left, it is the total lack of joy with which the True Believers in Barry Goldwater clobber their enemies and influence their friends. The Left, on the other hand, partly because its members are younger, goes about its business more spiritedly. After all, trampling out the grapes of wrath is much more fun when done to music.

But if the Left is learning to play old instruments, the Right is teaching the new tricks. There is humor in stealing a book that one disapproves of (books used to be stolen because they were enjoyed); and stolen not just once, but over and over as replacement copies are put on the shelves. There is humor in a syndicate of card-carrying borrowers who make sure the books they don't like are always out on loan. Formerly, one boycotted the objectionable. The rationale seems to be: If the book offends thee, pluck it out.

[8] From "Teaching Librarians to Fight Back," by David Dempsey, novelist and free-lance writer. *Saturday Review*. 48:20-1+. F. 27, '65. Reprinted by permission.

There is humor, too, in discovering just what kinds of books are symbolically burned by being symbolically borrowed. The offending work may simply be *Lolita,* which, at worst, gets thrown out and, if it is lucky, is promoted to the "adults only" shelf. (Where, as Eric Moon, editor of the *Library Journal* insists, *Lolita* really *is* a dangerous book.) Miss Blanche Collins, the librarian from Long Beach, California, told the conference that her "most frequently stolen" items were those dealing with narcotics, extrasensory perception, and almost anything critical of the extreme Right. Along with works on hypnotism and sex, they are now safely behind lock and key in Long Beach—for their own protection, not the reader's. . . .

[In 1964] a group of Long Beach, California, citizens calling themselves the Education Society of Long Beach demanded that Nikos Kazantzakis's *The Last Temptation of Christ* be withdrawn from the public library as "blasphemous." Miss Collins refused. She refused, also, to arbitrarily stock her shelves with Right-wing material insisted upon by the Education Society. (The library had already obtained some of this material through its normal acquisition procedures.) The society thereupon took the matter to the city council.

To the council's credit, after a turbulent session it backed the librarian's right to choose her own books. (Things ended less happily in Arcadia, California, where *The Last Temptation of Christ* split the town wide open and led to the librarian's resignation.) A sixtyish, gray-haired, mild-mannered woman, Blanche Collins exemplifies what she herself called "the quiet librarian who sees it through." The point is not only that she "saw it through," but that enough community support rallied to her side to make seeing it through possible.

How to strengthen the librarian's hand in similar situations was one of the major purposes of the two-day Intellectual Freedom conference. Financed by a $7,000 grant from the *World Book Encyclopedia,* the seventy-five invited participants included lawyers, an expert on juvenile delinquency, a regional director of the ACLU [American Civil Liberties Union], two ministers, writers, book industry spokesmen, teachers, and others in the direct line of fire.

Probably two thirds of those attending were professional librarians, and they came both from the big cities and from such smaller places as Oshkosh, Wisconsin. It was a serious group intent on hammering out, in a single weekend, a program of action for submission to the 28,000 members of the American Library Association. . . .

Conferences, of course, don't frighten bush-league Comstocks; and in any case the question of censorship is not easily solved by a set of abstract principles. One librarian said to me, "Between the high-minded intellectual dedication of this meeting and the problems of my little library in New Jersey, there is a wide gap indeed." The point is well taken. Under pressure from their communities, librarians today are expected to be guardians of public morals.

It may seem that they have always had this task, but not until after a succession of censorship decisions by the Supreme Court has the problem become really intolerable. The Court has, in effect, asked the librarian to be a libertarian as well. What was once proscribed is now legal, and the burden of choice has been shifted from the law to the school, the library, and the bookseller. By the same token, the frustrations of the censor have been deflected from the Court (impeach Earl Warren) to the house of books (fire Blanche Collins). The role is one which most librarians are not yet prepared to play.

The situation is complicated by the diverse bag of books that must now be defended: seldom the acknowledged classic *(Ulysses)* but rather the acknowledged trash *(Peyton Place)*. The prurient book may not be "utterly without redeeming social importance" (in the words of Justice Brennan)—hence not pornographic—but it may very likely be without any redeeming literary value. For as Dan Lacy, [then] director of the American Book Publishers Council, told the meeting, the social consequences of freedom from censorship are not altogether positive. One of the prices paid has been a mass of junk.

This in itself would not be so bad if it were only junk the librarian had to contend with—most of which, in any case, she leaves to the corner newsdealer. In her role as arbiter of public taste, she is also expected to neutralize the value conflicts that go deep into the roots of her community. She must offend no one, and if she is hep she may defend freedom of speech by hiding the offending books. (A library in California admitted a few years ago to having two thousand "controversial" books stashed away in a locked room.) Some librarians pine for the good old days when it was the chief of police, the American Legion, and members of the state legislature who did the censoring—people who ordinarily didn't read books and might easily be made to seem ridiculous. But today, the Civil Liberties Union's Charles Morgan declared, the pressure may come from high-minded liberals who sincerely believe that there are certain valid exceptions to freedom of expression.

Morgan read a policy statement issued by an outstanding public library in the North.

> The library may exclude a majority of the books presenting views that are regarded by a consensus of responsible opinion . . . as unsound. For the use of students and scholars, however, the collection may include a few representative and prominent books that, when published, favored practices which have since come to be regarded as either antisocial or positively illegal, e.g., it possesses a number of antebellum works in favor of slavery, which are of great value to students of the period. . . . These are usually kept "for reference only."

The unhappy deduction to be made from such a statement is that it was obviously devised by reasonable men who thought they were doing the right thing. This same historical double-think is seen in Philadelphia, where the schools use an "adapted" version of *Huckleberry Finn,* in which the violence, dialect, and derogatory references to Negroes are toned down. Or consider the selection policy of the library in a large southern city which excludes all religious books that "show partisanship or are destructively critical of another faith." . . .

The absence of censorship cases in many communities may be no cause for rejoicing, but simply an admission that the librarian has beaten the censors at their own game. The Fiske Report, *Book Selection and Censorship: A Study of School and Public Libraries in California,* published in 1959, testifies to the effectiveness of this do-it-yourself movement. Of the ninety libraries and 204 librarians sampled in twenty-six localities, two thirds of the respondents reported refusals to purchase based on the controversial nature of a book or its author, one third reported the permanent removal of some controversial materials, and a fifth reported an habitual avoidance of all controversial matter. An interesting footnote to the study (financed by a grant from the Ford Foundation) is that the project was first offered to the California Library Association, which ducked the issue as too hot. It was finally carried out by the School of Library Science at the University of Southern California.

If the findings of this report can be extrapolated nationally, the average American library is in danger of becoming a refuge for the middle-class, the middle-brow, and the middle-sexed. The conference, indeed, was deeply concerned with the failure of libraries to draw the "outsider"—the potential delinquent, for example, who, far from being corrupted by "dirty books," seldom reads any books at all. "Removing books from the reading shelf to save delinquents is a vain and futile gesture," Professor William C. Kvaraceus of Tufts University said.

The missionary may possibly be the local minister or priest, although more likely he is one of their flock who has been blown off course by the jet stream of "extremist" propaganda that howls these days from west to east. Dr. Theodore Gill, president of the San Francisco Theological Seminary, in a dazzling condemnation of the church's role in censorship, described the "content" Christian who knew "what had been, was, and always would be obscene."

How is this wisdom achieved?

> In the first place [Dr. Gill declared], since Christians seemingly had always been suspicious of "the world" and nervous about sex, obscenity generally would be in the sexual area and Christians would be against it. Second, because of the word fixation of Protestants, obscenity would have to do more with uttered words than with contextual attitudes.

In fairness to his address, I should add that Dr. Gill described another type of Christian—indeed, from the passion of his argument I suspect that he invented him—who is willing to resolve his moral doubts by subjecting them to the provisional, relative, and enlightened nature of modern taste. Is this asking too much? Yet, paradoxically, enlightenment in our society, not ignorance, has brought the libraries a good deal of their present grief. Professor Burress [Lee A. Burress of Wisconsin State College] could say: "There was nothing to censor in my small-town high school library.

In fact, there was nothing to read." Improvement in instruction during recent years—the use of books other than texts, for example—has produced a teen-age generation hungry for "real literature," a generation that wants to make its own choices. They are making the acquaintance of the library, seriously, for the first time; and it is here that they also make the acquaintance of the censorious mind and/or timid librarian. The books they have outgrown are frozen into a special "teen-age section," while the books they want to read are locked up. What a disappointment not to be able to see in print the words they have been using since the age of eight.

Our libraries should not get all the blame for this. It was the English teachers of the past, Professor Burress pointed out, who laid the groundwork for censorship by canonizing an "official" body of literature (and in some instances Bowdlerizing it as well). They left scant room in the curriculum for an apocrypha which, today, has become the new heresy. The more militant teacher—the man who assigns, or options, *The Catcher in the Rye* or even James Baldwin's *Another Country*—may be asking for trouble, but he is also asking his students to *take* the trouble to find out what contemporary literature is all about, and thus to go on being readers when they get out of school.

The risks here are considerable. To read one must understand—and, in the end, accept. This is no simple matter when it is easier to pretend that the writer, not his audience, is out of step in a cockeyed world. "There is a reluctance on the part of our culture to listen to what the writer has to say about that culture," Robert F. Lucid of the American Studies Association summed up. The problem is not only legal but psychological—and even medical (as Dr. Gill suggested). The "alienated" writer hurts because he is saying unpleasant things, and one suspects that it is not sex after all that bothers the typical censor, but rather the deeper and unadmitted maladies in our society of which the obsession with sex is a symptom, and the literature of sex an analgesic. "When you really succeed in getting people to read, there is going to be trouble," Mr. Lucid predicted.

If things get worse, it means that the librarian is going to have to get better. This is not easy when you are on the firing line, and the conference recognized the librarian's vulnerability when it adopted a recommended plan of action. This includes setting up a special "intellectual freedom" office within the ALA [American Library Association], the employment of full-time legal counsel to defend librarians involved in censorship cases, and the establishment of a defense fund to assist librarians who are fired for anticensorship activity.

The committee hopes to get the full membership of the ALA to work for a tenure plan for librarians, and to come out flatly against "closed shelves" for adult borrowers, as well as all varieties of book labeling. A model selection procedure would discourage the tendency to shy away from the "controversial" book, no matter how extreme. Finally, the conference urged the librarian to line up her friends in the community before the trouble starts—to "get the wagons in a circle," as someone put it.

V. CENSORSHIP AND EDUCATION

EDITOR'S INTRODUCTION

The tradition of academic freedom in universities and colleges is an ancient one. Until recently, however, academic freedom has never been affirmed as a form of free speech by the United States Supreme Court. The Court has now reaffirmed that academic freedom is equivalent to free speech in striking down laws that require New York State teachers to sign "loyalty oaths" disavowing Communist party membership. The power of state authorities and university and other school administrators, and even the force of public opinion, to silence teachers, to alter school curricula, and to suppress protest must still be reckoned with. Nevertheless, academic freedom has now gained the status of a constitutional right, the right of free speech. As such it should be better sheltered from attack in the future.

Discussion of the nature of academic freedom is here taken up by the American historian Henry Steele Commager, and by former Vice President Richard M. Nixon. Fred P. Graham, of the New York *Times* Washington Bureau, examines the decision on the New York case referred to above. Closing the compilation is an article by Philip Gleason, professor of history at the University of Notre Dame, on the special problems bearing on academic freedom in Catholic colleges and universities.

THE NATURE OF ACADEMIC FREEDOM[1]

Let us begin with the academy itself, and then consider the nature of the freedom which it enjoys. What is a university, and what are its functions?

A university is a place where young and old are joined together in the acquisition of knowledge and the search for truth.

[1] Article by Henry Steele Commager, Winthrop H. Smith Professor of American History at Amherst College, and co-author of *Growth of the American Republic*. *Saturday Review*. 49:13-15+. Ag. 27, '66. Reprinted by permission.

Its functions are threefold. First, to transmit knowledge imaginatively from one generation to the next. Second, to provide society with a body of trained professionals—originally priests, doctors, lawyers, and scholars—which is why Old World universities still have only four faculties. In modern times, and particularly in the United States, the university is expected to train for many other professions as well—architecture, journalism, teaching, forestry, engineering, and so forth—but the purpose is the same. The third function of the university is rapidly becoming the most important: to expand the boundaries of knowledge through research and to discover new truths.

Now, these functions imposed on the university by history and by circumstances mean that the university is to be a special kind of institution. It is the only institution in Western society whose business it is to search for and transmit truth regardless of all competing or conflicting pressures and demands: pressures for immediate usefulness, for social approval, pressures to serve the special interests of a government, a class, a professional group, a race, a faith, even a nation. If the university performs its duty it will, of course, serve all of these interests, for we must believe that the search for truth is useful to all groups, but this is a by-product of the larger achievement of the training of the young to wisdom and the search for truth.

The university is the chief instrument whereby society provides itself with independent criticism and advice, and with a continuous flow of ideas. It maintains the university as it maintains scientists, doctors, judges, and priests, not to minister to its passions but to serve its deeper and more permanent needs. Society does not impose its will on scientists because it wants to discover the secrets of the universe; it refrains from bringing pressure on judges because it wants to see justice done; it leaves doctors alone because it wants to discover the causes of and the cure for diseases; it permits religious freedom because it wants spiritual solace. Society provides freedom for scholars and for the university as an institution for the same elementary reason, because it wants to discover truth about as many things as possible.

It is out of this situation that the concept and the practice of academic freedom emerges, and on these principles that it rests. If society is to assure itself of a new generation trained to understand the world in which it will live, it must leave teachers free to transmit truth as they see it; if society is to have the benefit of disinterested advice, it must protect scholars who give that advice even when it is unpalatable; if society is to have the advantage of a flow of new ideas and discoveries, it must leave scholars to carry on research in their own way. At its peril does any society interfere in any way, at any time, through pressure, intimidation, distraction, or seduction, with these sovereign functions of the academy.

Once the nature of the university is clear, particular problems of "academic freedom" present few real difficulties. Consider, for example, two questions which have greatly agitated our society of late: the problem of student rebellion and student discipline, and the larger problem of alleged subversives on university faculties who justify their advocacy of unpopular causes—Negro rights in the South, opposition to the war in Vietnam, the recognition of Communist China—by the plea of academic freedom. The principles which must control our attitude toward these problems are rooted in the nature and function of the university.

We can dispose briefly of what now troubles a good many well-meaning people—manifestations of student freedom that seem (or are) excessive, bad-mannered, or unpatriotic. It should be remembered that academic freedom was born, some seven centuries ago, as student freedom, with the insistence by students in Italian and French universities on the right to have a decisive voice in choosing professors, arranging for courses of lectures, controlling all their housekeeping affairs, and securing certain political rights in their communities. The notion that the university should act *in loco parentis* to its students is a relatively new and limited one; to this day it is confined pretty much to English-speaking countries, and unknown elsewhere. The principle of *in loco parentis* was doubtless suitable enough in an earlier era, when boys went to college at the age of thirteen or fourteen; it is a bit ridiculous in a society where most students are mature enough to marry and raise families.

No one will deny that manifestations of student independence occasionally get out of hand, just as manifestations of adult independence get out of hand; we should remember, however, that if there is to be excess, it is far better to have an excess of interest and activity than an excess of apathy. But the solution for student intemperance is not for the university authorities to act in the place of parents. It is not the business of the university to go bustling around like some Aunt Polly, censoring a student paper here, cutting out indelicacies in a student play there, approving this club or that, accepting or rejecting speakers invited by student organizations, snooping into the private lives of students. These matters are the responsibility of the students themselves.

If they perform their duties badly, so much the worse for them—perhaps they will learn by experience. If they go to excess and violate the law, let them be subjected to the penalties of the law. Where they violate reasonable academic rules—rules designed to protect the integrity of the academic enterprise, they should be subjected to whatever penalties are provided for such violations. But they should not be treated as if they were children, nor should the university be expected to turn aside from its proper job, which is education and research, to the petty pursuit of discipline.

Granted that the expression of student independence sometimes causes pain or chagrin. But to those who deplore or denounce students who ostentatiously depart from commencement exercises when a member of the Johnson Administration is given a degree, we can put a very simple question. Would you rather have the kind of society where students were so indifferent that they lacked interest in politics, or the independence to differ with the administration? Would you rather have the kind of society where no student would dare assert his independence for fear of reprisal? If not, you must take your chance on independent thinking running to what you consider bad manners, just as adult independence often runs to bad manners: when members of UN delegations walk out, for example, or when mayors of New York cancel dinner invitations.

Turn, then, to the far more important question of "subversives" on university faculties, or subversion in teaching: It is the fear of these which induced infatuated legislatures to require special loyalty oaths for teachers in the McCarthy era, and which accounts for the harassment of universities in backward states such as Massachusetts and California.

We may observe that there is no evidence of subversives on college faculties, or that the term "subversion" is so vague as to be drained of meaning, or that neither loyalty oaths nor inquisitions can prevent the contagion of ideas. But these observations, though just enough, are not really relevant to our central problem. What is of crucial relevance to that problem is quite simply that the academic community, if it is to be free to perform its beneficent functions, must be free to fix its own standards and determine its own credentials. No other bodies, certainly not an inflamed public nor an election-minded legislature, are competent to fix these standards or to determine whether or not scholars meet them. This responsibility is primarily one for specialists—fellow physicists, fellow historians—and ultimately one for the whole academic community, for sometimes specialists have a narrow or jaundiced view. But questions of fitness to teach and to carry on research are always academic questions.

Professional qualifications do sometimes involve questions of character, to be sure, but how, when, and where they do are matters for professional determination. And the reason for this is very simple. It is not merely that it is logical and just, but that it is the only method which can provide us with the kind of physicists and historians that we need. If other criteria than those of professional competence and the confidence of academic colleagues in the integrity of the scholar are invoked, the system itself will break down, just as medicine or justice will break down if surgeons or judges are selected by other than professional criteria. Needless to say, scholars will make mistakes in judgment, just as doctors and lawyers make mistakes in judgment. But the consequences of substituting irrelevant and pernicious criteria for professional ones in choosing academic colleagues are far more serious than any possible consequences of occasional incompetence in professional selection.

What shall we say of university teachers and scholars who outrage public opinion by advocacy of doctrines that seem to the great majority to be erroneous? What shall we say of teachers who persistently flout the public will as expressed by resounding majorities? Once again the underlying principle is simple enough. If scholars, or students, violate the law, the law should deal with them as it deals with any other members of society who violate the law. No scholar may claim that academic freedom gives him some special immunity from the law. But if what a scholar does or says does not violate any law, but merely outrages public opinion, then it is not the business of the university to do what civil authorities are unable to do.

The spectacle, common enough in the McCarthy era, of regents and trustees rushing in to punish teachers for conduct for which the civil authorities were unable or unwilling to prosecute—"taking the Fifth Amendment" for example—was a shameful one. In so far as trustees join with public opinion to intimidate or silence scholars, however much they may be misguided, they violate and betray their trust.

So it is with the punishment, by whatever means, of those who exercise their right to express ideas that are unpopular and seem dangerous—advocacy of the cause of the Vietcong, for example, or of the propriety of mixed marriages, or of the harmlessness of pornography. No doubt it is deplorable that otherwise intelligent men should entertain, let alone champion, notions of this sort, but how much more deplorable if we had the kind of society where they could not. A university is an institution where scholars are not only permitted but encouraged to think unthinkable thoughts, to explore intolerable ideas, and to proclaim their findings. There are risks here, to be sure. The Church saw that when it forced Galileo to recant, or forbade the teaching of the circulation of the blood, or the Linnaean system of botanical classification. But these are risks that society must learn to take in its stride if it expects progress in the realms of knowledge and of science.

If we are to have the kind of society where thought and expression are free, we must take our chances on some thoughts being, in the words of Justice Holmes, "loathsome and fraught with death." Nor is the danger really a desperate one. Those who disagree with the loathsome thoughts are equally free to express thoughts that are beautiful.

Let us not suppose that all this is but a matter of theory. We have ample evidence, in our own history, and in the history of other nations, of what happens when government or society silences, by whatever means, dangerous or loathsome ideas. And we know, too, that ideas which one generation thinks dangerous are regarded by the next as salutary; ideas which one society thinks loathsome are accepted by another as noble.

The Old South persuaded itself that slavery was not only good but a positive blessing, and that those who criticized slavery or sought to undermine it were enemies to the Southern way of life. As the slave interest had things all its own way, it proceeded to dispose of its enemies. To protect the "peculiar institution," teachers who questioned the historical or ethnological credentials of slavery were dismissed, preachers who denied the biblical justification of slavery were expelled from their pulpits, editors who criticized slavery or the slaveocracy lost their posts, books and magazines which contained antislavery propaganda were burned. To counter the abolitionist argument which seemed to Southerners as pernicious as communism seems to members of the John Birch Society—they formulated a proslavery argument and invested it with moral authority. Thus the South silenced serious discussion of its major problem; thus it foreclosed every solution to that problem but the ultimate solution of violence; thus it laid the foundations for a century of hatred and violence.

More familiar to most of us is the dark and tragic history of Hitler's Germany. The Nazis not only convinced themselves of Aryan superiority and of Jewish inferiority; they were so sure they were right that they looked upon anyone who spoke up for the Jews or who opposed Nazi policies as an enemy of the Fatherland. More systematically and more savagely than Southerners of the 1850's, they purged the universities, silenced the clergy, closed down the press, burned offending books, and wrote new books to replace them, and killed, exiled, or silenced all who dared question the justice of what they did. They destroyed not only dissent but free inquiry and discussion, and—like the Southerners—left no remedy for their errors but that of violence. Nor can we reassure ourselves that these manifestations of hostility to the university and to intellectual independence, are a thing of the past. Even now, in South Africa, in Rhodesia, in the Argentine, those who fear freedom and democratic processes, move with sure instinct to control the universities and to destroy academic freedom.

Those who today assure us that academic freedom is all right in ordinary times, but that in time of crisis it must give way to the importunate demands of national unity, those who argue that academic freedom is all very well in time of peace but a pernicious indulgence in time of war, are like the Southern slaveocracy and the Nazis and the white supremacists of South Africa, if not in conduct, then in principle. They are saying in effect that discussion and debate are all very well when there is nothing to discuss, but that they must be abated or suspended when there are serious matters before us. They are saying that we can tolerate freedom when there are no issues that threaten it, but that we cannot tolerate it when it is in danger.

Do those who would suspend academic freedom in time of crisis because it imperils national unity really understand the implications of their argument? Are they prepared to decry those Englishmen who in the 1770's stood up for the American cause—men like Tom Paine and Dr. Price and Joseph Priestley and Lord Jeffrey Amherst, whom we have so long honored as friends of liberty? Are they prepared to assert that those Southerners who, in the crisis of 1861, rejected the claims of Southern unity and preferred instead to go against the stream of public opinion and stand by the Union, deserve only obloquy? Are they prepared to say that Germans who revolted against the iniquities of the Nazi government and sought to overthrow Hitler were traitors and deserve the detestation of mankind? Do they really think that the only test of true patriotism is support of a government, no matter what it does?

These considerations go far beyond the confines of the academy, but they bear with special force on the academy. For the university has a special obligation to act as the critic and the conscience of society. Society has indeed created it to play this role. It has said to the scholars who constitute the academy:

> It is your business to think and investigate and fearlessly to announce your findings. It is your business to be independ-

ent and scientific and impersonal, to stand aside from the awful pressures of public opinion and of interest, the persuasive pressures of nationalism and the compelling pressures of patriotism, and consider scientifically the validity of what your society does. It is your business to study politics and economy and history as scientists study physics and astronomy and geology. It is your business to look and to think far ahead, to look not to the immediate effects but the ultimate consequences of conduct.

We require you, therefore, if you would not betray your historic function, to avoid all that is merely parochial, all that is interested, all that is prejudiced. We require you to avoid the temptation to serve those who may suppose themselves your masters, and devote your affluent talents to your true masters—the whole of society, the whole of humanity, the great community of learning, the sacred cause of truth. In order that you may do this we give you the precious boon of independence which is academic freedom. We know that some of you will abuse this independence, that some of you will fail to use it in the larger service of mankind, and that many of you will be mistaken in your findings. These are chances we are willing to take because we know that if we do not protect those whose task it is to search out truth, we may fall into irreparable error and thus lose everything that we hold dear.

FOUR ACADEMIC FREEDOMS [2]

The war in Vietnam has triggered a crisis throughout America's academic community. The University of California at Berkeley has been rocked by riots and demonstrations; at the University of Chicago, students seized the administration building in a draft protest; at Amherst and NYU, Defense Secretary McNamara watched students walk out on commencement speeches. In many cases, demonstrations were incited by faculty members.

[2] From "The Four Academic Freedoms," by Richard M. Nixon, former Vice President of the United States. *Saturday Review.* 49:12-13+. Ag. 27, '66. Reprinted by permission.

One natural reaction is to demand a "crackdown" on those responsible; the opposite reaction is to consider any outburst to be an expression of academic freedom and therefore sacrosanct. Now is the proper time to examine the guarantees and the limitations of academic freedom.

Academic freedom is no "academic question"; it is one of the most powerful forces in human history. Princes, presidents, even generals tremble in its presence. Academic freedom is a free society's greatest single advantage in its competition with totalitarian societies. No society can be great without the creative power it unleashes. Yet while it can create, it can also destroy and it can consume itself.

A generation ago, "Four Freedoms" became a rallying cry for the forces of democracy: freedom of speech and of worship, and freedom from fear and from want. Today let us examine the Four Academic Freedoms.

There is the academic freedom of the student to investigate any theory, to challenge any premise, to refuse to accept old shibboleths and myths.

There is a second academic freedom of the student to espouse any cause, to engage in the cut and thrust of partisan political or social debate, both on and off campus, without jeopardy to his or her academic career.

The third academic freedom is that of the teacher—freedom from fear of reprisal while speaking or publishing the truth as he sees it, governed by the dictates of his own intellect and of the disciplines of scholarship.

Finally, there is a fourth academic freedom—this one within the academic community—that is, the freedom of the student from tyranny by the faculty, and, conversely, freedom of the faculty from student tyranny.

These four academic freedoms underlie the concept of American education; without these freedoms, teaching becomes indoctrination—a mockery of education. Wherever academic investigation has been suppressed or a climate hostile to scholars created, society has suffered. On the other hand, those societies that protect academic freedom are able to mine human resources most effectively. . . .

A paradox confronts the academic community today and presents all of us with real problems of choice. The power of the scholar in the United States has never been greater. Yet that enormous power of the academic community, which is the product of academic freedom, potentially threatens academic freedom.

Let us remember that we are considering here a freedom that derives its protection not from the law but from the respect and confidence the academic institution enjoys in the community in which it is located. Members of the academic community have a special status in our society for two reasons. One, a determination by society that the recipient must enjoy a maximum freedom of expression to serve society effectively; and, two, a respect by society for the judgment of the particular group, a confidence on the part of society that the privilege will not be seriously abused.

I believe that academic freedom in the United States is now so strongly supported that it will never be destroyed by its enemies—but it may be endangered by those who claim to be its friends.

Teachers must, of course, be free to take positions on all issues. But the position they hold in our society requires them to act with self-restraint. To illustrate that point, let me turn to the controversy that developed when a Rutgers professor declared that he would welcome a victory for the Vietcong over our forces in Vietnam. The question at issue is—what limits, if any, should be placed on academic freedom during wartime? . . .

America's greatest jurists have often been divided deeply and sometimes bitterly on where to draw the line between freedom and security.

The war in Vietnam presents this problem in even more difficult terms. Like the war in Korea, it began without a formal declaration of war approved by the Congress. There is confusion and uncertainty as to what America's war goals are. This is the first war in America's history in which a President has been unable to unite his own party behind the war. This is America's first foreign war in which our European allies have not only refused to assist us in fighting the enemy, but have continued to aid the enemy by trading with him.

In the light of these circumstances, to what extent should academic freedom protect those who protest the war effort? I do not agree with those who would curtail the right of dissent on our college and university campuses on the ground that such demonstrations give aid and comfort to the enemy. I do not question the patriotism of the protesters. I do not question their academic freedom to be against war, to be against this war, to be against the way this war is conducted, to be against the inequities in the draft. I believe also that academic freedom should protect the right of a professor or student to advocate Marxism, socialism, communism, or any other minority viewpoint—no matter how distasteful to the majority—provided he does so openly and is not in violation of the law.

But there is a far more difficult question: Should academic freedom protect a professor when he uses the forum of a state university to welcome victory for the enemy in a war in which the United States is engaged? I know that in answering no to that question I am expressing disagreement with a great many students and teachers. However, since academic freedom includes the right to espouse an unpopular cause, let me tell you how I reached this conviction.

To those who would welcome victory for the enemy I respectfully suggest that they do not know the enemy. I am convinced that victory for the enemy in South Vietnam would mean not only the blotting out of freedom for fifteen million South Vietnamese but an immense escalation of the danger of World War III. I am convinced that history will record that what many believe to be a "quicksand war" was the war that had to be fought to prevent World War III.

In the light of these convictions I could not take the more expedient course of refusing to comment on a point of such importance. I believe that any teacher who uses the forum of a university to proclaim that he welcomes victory for the enemy in a shooting war crosses the line between liberty and license. If we are to defend academic freedom from encroachment we must also defend it from its own excesses.

Examine the spectrum of freedom. At one extreme is anarchy—too much freedom, where nobody is really free at all. At the other end of the spectrum is tyranny—the totalitarian state which stresses order to the exclusion of personal liberty. In the center is limited freedom, with its very limits posing a kind of defense perimeter against the extremes of anarchy and tyranny....

The hard choices, the delicate balances along the perimeter of limited freedom, are the ones each of us must face. Not one of us will be right in his choice every time—but we will always be right to face the hard choices of where to draw the line. Most members of the academic community agree that a line must be drawn somewhere.

I submit that no one person, and no single group, has the right or the power to draw that line by itself. Only through the interplay of free discussion can a balance be struck, with each of us willing to speak out on our interpretation of the line that not only limits—but defends—academic freedom.

When the American experiment in government began two centuries ago, it was predicted that all order would disappear under the strain of our drastic guarantees of freedom. The expectation of our collapse can be traced to the basic belief that freedom and order are mutually exclusive. The wisdom of our people to limit freedom so as to ensure freedom has kept our nation strong.

This is the paradox of our Government. For as we criticize, debate, and disagree, in the final analysis we must support the actions taken by our duly elected representatives. We cannot, for instance, refuse to pay our taxes if we disagree with the law that imposes them or the purposes for which they are used; we cannot refuse to enroll in Social Security or evade jury duty; and, should our Government decide to wage war, we may criticize that decision, we may try to convince others of its inadvisability, we may even call for a change in leadership; but we should not root for the other side; we should not refuse to participate if called; we should not create the impression abroad that our Government has been deserted by its people.

We must demonstrate to the world that while among ourselves we speak with many voices, we are as one; that even though we may disagree with our Government we still do not support the enemy; that although we may not agree with the decision to wage war, we will not publicly pray for the defeat of our country, we will not give active assistance to the other side, we will not refuse to serve in our country's armed services; that instead, we will confine our opposition to those avenues provided by the system itself—criticism, demonstrations, and elections.

A generation has passed since President Roosevelt spoke of the Four Freedoms. Despite three major wars since then, the world is still not free from fear or from want, and millions of human beings are still denied the freedom to speak and to worship as they choose. Let us hope that the Four Academic Freedoms, in this coming generation, will fare better. For students, the freedom to challenge myths and the freedom to debate; for teachers, the freedom to responsibly express unpopular points of view; for both student and teacher, freedom from tyranny by the other.

On this we can all agree: The more the academic freedoms deepen and spread their roots, the greater are the world's chances to achieve all the other basic human freedoms.

ACADEMIC FREEDOM IS FREE SPEECH [3]

Academic freedom, a Johnny-come-lately to constitutional law, [has] won an impressive and perhaps decisive victory . . . over its traditional opposing concept, loyalty-security legislation. For a concept that was not even recognized as a constitutional right until a decade ago, academic freedom received a surprisingly strong endorsement from the Supreme Court.

In a decision that is certain to become a rallying point for academicians in future conflicts over antisubversive measures, the High Court struck down the entire New York teacher "loyalty" program and rejected the theory that teachers' rights are secondary to considerations of internal security.

The vote was close—5 to 4—but the majority declared unconstitutional New York's "complicated and intricate scheme" of antisubversive laws in a sweeping decision that appeared to doom similar laws in at least twenty-six other states.

[3] From article by Fred P. Graham, member, New York *Times* Washington Bureau. New York *Times*. p. E 12. Ja. 29, '67. © 1967 by The New York Times Company. Reprinted by permission.

New York's antisubversive scheme was typical of many that were created during the antisubversive hysteria of the McCarthy era. It required public school and college teachers to sign statements that they were not Communists, and provided for the discharge of those who uttered "treasonable or seditious" words or endorsed writings that advocated the violent overthrow of the Government. School officials were required to report whether any members of their staffs were "subversive."

When the University of Buffalo became a state college in 1962, five teachers refused to sign the non-Communist disclaimer and challenged the entire scheme in court. In a broad constitutional attack, they said it violated the First Amendment by attempting to impose political orthodoxy on teachers.

More Freedom

The Supreme Court, in deciding the Buffalo teachers' suit . . . [on January 23, 1967], accepted this argument in terms that should vastly strengthen the freedom of teachers to express their views.

It is well established in constitutional law that the First Amendment's guarantee of freedom of speech is a preferred right, to be given precedence over conflicting considerations. In . . . [its] decision, the Supreme Court went beyond this and declared that teachers have even greater First Amendment protection than ordinary citizens. Speaking for the majority, Justice William J. Brennan, Jr., said:

> Our nation is deeply committed to safeguarding academic freedom, which is of transcendent value to all of us and not merely the teachers concerned. That freedom is therefore a special concern of the First Amendment, which does not tolerate laws that cast a pall of orthodoxy over the classroom.

Although the Court specifically recognized the right of a state to protect its school system from subversion as long as the methods used did not have a "stifling effect on the academic mind," it flatly rejected two ideas that constitute the underpinning of most loyalty-security programs. One is the old doctrine that teachers bargain away some of their rights as citizens when they go on a public payroll. This doctrine has been undermined by recent decisions, but . . . [in the present decision] the majority put it finally to rest.

It also squarely rejected the idea that teachers can be fired for refusing to state whether they are members of the Communist party, or any other subversive group.

The High Court had made it clear in earlier decisions that mere membership in such a group cannot be grounds for dismissal. Otherwise, teachers might shy away from any unorthodox movement for fear it might be held to be subversive. . . . [In 1966], for example, in voiding Arizona's teachers' loyalty oath, the Court hinted that a much stricter standard than even this might be required. . . . In the New York case, it dropped the other shoe and stated flatly that loyalty oaths are unconstitutional unless they apply only to those who are active members of a subversive group, or who specifically intend to carry out its illegal aims.

Amendments Not Likely

This comes close to saying that a teacher's dissent must be virtually at the bomb-throwing stage before it is grounds for dismissal. Apparently he can be made to swear that he is not of such a mind, but it is doubtful that many states will bother to amend their laws to require their teachers to make such a pledge.

The decision was a historic victory for academic freedom by any standard, but it was particularly impressive in view of the fact that it was only about ten years ago that the Supreme Court recognized academic freedom as a constitutional right.

Until then, the courts had always ruled that public employees, including teachers, sacrifice certain of their rights as citizens as the price of holding their public jobs. The Supreme Court specifically reaffirmed this doctrine in 1952 when it upheld the constitutionality of the same New York laws that fell . . . [with this decision].

If the state's teachers did not like the loyalty program, Justice Sherman Minton said then, "they are at liberty to retain their beliefs and associations and go elsewhere."

But in 1957, when the Court threw out the contempt conviction of a New Hampshire professor who refused to answer questions about views expressed in his lectures, a majority of the justices declared that a constitutional right of academic freedom did exist, although they left it undefined.

New Standard

Now, in view of . . . [the present] decision, it is difficult to believe that any of the existing state loyalty oaths could survive a court test under the new standard.

With the Supreme Court throwing its power heavily behind the teachers, it is likely that many states will simply abandon their efforts to enforce "loyalty." This is already happening in New Hampshire, where Attorney General George Pappagianis is asking the state supreme court to declare that the state's loyalty oath cannot be constitutionally enforced.

Civil libertarians have always insisted that truly subversive persons would not blanch at signing loyalty oaths. And, as Justice Hugo L. Black once put it, "Loyalty must arise spontaneously from the hearts of people who love their country and respect their government."

THE PROBLEM FACING CATHOLIC COLLEGES [4]

The explosion at St. John's University [where faculty disturbances occurred over academic freedom issues] furnishes dramatic evidence that American Catholic institutions of higher education are entering a critical period in respect to academic freedom. In the practical order, it shows that an academic freedom issue can profoundly disrupt the functioning of a university, jeopardize its accreditation and endanger its very life. In the speculative order, the St. John's case demonstrates that controversies over academic freedom are only too likely to lead to denials that a true "Catholic university" can or should exist. Academic freedom is therefore a critical issue for Catholic institutions, because it can engender passions capable of crippling them in practice, while denying in theory their right to existence.

[4] From "Academic Freedom," by Philip Gleason, professor of history at the University of Notre Dame. *America*. 115:60-3. Jl. 16, '66. Reprinted with permission from *America*, The National Catholic Weekly Review. 106 W. 56th St. New York 10019.

This is a new state of affairs for American Catholic higher education. Until very recently, Catholic educators have looked upon academic freedom more or less from the outside. They have ordinarily viewed it as something having to do with secular universities, but with no vital bearing on the life of their own institutions. Although there were some keen and sympathetic articles on academic freedom by Catholic scholars in the 1950's, when it was so prominent an issue, even at that late date the predominant feeling seemed to be that academic freedom was not really a live issue for Catholic institutions. Thus Lazarsfeld and Thielens report in *The Academic Mind* that, at the height of the McCarthy period, Catholic professors in the sensitive areas of the social sciences were less apprehensive over threats to academic freedom than any other comparable faculty group in the whole spectrum of American higher education.

Obviously, the situation has radically changed in a very short time—or, more accurately, changes have been under way for some time whose implications for academic freedom have only recently become unmistakably visible. As a consequence, academic freedom has now become perhaps the most important single issue confronting Catholic higher education in the United States. . . .

Since, however, American Catholics have only recently begun to look upon it as a live issue, they still have no clear understanding of what academic freedom is, of what sort of modifications in our thinking its claims may entail, or whether anything will be left of the "Catholic" character of colleges and universities that embrace it unreservedly.

It was with the aim of initiating a serious investigation of questions like these, on as scholarly a level as possible, that a symposium on Academic Freedom and the Catholic University was held at the University of Notre Dame on April 22 and 23 [1966].

The symposium, the first of its kind ever held, was arranged by the Notre Dame chapter of the AAUP [American Association of University Professors] in cooperation with several student groups, and with the full support of the university administration. Four of the eight principal speakers were from Notre Dame, and included Fr. John E. Walsh, C.S.C., the vice president for academic affairs.

Speakers from outside the university were Professor David Fellman, political scientist from the University of Wisconsin and national president of the AAUP; Daniel Greenberg, writer on politics and education for *Science* magazine; Fr. John L. McKenzie, S.J., biblical scholar; and Daniel Callahan of *Commonweal*.

The papers included a sketch of the historical background of the present situation (my own contribution); a philosophical discussion of Academic Freedom and the Committed University (Professor Frederick Crosson); an administrator's view of the problem (Fr. Walsh); an analysis of the situation of the priest-scholar (Fr. McKenzie); a discussion of academic freedom as it relates to the drive for excellence (Mr. Greenberg); an explication of the AAUP's stand (Professor Fellman); and two perspectives on the subject of freedom for students (Mr. Callahan and Professor Robert Hassenger). Since the papers are to be published as a book, I will not attempt to summarize them here in a systematic way; but I would like to comment on some of the leading themes that emerged from the discussions, and to record general impressions.

What impressed me most forcibly was the way the issue of academic freedom brings together in a sort of omnium-gatherum practically all the new trends and disputed points of American Catholic life. Religious liberty, ecumenism, the new status of the layman, the reexamination of ecclesiastical authority, the questions of clerical obedience and priestly witness, the widespread student unrest, the reorientation of Catholic thinking on secularization, the general "identity crisis" of Catholic higher education—all these themes, and others as well, arose during the discussions or were clearly implied by them. This omnibus quality is one of the reasons that academic freedom is so critical an issue: when it comes up, one is likely to find in addition that a whole galaxy of perplexing questions are suddenly before the house.

A second and closely related point concerns the imprecision of the notion of academic freedom and the confusion as to what it is and how it applies. The matter of student freedom offers the best illustration of this ambiguity of meaning. Two of the papers were devoted to aspects of student life as related to academic freedom, and Professor Fellman likewise spent some of his time outlining the

AAUP's position on academic freedom for students. (Yet another speaker confessed he was unable to see that academic freedom had any relevance at all to student life.) Mr. Callahan, though he made an eloquent case for liberalization of disciplinary regulations and freedom for student organizations and publications, failed to persuade all his listeners that what he was talking about properly fell under the heading of academic freedom. Professor Hassenger, a Notre Dame sociologist, who gave the other paper on student life, defined academic freedom in "rather broad, social-sciency terms . . . to mean 'the freedom to become,'" and then proceeded to argue that Catholic colleges and universities should deliberately aim to bring about a change in the attitudes and values of their students by the manipulation of their emotional lives. While there were certainly a number of interesting implications for academic freedom in this talk, it did little to pin down the term's meaning.

It would be misleading, however, to give the impression that the symposiasts flailed away for two days without at least clearing the ground for a more adequate understanding of the notion of academic freedom and how it applies to Catholic universities. As I see it, three levels of meaning of the term academic freedom emerged from the symposium. Simply for the sake of having some distinguishing labels, I will call them the level of operational precision, the level of vague abstraction and the level of ideology.

Professor Fellman's paper offers the best approach to academic freedom on the level of operational precision, although it was not confined to that dimension alone. That is to say, the professor spelled out clearly what academic freedom means in terms of specific requirements, and prescriptions designed to shield professors from arbitrary action on the part of administrators, and students from arbitrary action by professors or administrators. He discussed the function of tenure provisions in safeguarding the professor's position, and he insisted on the importance of "academic due process" (written charges, hearings, appeals, etc.) whenever dismissal action is undertaken in the case of tenured professors. Although Professor Fellman made no explicit reference to it, the St. John's case obviously involved the most glaring violation of academic due process.

No Catholic participant in the symposium suggested that there was the least incompatibility between Catholicism as an institutional religious commitment and the fullest acceptance of academic freedom on the level of operational precision. On the contrary, the consensus seemed clearly to be that Catholic universities should embrace and follow academic due process, tenure prescriptions and other procedural rules worked out by the AAUP to safeguard academic freedom.

On the level of vague abstraction, academic freedom is another matter. The difficulty here is that when academic freedom is not specified by a set of operational requirements, it is so general a notion that it can mean almost anything. So broad and universalistic a concept can be applied in one way or another to practically any concrete situation.

After all, there are few matters that cannot, with a little ingenuity, be construed as having something to do with freedom, and the danger is that academic freedom will become merely a slogan if it is called upon to justify every claim that can possibly be associated with the name of freedom in the academic world. (It makes a very good slogan, of course, for few of us willingly admit to being opposed to freedom, academic or otherwise.) But while it is rhetorically advantageous to link freedom with whatever causes one is interested in, it is a questionable service to the cause of academic freedom itself to treat it thus. For if, as a result of its almost universal applicability and its rhetorical utility, academic freedom is invoked too often, it will soon mean so many different things that in itself it will mean nothing.

How meaningful, we may ask, is a concept that can be invoked to justify, on the one hand, the professor's demand for sabbaticals for the purpose of more research, and on the other hand, the student's demand that his professor stay home and direct his attention to teaching rather than to research? . . .

Yet it is equally true that academic freedom must legitimately be granted a very broad applicability. For while the interests of some are served by identifying academic freedom with every position they wish to defend or promote, there are others whose interests are served by refusing to grant that it ever applies to *any* matter at issue.

I do not think there is any way to "solve" this sort of problem, or to guarantee that academic freedom will always be understood "properly" and applied "legitimately." All one can hope for is that those involved in academic contentions will exercise responsibility, and perhaps even a little rhetorical self-denial, in dealing with academic freedom....

For a variety of reasons, however, it seems certain that in the coming years Catholic universities are going to be much more deeply concerned about academic freedom than they have been heretofore.

A number of other changes are also bound to come, changes in policy and administrative procedure, that will involve academic freedom only indirectly or not at all. There will doubtless be disagreement about these matters, and in many cases heated disputes. It would be most unfortunate, in my opinion, if the issue of academic freedom were needlessly injected into these disputes, even though (as we have noted) it is nearly always possible to find some plausible connection between academic freedom as a vague abstraction and any one concrete issue.

It would be unfortunate because the effect would be to raise the temperature and noise level of the discussion, obscure the substantive issues and make it more difficult to reach some common ground of agreement or compromise. When academic freedom comes up, attitudes tend to grow rigid: a great principle is at stake, and there is a temptation for each side to begin asking questions about the motives of those in the opposite camp. After matters reach this pass, it is only a step to the conclusion, on the part of all concerned, that academic freedom and the Catholic university are mutually exclusive terms. I do not intend these remarks to apply to the St. John's situation, because there is no question that a genuine issue of academic freedom is central to the problem there as it presently exists. But the case certainly does illustrate the unhappy consequences that can follow when a number of procedural and policy disagreements become focused primarily in a dispute over academic freedom.

This brings us to the third level of meaning of academic freedom —the ideological. It is a new thing for a Catholic professor to say, as

Dr. Rosemary Larer did, that institutional religious commitment is incompatible with the proper functioning of a true university. But if there is anything that is *not,* in itself, a novel conclusion, it is that academic freedom and Catholic universities "don't mix." On the contrary, it is a quite commonplace *a priori* affirmation among those who have been identified with the tradition of academic freedom in the United States. For although Catholic educators may have had other things on their minds, academic freedom has been developing in this country for over a century; and it has been developing in a climate not merely removed from the influence of traditional religion, but for the most part actively hostile to it. Consequently, academic freedom stands within the decidedly secular tradition, and has become associated with a world view that leaves little room for revealed religion. . . .

No elaborate argument is needed, one might assume, to show that academic freedom on the ideological level confronts Catholic universities with speculative problems of the profoundest sort—with difficulties that go straight to the heart of the ancient problem of faith and reason, of the relationship between divine truth and human knowledge. Yet, if I interpret the reactions of some of my colleagues correctly, there are Catholic scholars who do not believe that ideological academic freedom poses any real difficulty for Catholic institutions. They might grant that this variety of academic freedom is part of a *Weltanschauung* that has assumed something of the character of a rival faith, but, as Professor Edward Manier of the Notre Dame philosophy department puts it, they find it "difficult to see why contemporary Catholicism should regard this 'rival faith' as inimical or contrary to its spirit." Presumably, they would argue that, although academic freedom arose in a secularist context, it is simply another of those achievements of the secular world that we should accept wholeheartedly, without all this quibbling about how it may affect the "deposit of faith."

No doubt this jaunty confidence is a good deal more emotionally satisfying than fuss-budgeting about with doubts and reservations; and we have certainly had in the past more stern censors of academic freedom than glad affirmers of it. So perhaps the affirmers deserve our unqualified encouragement. Yet it is doubtful that rashness, in itself, is preferable to timidity. And to assume that Catholic institutions of higher education can and should buy the whole ideological package that, in the minds of many people, accompanies academic freedom is, in my opinion, not only rash but simplistic.

Academic freedom as an operational principle—a set of procedural rules and safeguards—Catholic institutions can and should accept to a greater degree than they have in the past. But I do not think it necessarily follows that they have to accept all the theoretical underpinnings and ideological trappings with which academic freedom has come to be associated—as a result of its long developmental association with Germanic *Wissenschaft,* rationalistic and doctrinaire liberalism and positivistic scientism. After all, people can agree that freedom of research, teaching and so on are good and desirable things in the practical order without necessarily agreeing on the theory that provides their rationale.

Professor Fellman developed in his paper the analogy between political freedom and academic freedom. "Academic freedom," he asserted, "rests on assumptions concerning the nature of the pursuit of truth and knowledge which are quite comparable to parallel pursuits in the political field." This suggests a further analogy along the lines of Maritain's remarks about democracy in *Man and the State*. . . . In this work, Maritain distinguishes between common agreement on a "set *of practical conclusions*" as to how a democratic society should function, and, on the other hand, the "*theoretical justifications,* the conceptions of the world and of life, the philosophical or religious creeds which found, or claim to found, these practical conclusions in reason" (Maritain's italics).

It is much the same with academic freedom. There are few in any camp who would claim that academic freedom must be absolute; and Catholics can surely agree with the most naturalistically inclined rationalist or positivist that the greatest possible freedom in scholarship, teaching, etc., is desirable and good. But I cannot see that Catholics must accept a good version of academic freedom that would require them to become naturalistic rationalists or positivists, themselves, in order to qualify as true believers in it. Are we to exchange one inflexible orthodoxy for another equally rigid? . . .

There are, to be sure, very great difficulties in working out just how academic freedom is to be understood in Catholic universities, in determining its applications and in exploring its theoretical grounding. Faith does indeed mean a commitment; it does assume that there is such a thing as revelation; and it does claim that there is a sort of knowledge that is valid although it is not publicly verifiable through empirical tests. . . .

For my part, . . . I can think of two . . . responses that Catholic universities should strenuously endeavor to avoid: (1) simply to insist that things remain as they always have been, and that academic freedom fit itself into the interstices of a paternalistic and authoritarian Catholicism; and (2) to insist with equal dogmatism on academic freedom of the most doctrinaire ideological sort as the only "true" variety.

BIBLIOGRAPHY

An asterisk (*) preceding a reference indicates that the article or a part of it has been reprinted in this book.

Books, Pamphlets, and Documents

American Bar Association. Advisory Committee on Fair Trial-Free Press. American Bar Association project on minimum standards for criminal justice: fair trial and free press. mimeo. The Association. 1155 E. 60th St. Chicago. 60637. '66.
Excerpts: New York Times. p 81. O. 2, '66.

American Civil Liberties Union. Academic freedom, academic responsibility, academic due process; statement of principles. The Union. 156 Fifth Ave. New York 10010. S. '66.

American Civil Liberties Union. Tension, change and liberty; 45th annual report. The Union. 156 Fifth Ave. New York 10010. '65.

*American Civil Liberties Union. Board of Directors. Statement on fair trial and free press. mimeo. The Union. 156 Fifth Ave. New York 10010. D. '66.

American Library Association. Intellectual Freedom Committee. Freedom of inquiry: supporting the Library Bill of Rights; proceedings of the Conference on Intellectual Freedom, January 23-24, 1965, Washington, D.C. The Association. 50 E. Huron St. Chicago 60611. '65.
Same: ALA Bulletin. 59:469-533. Je. '65.

American Newspaper Publishers Association. Committee on Free Press and Fair Trial. Committee report. The Association. 750 Third Ave. New York 10017. '67.
Excerpts: New York Times. p 20. Ja. 5, '67.

Association of the Bar of the City of New York. Special Committee on Radio, Television, and the Administration of Justice. Freedom of the press and fair trial; final report with recommendations; Harold R. Medina, chairman. Columbia University Press. New York. '67.

Bell, Daniel, ed. Radical right. Doubleday. Garden City, N.Y. '64.

Broyles, J. A. John Birch Society: anatomy of a protest. Beacon. Boston. '64.

Cain, E. R. They'd rather be right. Macmillan. New York. '63.

Carmen, I. H. Movies, censorship, and the law. University of Michigan Press. Ann Arbor. '66.

Chandos, John, ed. To deprave and corrupt. Association Press. New York. '62.

Cohen, M. L. ed. Your right to dissent in a time of crisis. American Civil Liberties Union. Greater Philadelphia Branch. 260 S. 15th St. Philadelphia 19106. '66.

Commager, H. S. Freedom and order. Braziller. New York. '66.

Cowen, Zelman and others. Fair trial vs. a free press. Center for the Study of Democratic Institutions. Santa Barbara, Calif. '65.

Craig, Alec. Suppressed books. World Publishing Co. Cleveland. '63.

Crowther, Bosley. Movies and censorship. (Public Affairs Pamphlet no 332) Public Affairs Committee. 381 Park Ave. S. New York 10016. '62.

Daniels, W. M. ed. Censorship of books. (Reference Shelf. v 26, no 5) Wilson. New York. '54.
Bibliography. p 191-202.

Douglas, W. O. Freedom of the mind. Doubleday. Garden City, N.Y. '64.

Downs, R. B. ed. First freedom; liberty and justice in the world of books and reading. American Library Association. 50 E. Huron St. Chicago 60611. '60.

Emerson, T. I. Toward a general theory of the First Amendment. Random House. New York. '66.

Ernst, M. L. and Schwartz, A. U. Censorship: the search for the obscene. Macmillan. New York. '64.

Felsher, Howard and Rosen, Michael. Press in the jury box. Macmillan. New York. '66.

Forster, Arnold and Epstein, B. R. Danger on the right. Random House. New York. '64.

*Freedom of Information Center. Attempt to rewrite history. (Publication no 172) The Center. School of Journalism. University of Missouri. Columbia. D. '66.

*Freedom of Information Center. Obscenity and the Supreme Court, by R. I. Lowenstein. (Publication no 154) The Center. School of Journalism. University of Missouri. Columbia. F. '66.

Friendly, Alfred and Goldfarb, R. L. Crime and publicity. Twentieth Century Fund. New York. '67.

Gillmor, D. M. Free press and fair trial. Public Affairs Press. Washington, D.C. '66.

Hewitt, C. R. ed. Does pornography matter? Routledge. London. '61.

Hofstadter, Richard. Academic freedom in the age of the college. Columbia University Press. New York. '66.

Hyde, H. M. History of pornography. Farrar. New York. '64.

Jennison, P. S. Freedom to read. (Public Affairs Pamphlet no 344) Public Affairs Committee. 381 Park Ave. S. New York 10016. '63.

Kauper, P. G. Civil liberties and the Constitution. University of Michigan Press. Ann Arbor. '66.

Konvitz, M. R. Expanding liberties: freedom's gains in postwar America. Viking. New York. '66.

Kronhausen, Eberhard and Kronhausen, Phyllis. Pornography and the law. Ballantine. New York. '60.

Lacy, Dan. Freedom and communications. University of Illinois Press. Urbana. '61.

Lazarsfeld, P. F. and Thielens, Wagner. Academic mind: social scientists in a time of crisis; with a field report by David Riesman. Free Press. Chicago. '58.

Lipset, S. M. and Wolin, S. S. eds. Berkeley student revolt. Doubleday. Garden City, N.Y. '65.

Lofton, John. Justice and the press. Beacon. Boston. '66.

McClellan, G. S. Civil rights. (Reference Shelf. v 36, no 6) Wilson. New York. '64.
Bibliography. p 188-92.

McCormick, John and MacInnes, Mairi, eds. Versions of censorship. Doubleday. Garden City, N.Y. '62.

Metzger, W. P. Academic freedom in the age of the university. Columbia University Press. New York. '66.

Nelson, H. L. ed. Freedom of the press from Hamilton to the Warren Court. Bobbs-Merrill. Indianapolis. '67.

Nelson, Jack and Roberts, Gene, Jr. Censors and the schools. Little. Boston. '63.

Paul, J. C. N. and Schwartz, M. L. Federal censorship; obscenity in the mail. Free Press of Glencoe. New York. '61.

Reston, James. Artillery of the press. Harper (for Council on Foreign Relations). New York. '66, '67.

Roberts, E. A. Jr. Smut rakers. (Newsbook) National Observer. Silver Spring, Md. '66.

Rourke, F. E. Secrecy and publicity. Johns Hopkins Press. Baltimore. '66.

Schumach, Murray. Face on the cutting room floor. Morrow. New York. '64.

*Sigma Delta Chi. Report of the 1966 Sigma Delta Chi Advancement of Freedom of Information Committee. Sigma Delta Chi. 35 E. Wacker Dr. Chicago 60601. Fall '66.

United States. Congress. House of Representatives. Committee on Post Office and Civil Service. Circulation of obscene and pornographic material; hearing before the Subcommittee on Postal Operations, May 27, 1960. 86th Congress, 2d session. Supt. of Docs. Washington, D.C. 20402. '60.

*United States. Supreme Court. United States Reports. 383 U.S. 463 (1966). Ralph Ginzburg et al, Petitioners, v. United States. Supt. of Docs. Washington, D.C. 20402. '67.

Walker, B. R. Christian fright peddlers. Doubleday. Garden City, N.Y. '64.

PERIODICALS

ALA Bulletin. 59:27-33. Ja. '65. Climate of intellectual freedom: why is it always so bad in California? Edwin Castagna.

ALA Bulletin. 60:57-62. Ja. '66. Bias in book reviewing and book selection. Henry Regnery.

America. 113:136-40. Ag. 7, '65. Academic revolution at St. John's. F. P. Canavan.

America. 113:184-5. Ag. 21, '65. This flood of filth; New York City citizens' anti-pornography commission's steps to curb pornography. E. F. Cavanagh, Jr.

America. 114:122-4. Ja. 22, '66. St. John's University: the issues. F. P. Canavan.

*America. 114:430. Ap. 2, '66. Confusion on obscenity.

*America. 115:60-3. Jl. 16, '66. Academic freedom. Philip Gleason.

America. 115:411-13. O. 8, '66. Censorship in the church. E. C. Bianchi.

American Scholar. 36:71-91. Winter '66-'67. Ginzburg decision and the law. Leon Friedman.

*American Scholar. 36:93-103. Winter '66-'67. Public custody of the high pornography. Kathleen Molz.

Annals of the American Academy of Political and Social Science. 364:37-49. Mr. '66. Controversies about the mass communication of violence. O. N. Larsen.

Atlantic. 217:77-81. F. '66. Unbanning of the books. Harry Levin.

*Atlantic. 218:56-60. Ag. '66. Obscenity business. Jason Epstein.

Atlantic. 218:72-82+. S. '66. Decline of freedom at Berkeley. L. S. Feuer.

Atlantic. 219:74-8. Ja. '67. Pornography and the new expression. Richard Schechner.

Catholic Library World. 38:291-4. Ja. '67. Intellectual freedom for seminarians. Ruth Warncke.

Christian Century. 82:769-72. Je. 16, '65. Literature and obscenity. Robert Tracy.

Discussion: 82:993. Ag. 11, '65.

Christian Century. 82:772-5. Je. 16, '65. Morality of Catholic censorship. B. A. Curtis.

Christian Century. 82:1244-5. O. 13, '65. Right to read.

*Christian Century. 83:451-2. Ap. 13, '66. Court stirs a hornet's nest.

*Christian Century. 83:608-9. My. 11, '66. Index becomes an appendix.

Christian Century. 83:645-7. My. 18, '66. Burgeoning big brotherism; fight to halt a subtle, persistent growth in violations of the individual's right to privacy. E. V. Long.

Christian Century. 83:1372-4. N. 9, '66. Freedom and restraint in the Christian college. W. B. Martin.

*Christianity and Crisis. 24:284-8. Ja. 25, '65. Toward a new definition of obscenity. Howard Moody.

Commentary. 42:76-8+. N. '66. An end to pornography? Dan Jacobson.

*Commonweal. 81:701-3. F. 26, '65. Let it be printed. Elizabeth Bartelme.

Commonweal. 83:601-3+. F. 25, '66. Censorship in the church. J. V. Schall.

Commonweal. 84:94-5. Ap. 15, '66. Obscenity ruling.

*Crane Review. 8:118-24. Spring '66. Persistence of pornography. J. A. Schneiders.

Editor & Publisher. 100:13. My. 6, '67. Bar group modifies fair trial proposals.

Editorial Research Reports. 1, no 24:461-78. Je. 28, '61. Peacetime censorship. W. B. Dickinson, Jr.

*Encounter. 25:14-19. O. '65. Night words. George Steiner.

*Foreign Affairs. 44:553-73. Jl. '66. Press, the president and foreign policy. James Reston.

George Washington Law Review. 35:85-92. O. '66. Obscenity, advertising and publishing: the impact of *Ginzburg* and *Mishkin*. C. D. Ablard.

*Harper's Magazine. 230:51-60. Mr. '65. Against pornography. G. P. Elliott.
Discussion: 230:6+. My. '65.

Journalism Quarterly. 42:363-72. Summer '65. Puzzle of pornography. D. M. Gillmor.

Law and Contemporary Problems. 28:429-671. Summer '63. Academic freedom; ed. by R. O. Everett.

Library Journal. 90:2473-8. Je. 1, '65. Censorship and cultural rebellion; excerpts from address, October 1964. H. E. Fey.

Library Journal. 90:2479-83. Je. 1, '65. Who shall silence all the airs and madrigals? a bookseller looks at censorship. Jake Zeitlin.

Library Journal. 90:2486-90+. Je. 1, '65. Ordeal at Long Beach. Blanche Collins.

Library Journal. 90:2495-8. Je. 1, '65. They play it safe. E. W. Tamblyn.

Library Journal. 90:2499-503. Je. 1, '65. Crucial battle for the minds of men. H. W. Axford.

Library Journal. 90:2774+. Je. 15, '65. Intellectual Freedom Committee reports busy year of censorship in New Jersey. Zoia Horn.

Library Journal. 90:3681-5. S. 15, '65. Clear and present danger: the books, or the censors? Harry Bach.

Library Journal. 91:624-8. F. 1, '66. Birch tree grows. Janet Freedman.

Library Journal. 91:629-32. F. 1, '66. Fallacy of balance in public library book selection; excerpts from address, October 1965. R. A. Landor.
Discussion: 91:1952+, 2734. Ap. 15, Je. 1, '66.

Library Journal. 91:1038. F. 15, '66. NEA study shows censorship, criticism of schools increased.

Library Journal. 91:2016. Ap. 15, '66. Titillation's a crime: cases considered by the U.S. Supreme Court. Eric Moon.

Library Journal. 91:2118. Ap. 15, '66. Sex education and the censor. Evelyn Geller.

Library Journal. 91:2768-73. Je. 1, '66. Pornographic convention. J. R. Coyne, Jr.

Library Journal. 92:53-5. Ja. 1, '67. Of obscenity and such [review of and commentary on events of 1966].

Library Journal. 92:83-5. Ja. 1, '67. *CLEAN* down the drain. E. T. Moore.

Library Journal. 92:984-5. Mr. 1, '67. Library bill of rights. E. J. Gaines.

Life. 60:26. Ap. 22, '66 Dissent to the High Court's harsh verdict: R Ginzburg case. Loudon Wainwright.

NEA Journal. 54:17. S. '65. Danger of extremism. Jennelle Moorhead.

Nation. 201:5-10. Jl. 5, '65. Censorship: fanatics and fallacies. Norman Mark; Elmer Gertz.

Nation. 201:358-60. N. 15, '65. Smut hunters; new jurisprudery; activities of Citizens for Decent Literature, Inc. Howard Junker.

Nation. 202:421-4. Ap. 11, '66. Open court & fair press. Raymond Spangler.

Nation. 202:456-9. Ap. 18, '66. California's dirty book caper; the politics of smut. William Wingfield.

*National Review. 18:346. Ap. 19, '66. Ginzburg & pornography: Supreme Court's ruling.

New Leader. 49:15-17. Ap. 11, '66. Court and obscenity. Richard Morgan.

New Republic. 153:9-10. D. 18, '65. May it please the Court. A. D. Kopkind.
Reply. 154:37. Ja. 29, '66. D. Macdonald.

*New Republic. 154:5-6. Ap. 2, '66. Obscenity and the law.
Reply with rejoinder: 154:28. Ap. 23, '66. S. Kipperman.

New Republic. 155:21-4. D. 10, '66. Apology for pornography. Peter Michelsen.

New Republic. 156:15-17. My. 27, '67. Obscenity cases. A. M. Bickel.

*New York Post. p 5+. F. 23, '67. Book firm spells out CIA ties. Arthur Greenspan.

New York Times. p 1+. My. 3, '66. Ginzburg denied a review of sentence for obscenity.

*New York Times. p 14. Je. 2, '66. Excerpts from speech on coverage of Bay of Pigs buildup. Clifton Daniel.

*New York Times. p 12E. Je. 5, '66. Freedom and the press.

*New York Times. p 25. Jl. 5, '66. Johnson supports greater access to U.S. data. J. D. Pomfret.

*New York Times. p 1+. S. 21, '66. New movie code ends some taboos. Vincent Canby.

*New York Times. O. 2, '66. p 1+. Bar report urges curbs on news about suspects. F. P. Graham.

New York Times. p 12E. O. 16, '66 Fair trial and free press.

*New York Times. p 46. D. 6, '66. Court speaks for freedom.

New York Times. p 52. D. 14, '66. Defense is wary. S. E. Zion.

*New York Times. p 1+. Ja. 5, '67. Publishers and city bar group oppose crime news restrictions.

Report by A.N.P.A. [American Newspaper Publishers Association]. S. E. Zion. p 1+; Study by lawyers [Association of the Bar of the City of New York]. Edward Ranzal. p 1+; Excerpts from report by publishers. p 20.

*New York Times. p 12E. Ja. 29, '67. Academic freedom is free speech. F. P. Graham.

New York Times. p 15. F. 18, '67. Widening C.I.A. debate.

New York Times. p 1+. F. 24, '67. C.I.A. aid backed by White House as legal policy. B. A. Franklin.

*New York Times. p 1+. F. 24, '67. City bar advocates tight restriction on trial publicity. S. E. Zion.

New York Times. p 1+. Mr. 30, '67. President orders C.I.A. to halt aid to private groups. Roy Reed.

Texts of statement and report on covert C.I.A. aid. L. B. Johnson; N. deB. Katzenbach. p 30.

New York Times. p 1+. My. 9, '67. High court voids obscenity charges in 3 test cases. F. P. Graham.

New York Times. p 1+. My. 26, '67. History of Frick upheld in court.

New York Times Magazine. p 14-15+. D. 19, '65. Study in academic freedom: Genovese case. Arnold Beichman.

Newsletter on Intellectual Freedom.

Bimonthly published by American Library Association.

Newsweek. 67:59-60. Ja. 10, '66. Universities, free style.

*Newsweek. 67:54-5. Ja. 24, '66. Time of the bloop; TV's self-censorious attitude.

Publishers' Weekly. 189:77-9. Ja. 17, '66. Censorship and the freedom to read; 1965 in review.

Publishers' Weekly. 189:43-4. Mr. 28, '66. U.S. Supreme Court rules pro-censorship in two of three cases involving books.

*Publishers' Weekly. 191:50-2. Ja. 30, '67. Censorship and the freedom to read.

Publishers' Weekly. 191:43. My. 29, '67. Supreme Court overturns Warren Spahn decision.

Publishers' Weekly. 191:144+. Je. 5, '67. Stevens' book vindicated by Pennsylvania Court; judge terms book "true" and "excellent history."

Reader's Digest. 87:177-8+. S. '65. Fight against the smut peddlers; newsstand and mail-order pornography. O. K. Armstrong.

*Reader's Digest. 88:73-6. Mr. '66. Filth for profit: the big business of pornography. O. K. Armstrong.

Religion in Life. 35:170-229. Spring '66. New morality: what, why—and why not?

Reporter. 33:10. D. 16, '65. Dissent, consensus, and McCarthyism. J. P. Roche.

Saturday Evening Post. 238:27-32+. My. 8, '65. Explosive revival of the far left. Richard Armstrong.

Saturday Evening Post. 240:8-10. Ja. 14, '67. We need more censorship. P. H. Johnson.

*Saturday Review. 48:20-1+. F. 27, '65. Teaching librarians to fight back. David Dempsey.

Saturday Review. 48:12. N. 6, '65. Manner of speaking; right to read: New Jersey committee activities. John Ciardi.

*Saturday Review. 49:12-13+. Ag. 27, '66. Four academic freedoms. R. M. Nixon.

*Saturday Review. 49:13-15+. Ag. 27, '66. Nature of academic freedom. H. S. Commager.

*Saturday Review. 50:18-29. Ja. 21, '67. Kennedy-Manchester book controversy: symposium.

Reprinted in this book: Author's right to write. Irwin Karp. p 28-9.

Science. 150:1559-63. D. 17, '65. Academic freedom and political liberty. Albert Lepawsky.

Reply. 151:1034. Mr. 4, '66. S. K. Escalona.

*Social Education. 30:633-44. D. '66. Fair trial vs. free press.

*Stanford Today. p 14-17. (Series 1, no 17) Autumn '66. Fear of books. J. H. Merryman.

Teachers College Record. 66:574-8. Ap. '65. Intellectual freedom and censorship. A. L. McNeal.

Time. 85:52. Je. 4, '65. Free mail and free speech: Supreme Court decision to end censoring of Communist political propaganda by Post Office.

U.S. News & World Report. 60:42-3. Ja. 31, '66. Back of the uproar about LBJ managing the news.

U.S. News & World Report. 60:69. Ap. 4, '66. End of the boom in smut?

UNESCO Courier. 18:22-6. F. '65. What TV is doing to our children: summary of Effects of Television on Children and Adolescents. Wilbur Schramm.

Washington Post. p A 24. O. 5, '66. Reardon committee.

Washington Post. p G 1. Ja. 22, '67. M.G.M.'s release of "Blow-Up" without seal challenges code. L. F. Aarons.

Washington Post Book Week. p 1+. My. 15, '66. Curbing obscenity. J. W. Grossman.

*Washington Post Book Week. p 2+. F. 5, '67. Government book control. Geoffrey Wolff.

Reply: Letter to editor. Washington Post. p A 20. F. 9, '67. Reed Harris.

Wilson Library Bulletin. 39:638-72. Ap. '65. Full freedom of expression; symposium.

Wilson Library Bulletin. 39:720+. My. '65. Stand on censorship: statement of position of California Library Association and California Association of School Librarians.

Wilson Library Bulletin. 40:173-5. O. '65. In defense of academic freedom. E. J. Josey.

Wilson Library Bulletin. 40:795+. My. '66. Supreme Court rulings on obscenity cases.

Wilson Library Bulletin. 40:941-7. Je. '66. Implications of the Ginzburg affair. Kathleen Molz.

Yale Law Journal. 75:1364-1405. Jl. '66. More ado about dirty books. L. H. Becker.

Yale Law Journal. 76:127-57. N. '66. Obscenity, 1966: the marriage of obscenity per se and obscenity per quod. H. P. Monaghan.

(3423)